MINDREADING

Also by Sanjida O'Connell

fiction
Theory of Mind

MINDREADING

*An investigation into how we
learn to love and lie*

SANJIDA O'CONNELL

DOUBLEDAY
New York London Toronto Sydney Auckland

PUBLISHED BY DOUBLEDAY
a division of Bantam Doubleday Dell Publishing Group, Inc.
1540 Broadway, New York, New York 10036

DOUBLEDAY and the portrayal of an anchor with a dolphin
are trademarks of Doubleday, a division of
Bantam Doubleday Dell Publishing Group, Inc.

Mindreading was originally published in the United Kingdom by William Heinemann.
The Doubleday edition is published by arrangement with William Heinemann.

Library of Congress Cataloging-in-Publication Data
O'Connell, Sanjida, 1970–
Mindreading: an investigation into how we learn to love and lie /
Sanjida O'Connell. — 1st ed.
p.   cm.
Includes bibliographical references.
1. Philosophy of mind—Popular works.   2. Other minds (Theory of knowledge)—
Popular works.   3. Thought and thinking.   4. Mind and body.   I. Title.
BD418.3.O27   1998
128'.2—dc21   98-5648
CIP

To Guy

The publishers would like to thank the following for permission to quote from their books:

Hitch Hiker's Guide to the Galaxy by Douglas Adams, published by Macmillan General Books 1992.

Complicity by Iain Banks, published by Little Brown 1994.

Do Androids Dream of Electric Sheep? by Philip K Dick, published by Victor Gollanz Ltd 1968. Permission granted by the author and his agent, Russell Galen.

Immortality by Milan Kundera, published by Faber and Faber 1991.

An Anthropologist on Mars by Oliver Sacks, published by Picador 1995

Every effort has been made to trace the copyright holders of the quoted material. If there are any inadvertent omissions, however, these can be rectified in any future editions.

For I have learned
To look on nature, not as in the hour
Of thoughtless youth; but hearing oftentimes
The still, sad music of humanity,
Nor harsh nor grating, though of ample power
To chasten and subdue. And I have felt
A presence that disturbs me with the joy
Of elevated thoughts; a sense sublime
Of something far more deeply interfused,
Whose dwelling is the light of setting suns,
And the round ocean and the living air,
And the blue sky, and in the mind of man.

William Wordsworth, 'Tintern Abbey'

CONTENTS

ACKNOWLEDGEMENTS

My Ph.D. thesis on Theory of Mind in Chimpanzees formed the backbone of this book and I owe a debt of gratitude to many people who helped me during my years as a post-graduate student. Three scientists in particular inspired me and gave me practical advice and help: Robin Dunbar, Francesca Happé and Simon Baron-Cohen. Simon has also patiently put up with many queries regarding the book and read one of the chapters. I am grateful to John Sweetenham and Inman Harvey for taking the time to read and comment on various chapters.

I would like to thank the following scientists for answering my questions and sending me references: Michel Aube, Dave Barnes, Simon Baron-Cohen, James Blair, Dave Cliff, Rhiannon Corcoran, Kerstin Dautenhahn, Daniel Dennett, Roger Fouts, Chris Frith, Uta Frith, Norman Freeman, Juan Carlos Gómez, John Gory, Francesca Happé, Paul Harris, Inman Harvey, Horst Hendrik-Jansen, Sue Leekam, Alan Leslie, Anil Mahotra, Mary Minihan, Adam Pack, Irene Pepperberg, Josef Perner, Daniel Povinelli, Esteban Rivas, Aaron Sloman, Toby Simpson, Emmet Spier, John Sweetenham, Frans de Waal, Henry Wellman, Shelly Williams, Matt Williamson and Mark Xitco.

I am also indebted to Patrick Walsh, my agent, for his tireless enthusiasm, Richard Dale for his comments, Victoria Hipps for her editorial help and my family for their love and support and for reading and commenting on the book.

A PERSON IS A PERSON
THROUGH OTHER PEOPLE

In our African language we say 'a person is a person through other people'. I would not know how to be a human being at all except I learnt this from other human beings. We are made of a delicate network of relationships, of interdependence. We are meant to complement each other. All kinds of things go horribly wrong when we break that fundamental law of our being.

Archbishop Desmond Tutu

In Shakespeare's *The Winter's Tale*, Leontes, King of Sicilia, and his brother, Polixenes, have fallen out with each other. Hermione, Leontes's wife, persuades Polixenes to stay with her and the King in the hope that their friendship will be repaired. The King, as he watches the Queen speaking to his brother, is overcome with jealousy. He misinterprets her actions and believes she is having an affair with Polixenes. He tells his friend, the Lord Camillo, of his fears.

Ha'not you seen, Camillo,
(But that's past doubt; you have: or your eye-glass
Is thicker than a cuckold's horn) or heard,
(For, to a vision so apparent, rumour
Cannot be mute)

Leontes asks Camillo to kill Polixenes. Camillo agrees, with many misgivings for he does not believe the King. He warns Polixenes of the King's feelings and tells him to flee. Again, the King catches them talking and interprets this and his brother's imminent departure with Camillo (who can no longer risk staying) as proof of his brother's adultery and Camillo's treachery. He locks his wife up in prison and, even though she is pregnant, refuses to release her. He naturally thinks that the child is his brother's and when Hermione gives birth, he decides to kill the baby girl.

It is an unfortunate tale. The fate of these characters, Polixenes, Hermione and Camillo, hinges on two conversations and the hasty departure of Polixenes and Camillo. But the King has read volumes into their behaviour. The whole scenario takes place not in reality, but in the mind of the King.

> . . . for cogitation
> Resides not in the man that does not think it.

To a greater or lesser extent, and with consequences which are usually not quite as devastating, this is what we all do. We do not interact with other people by looking at how they behave, rather, we think about what they are thinking and respond to them on that basis.

This book is about the mechanism we use to understand what is going on in other people's heads. How we react to one another socially is the most important aspect of our lives. Without an understanding of what people think, what they want and what they believe about the world, it is impossible to operate in any society. Theory of Mind is the name given to this understanding of others. It is the basic necessity of humanity and is understood the same way the world over, from Japanese school children to the Baka pygmies of Cameroon.

The extent to which our thoughts colour our experiences can be seen in this very simple example. Imagine you are in a bar and you see two women leaning on the counter drinking. One of them looks round, then turns to the other and nudges her. The second woman looks in the direction the first looked in, smiles at her companion and the two of them start to walk towards a man sitting on his own in the corner.

This is a bare description of their behaviour, but if you were in the bar you might think that one woman had seen someone whom she found rather attractive, or knows that her companion will find attractive, and the two of them want to chat the guy up. Alternatively, he might have been a friend of theirs whom they had arranged to meet in the bar. Perhaps they had seen him come in and wondered how long it would take him to notice them, but now their patience has run out and they are going to surprise him.

In each case, the scenario is interpreted in terms of what the people involved think and want. We use these terms – want, think, know – about states of mind and emotions on such a regular basis that they have become invisible. We interpret people's actions using words that describe their mental states so often that we cease to think about what it is we are actually doing. As Daniel Dennett, a philosopher from Tufts University, Boston, says, 'Every time we venture out on the highway we stake our lives on the reliability of our general expectations about the perceptual beliefs, normal desires and decisions of the other motorists.' He gives another everyday example of how we continuously and unconsciously use Theory of Mind: 'Watching a film with a highly original and unstereotyped plot, we see the hero smile at the villain and we all swiftly and effortlessly arrive at the same theoretical diagnosis: "Aha!" we conclude (but perhaps not consciously). "He wants her to think he doesn't know she intends to defraud her brother!" '

We are social animals. The vast majority of us interact with people every day of our lives. Our relationships are informed by the mind, by what we think others are thinking. We are by no means telepathic but we use our powers of imagination to help us 'mindread'. Mind-reading allows us to predict other people's behaviour. The unhappy King Leontes in *The Winter's Tale* predicted his Queen's behaviour (she would have an affair with his brother) and Camillo's behaviour (he would betray the King). Leontes's predictions were totally wrong. Sometimes we, too, misinterpret the actions of others and for a very simple reason: we cannot ever know for certain what another person is thinking. We cannot get inside another's head.

Misunderstandings are commonplace, yet they stand out because most of the time we are highly accurate in predicting what other people will do on the basis of what we believe they are thinking. We take mindreading so much for granted that we are blind to the fact that it is going on. We think that what we see is what we get, when really we are not *seeing*, rather, we are infusing scenes with our own expectations, thoughts, beliefs, hopes and desires.

We do not just watch other people as if we're anthropologists from Mars, we speak to them and they tell us what they're thinking. But even in conversation, we do not always say what we mean, or even mean what we say, and most people, again unconsciously, look at the underlying meaning, rather than the words themselves. People's speech rarely makes any sense unless you know what they are trying to say. An example given by Steven Pinker in his book *The Language Instinct* reads:

Woman: I'm leaving you.
Man: Who is he?

We know immediately whom the 'he' stands for, but we only know this because we guess what is going on in the minds of the man and the woman. Without this knowledge, or guesswork, their conversation would make no sense.

In *The Unbearable Lightness of Being* by Milan Kundera, Sabina, a painter, is having an affair with Franz, a married man. 'He listened eagerly to the story of her life and she was equally eager to hear the story of his, but although they had a clear understanding of the logical meaning of the words they exchanged, they failed to hear the semantic susurrus of the river flowing through them [. . .] While people are fairly young and the musical composition is still in its opening bars, they can go about writing it together and exchange motifs [. . .] but if they meet when they are older, like Franz and Sabina, their musical compositions are more or less complete and every motif, every object, every word means something different to each of them.'

Kundera illustrates his point with 'A short dictionary of misunderstood words' in which the simplest of words such as *woman* and *light* have opposing meanings to Franz and Sabina. The two of them are always destined to misinterpret each other because they do not understand what the other is thinking; or, rather, they think they know, which is far more dangerous.

We also intentionally deceive one another through our use of words, but the discerning can see through the tangled webs of other people's lies. A girl you meet at a party tells you that you are incredibly handsome. You might be flattered and immediately invite her out for a meal. But you happen to have a girlfriend who has just left you. And you happen to know that your ex-girlfriend is this girl's best friend. You are also painfully aware that the man your lover left you for was the boyfriend of the girl who is now complimenting you. Knowing all this, you hazard a guess that the woman who says she admires your looks might be hoping that you respond to her and make both her best friend and her ex-boyfriend jealous. At this point, you no longer believe her – but you might ask her on a date anyway.

This educated guesswork is called Theory of Mind and it forms the cornerstone of our interactions with people, no matter what their creed or their culture. It is the ability to understand that other people also have mental states such as thoughts, desires and beliefs about the world. Theory of Mind is the hallmark of humanity: knowing the workings of another person's mind allows us to be compassionate, cruel, concerned and conniving. We rarely respond to people solely on the basis of their words or their deeds, instead we use our understanding of what we believe others think to predict their behaviour. In this book we are going to look at how we develop a Theory of Mind and whether animals have an understanding of other minds. But first we will explore the main components of Theory of Mind.

Theory of Mind is independent of the real world, for you or I might have a belief that is wrong. I hear rain beating against the windows, so I decide to take my umbrella to work. But simply because I believe that it is raining, it does not mean that it is. The little girl next door has been throwing pebbles at my house again and I, mistakenly, think the sound of them scattering against the glass is a heavy shower. I have a logical but false belief about the world.

Theory of Mind is also independent of the mental states of others, because you and I can believe different things, even when we are both participating in the same event. Thinking of other people's mental states means that you are thinking *about* what is going on in their head. This is known as intentionality. To understand another person fully, you need to know what they are thinking *about* because they may perceive the same object or event in the real world differently from you. For example, think of the statement: Helen was bitten by her pet iguana. Now, an iguana is a cold-blooded reptile so it follows logically that Helen was bitten by a cold-blooded reptile. But although Helen knows she was bitten, she may not realise that the iguana is a cold-blooded reptile. Therefore, she *doesn't know* that she was attacked by a cold-blooded reptile, even though that is what happened. Suppose a second person were witnessing the attack. He might know that Helen was holding a cold-blooded reptile, but not realise that the lizard was an iguana. Helen's friend knows that she was bitten by a reptile, but paradoxically he doesn't know she was bitten by an iguana. Intentionality depends very much on what people think and know, which may not bear much resemblance to another person's reality.

As another example, imagine that Helen's lizard has escaped. She hears a rustling sound coming from behind the sofa. In fact, her baby brother has hidden behind the sofa. We would not want to say that Helen thinks her brother is a lizard, although in a strange sense that is what Helen does think! Intentionality is concerned with how people see or think about events. A classic example of intentionality comes from the Greek myth on Oedipus. Oedipus wants to marry Jocasta. Although he does not realise it, Jocasta is his mother. If Oedipus had been asked, he would have emphatically denied that he wanted to marry his mother, yet marry his mother is exactly what he does. Shakespeare was wrong: in the mind, what you call a rose does make a difference to how it might smell. Intentionality is thus a good tool to use when talking about what people think.

Intentionality comes in various levels, depending on what you think other people are thinking. For example, the first level of intentionality (or first-order intentionality) is: Jason *knows* the sherry is hidden in the cupboard under the kitchen sink. 'Knows' is in italics because that is what Jason is thinking: knowing is Jason's 'mental state'. Second-order intentionality would be: Jason *knows* his sister *wants* a glass of sherry. Here, the first order of intentionality is that his sister *wants* a drink. However, this is one step removed: we don't know for sure that Jason's sister wants the sherry. We know what she wants through Jason: he *knows* she *wants* it. Hence, there are two mental states in Jason's mind.

Third-order intentionality is: he knows that he *thinks* she *wants* the sherry. Or she *knows* that he thinks that she *wants* the sherry. There are three mental states embedded in the one sentence. One could go on making up more levels. Daniel Dennett was the first person to write about levels of intentionality, but he says, ' . . . you wonder whether I realise how hard it is for you to be sure that you understand whether I mean to be saying that you can recognise that I can believe you want me to explain that most of us can keep track of only about five or six orders under the best of circumstances.'

Three levels of intentionality is something we can cope with relatively easily and can deal with virtually automatically. As the levels increase, we have to concentrate far more and it does seem that there is a limit to the number of orders of intentionality any of us can understand. We are thought to hold these levels of meaning in our mind as pictures or representations. In our example, 'Jason's sister wants the sherry', Jason's sister represents her desire for a small measure of alcohol; she imagines a tumbler of sherry. A 'metarepresentation' is a representation of a representation, or a picture of a picture. Imagine Cezanne painting a picture of Van Gogh, who is painting sunflowers. Mentally, this is what Jason is doing. He imagines his sister imagining a drink. Therefore, Jason is metarepresenting.

Despite the complexity of pictures within pictures, and levels of understanding embedded in levels of understanding, we are capable of dealing with what people know, desire, think and want on an everyday basis. Most of us don't give a passing thought to the skill that we are lucky enough to possess. However, there are some people who have no Theory of Mind. They are 'mindblind'. They do not understand other people.

'Imagine yourself alone in a foreign land. As you step off the bus, the local people crowd towards you, gesticulating and shouting. Their words sound like animal cries. Their gestures mean nothing to you,' wrote Francesca Happé, a psychologist from the Medical Research Council's Cognitive Development Unit in London. We can imagine that level of helplessness in a foreign land but to be constantly surrounded by people with whom we cannot communicate, of whom we have no comprehension and whose actions mean nothing to us, would be a nightmare.

Henry Wellman, a child psychologist from the University of Michigan at Ann Arbor, wrote the following, 'Imagine a hypothetical being who knows nothing of internal mental states [. . .] Such a being might be able to remember, know and learn, but it would possess no understanding of these activities. The social world, the world of self and others, would be an impoverished place for such a creature [. . .] Persons would be seen and heard, but there would be no notion of [. . .] ideas and beliefs organising their actions and personalities. Indeed, for this hypothetical being, no one could be construed as possessing a private persona [. . .] The concept of a lie would be inconceivable, as would [. . .] notions such as illusions, beliefs, hunches, mistakes, guesses or deceptions. It is almost impossible to imagine [. . .] how such a creature would view the world.' When Wellman wrote this, he genuinely did not believe there was such an 'hypothetical being', but sadly these people do exist.

People with autism have no concept of what another person feels or thinks. Autism is an unusual hereditary disorder which affects a person for his or her whole life. It is incredibly hard to encapsulate the symptoms since each person who has autism is uniquely different. The people I am going to describe here all suffer from autism, but the particulars of each person are peculiar to themselves.

Sally did not speak until she was over three years old. At first, people thought she was deaf, but she could hear the rustle of a sweet paper. She would run around outside with almost no clothes on and would not seem to feel pain, cold or heat. Although these things did not make her cry, if someone took away her toy panda, she would scream for hours. Like many autistic people, she collected

8

things: she treasured leaves, plastic bottles and stones and would arrange them in special patterns.

One autistic young man asked everyone he met about the colour of the door to the juvenile magistrates' court in their area. Once, when he was asked why he never asked about doors to adult courts, he replied, 'They bore me to tears.' Despite the obsessive nature of their collecting, autistic people do not find the subject of their collection inherently interesting. Another young man learnt the name of every kind of carrot in the UK (there are at least fifty) but he himself did not like growing or eating carrots.

Paul, by the time he was one year old, became distressed if he saw a light bulb without a shade on and, by the age of ten, he had developed an intense fear of the sugar bowl. One girl would scream every time she was told she was going swimming. It wasn't until someone thought to say, 'And then we're coming back' that she stopped crying. This overwhelming literalness is characteristic of autistic people; the little girl didn't realise that implicit in the sentence 'We're going swimming' is the idea that afterwards everyone will go home again.

Autistic people have an overwhelming desire for things – from the layout of all the ornaments in the house to their daily routine – to stay the same. A further problem is communication. Often children with autism learn to speak at an older age than other children and use words in odd ways. One young man used to say, 'I wish to extract a biscuit from the tin' and another would always begin a phone call to his aunt by saying, 'This is Charles Smith, your nephew, speaking.' Many don't understand they are being boring when they talk incessantly about their private hobby to complete strangers, others have speech impediments and speak far too loudly and with a strange intonation. Some children express themselves by singing, but only their parents have learnt to tell whether a particular song means that they are happy or sad.

Autistic people have often been associated with idiots savants. Idiots savants, whilst being of subnormal intelligence, are able to perform some specialised task brilliantly. Stephen Wiltshire, who is autistic, has been an exceptional artist since he was a young child, capable of drawing buildings down to the finest detail. About one in ten autistic people have abilities that are way beyond their IQ and other skills. Sadly, the few who are blessed with these talents often lose them. One three year old could accurately sing Stravinsky's *The Rite of Spring*, but she lost her gift by the time she was ten. Worse, about three-quarters of autistic people are mentally retarded with an IQ below fifty-five.

The myth of the noble savage has also been applied to autism. The Wild Boy of Aveyron, a feral child, was discovered in a forest in France during the latter part of the eighteenth century. He was about twelve years old and did not seem to be able to speak. He had no clothes and was scarred from head to foot. Here, the people thought, was how human beings would develop in the absence of culture. However, according to Uta Frith from the Medical Research Council's Cognitive Development Unit in London, the wild boy could have been autistic. The boy was named Victor and a physician called Itard took on the arduous task of trying to educate him. Five years later, the boy communicated through gestures and showed stereotypical behaviour. He was good at manual work, but he never played imaginative games and he showed no awareness of noise (unless he heard someone cracking walnuts, which he loved; he would then immediately run and snatch the nuts). These traits are all hallmarks of autism. A scientific paper was written about him in 1800 by Professor Abbé Pierre-Joseph Bonnaterre. He wrote, 'His affections are as limited as his knowledge; he loves no one; he is attached to no one; he shows some preference for his caretaker, but as an expression of a need and not out of a feeling of gratitude.'

Frith says that autistic people would be relatively well able to survive in the wild compared to other children for they can tolerate extremes of cold, pain, hunger and a general lack of comfort. However, he was probably not abandoned in the forest before he was ten and local people might have fed him during the winter. After Itard had given up teaching him, Victor was no more 'tamed' than before. Once he and Itard were invited to the house of an aristocrat, Mme Récamier. She insisted that Victor sit next to her, but an eyewitness observed, 'Too occupied with the abundant things to eat, which he devoured with startling greed as soon as his plate was filled, the young savage hardly heeded the beautiful eyes whose attention he himself attracted. When dessert was served and he had adroitly filled his pockets with all the delicacies that he could filch, he calmly left the table.' Victor then ran into the garden, pulled his shirt off, ripped it in two, climbed up a tree and perched in the branches where he stayed until the gardener bribed him down with a basket of peaches.

Autism is not new. Folk tales abound of people who behave strangely and in very literal ways. One story from Malta describes a boy called Gahan. He did not like getting up early in the mornings, so when his mother told him one Sunday that she was going to church, he insisted on staying in bed. She replied that if he changed his mind, he should be sure not to forget to pull the door behind him. A little while later he arrived in church with a great banging and clattering. He had torn the door off its hinges and pulled it behind him all the way to the church. This story is reminiscent of a contemporary child who, when he arrived at a friend's house, was told to stick his coat anywhere and promptly started to search for some glue.

Holy or 'blessed' fools were venerated in Russia for centuries and it is likely that they were people suffering from autism. They often repeated words and phrases when people spoke to them, they had odd speech patterns and in many cases they did not reply when they were asked questions. One such 'fool', Pelagija Serebrenikova, would throw stones into a flooded pit one by one, then climb into the water, retrieve her stones from the bottom and recommence throwing them back in again. Typical of many autistic people, the blessed fools did not go out of their way to avoid others, but were always alone even when surrounded by a crowd, for they did not know how to relate to people.

Despite the long history of autism, it was not diagnosed until 1943 by Leo Kanner. A physician called Hans Asperger also described in very similar terms the disorder Kanner had written about and published his paper one year later. Neither man knew much about the other's work, yet, incredibly, both chose the word 'autism' to refer to the disorder they had described. Now we tend to use Asperger's name to describe a syndrome which is sometimes characterised as a milder form of autism. We will discuss 'Asperger's syndrome' in more detail in chapter eight.

In summary, autistic people have three core deficits:

- they cannot communicate
- they cannot imagine (and so show no pretend play)
- they are unable to deal with people socially

Many of us have not met an autistic person, but there is another group of people with whom all of us have come into contact at some point in our lives who also do not have the ability to mindread. They, like people with autism, cannot and do not act as if other people think. Neither do they know that they themselves have beliefs and desires. These people are children.

Before the age of four to five years old, children do not possess Theory of Mind. Even when they are older than five, they have difficulty understanding beliefs which involve high orders of intentionality. The mystery about children is that although we know that they will eventually understand what other people are thinking, we do not always know when they will develop Theory of Mind, or how they develop an understanding of what people think. For instance, by the age of two, children readily use words such as 'want', but it is unlikely that at such a young age they understand what they mean when they say, 'Daddy wants toast.' At this age, a child does not understand that she is referring to Daddy's desire; she only knows that he usually has toast and today he will too.

One of the standard ways of testing whether a child has Theory of Mind is the Smarties task. A child is presented with a tube of Smarties and asked what she thinks is inside. Any self-respecting child will say 'Smarties'. You open the tube and show her that it is actually full of birthday cake candles. You put the top back on and ask her what her friend thinks is inside the tube. You remind her that her friend is not in the room and did not see the tube being opened. Children younger than four or five will reply, 'Birthday cake candles.' They cannot understand that their friend will believe, as they did, that the tube is full of Smarties. They cannot understand that their friend has a false belief; because *they* know the tube is full of candles, surely *everyone* knows. Furthermore, if you ask the child what she thought was in the tube before you opened it, she will still say, 'Birthday cake candles.' A child's own false belief is as difficult for her to grasp as another person's is.

There is, however, another group of beings who are even more opaque to our queries, and whose minds are far more problematical to decipher: animals. As they possess even fewer words than young children, it is difficult to ask them if they think, what they think and whether they know that others can think. Why should we be concerned with whether animals have Theory of Mind? We are animals, too, so it is interesting to examine whether we share this trait with many species, or only those most closely related to us in evolutionary terms, or whether we are unique in possessing this ability.

As Woody Allen says, the brain is my second favourite organ, and it is the brain that is involved here. If the two-millimetre thick cerebral cortex that surrounds the outer surface of the brain were removed and flattened, a human's would occupy four sheets of A4 paper, a chimpanzee's would fit on one sheet, a monkey's would fill a postcard, and a rat's would be the size of a stamp. Primates – monkeys and apes – are the animals most likely to possess Theory of Mind, for they have large brains compared to other animals and are highly social (so it could be argued that they might need the ability to mindread and thus understand what their companions are thinking and planning). They are also evolutionarily very close to us: it is thought that chimpanzees share ninety-eight per cent of our genes and that we had a common ancestor as recently as four or five million years ago.

The term Theory of Mind was, in fact, coined by two primatologists and was first applied to a chimpanzee. In 1978 David Premack, currently at the Laboratoire de Psycho-Biologie at the Centre National de la Recherche Scientifique in Paris, and his colleague Guy Woodruff asked, 'Does the chimpanzee have a Theory of Mind?', by which they meant could apes do what humans could, namely attribute states of mind to others and use this to predict how others might act? They said, 'Does the ape wonder, while looking quizzically at another individual, "What does he really *want*? What does he *believe*? What are his *intentions*?" ' They specifically did not ask whether apes thought or had intentions. As they said, 'We took it for granted that the ape has [. . .] wants, beliefs, hopes, plans.'

Premack and Woodruff conducted several experiments on chimpanzees. They gave a chimpanzee called Sarah pictures which showed a person who had a problem. One picture showed her trainer locked in a cage, another showed him trying to reach some bananas that were hanging from the ceiling. They then presented her with a series of pictures, one of which had the solution: the trainer unlocking the cage, standing on a chair to reach the bananas and so on. Sarah correctly chose the right solution in each case. When she was given the same test, but with a trainer that she did not like, she chose pictures that would leave him in the lurch: locked in the cage and unable to reach the fruit. At first sight, this experiment seems to show that Sarah has a sophisticated understanding of what a person wants, and how he could satisfy his desire.

In the ten years after Premack and Woodruff posed the question of whether apes could understand what is going on in the minds of another animal, there was a flurry of work conducted on both children and other primates. Child psychologists launched a barrage of experiments, whereas the primatologists relied mainly on anecdotes. Anecdotes are simply descriptions of one-off events or notable moments and although they were used extensively by Victorian naturalists, contemporary scientists have been loath to trust them for the events described cannot be repeated in the laboratory. Nevertheless, the evidence from anecdotes points towards a peculiar form of intelligence seen in many species of primate.

When you look at gorillas in the jungle, they appear to do nothing except eat, sleep and mate. They have little to worry them and their food is plentiful. Yet, in captivity, they show great creativity and a high degree of intelligence. Some gorillas have even been taught how to use American sign language for the deaf. They can communicate with people and, according to their researchers, tell lies and crack jokes. Intelligence used to be viewed as technical expertise – how one deals with physical objects – however, primates and quite possibly other species treat other primates as objects to be manipulated mentally. Primate intelligence has been shaped by the need to deal with other individuals. After all, as primatologist Nicolas Humphrey says, 'If an ethologist had kept watch on Einstein through a pair of field-glasses, he might well have come to the conclusion that Einstein had a humdrum mind.' Humphrey goes on to add, 'This is just the point: Einstein, like [apes], displayed his genius at rare times in "artificial" situations – he did not use it, for he did not need to use it, in the common world of practical affairs.'

Close observation of primates has revealed a high degree of social intelligence. Primatologist Hans Kummer, from the University of Zurich in Switzerland, studied hamadryas baboons in Ethiopia. This particular species of baboon has a male who is head of the troop and who mates with all the females. While Kummer was watching from a cliff-top vantage point, he saw a female inch gradually over to a rock and then edge her way round it. The journey – a distance of about two metres – took her twenty minutes. Once she reached the rock, she started to groom a young male. The troop leader was on the other side of the rock. He could see her tail and the top of her head, but not her hands and very definitely not her occupation. Had he seen what the female was doing, it is likely that he would have punished her and chased away the male. Kummer commented, 'The only aspect that made me doubt that the arrangement was accidental was the exceptionally slow, inch-by-inch shifting of the female.'

Primate societies are characterised by rank. Each animal has its own place in the pecking order, although they all strive to progress further up the hierarchy. The key to this hierarchy is sex. Primates' social systems are governed by it. At the most basic level, this sex hierarchy determines whether a male ape will be able to have sex with a female. Frans de Waal, a primatologist from Yerkes Primate Research Centre at Emory University in Atlanta, spent some time watching a colony of chimpanzees at Arnhem Zoo, in Holland. On several occasions he saw a low-ranking male sitting with his arms resting on his knees, his hands hanging loosely, his legs apart and his penis erect. The males sat in front of females, openly inviting them, but viewed from the side, their hands and their legs were carefully positioned so that no one else could see the state of their member. The males also kept glancing at the dominant males to check that they had not shifted position and would thus be able to look at something they should not see.

On a more complex level, in a group of primates, there are several who are related to each other. In one type of monkey, the macaques, infants inherit rank from their mother. A baby monkey born to a high-ranking female can thus be more dominant than a much older monkey. Should one monkey attack another, the offender will have to contend with the monkey it fought with, as well as all its victim's kin. The cousins, brothers, sisters and aunts of the victim may not attack at that very moment, but at some point they will wreak revenge on the assailant. Primates need to have an advanced social knowledge to work out who is related to whom and how closely and whether it is more acceptable to steal food from X's third cousin than Y's aunt's brother.

One of the hallmarks of social intelligence witnessed in primates has been deceptive behaviour, but as we will see in chapter seven, apes, and in particular, chimpanzees, have to deal with individuals who are usually as clever as themselves and who might see that they are being duped and adopt countermeasures. For this reason, social intelligence has come to be called Machiavellian Intelligence, after Niccolò Machiavelli, a sixteenth-century political analyst and author of *The Prince*. His words are as true for primates as they are for people: 'Everyone realises how praiseworthy it is for a prince to honour his word and to be straightforward rather than crafty in his dealings; nonetheless, contemporary experience shows that the princes who have achieved great things have been those who have given their word lightly [. . .] For a prince, then, it is not necessary to have all the [virtuous] qualities, but it is very necessary to appear to have them [. . .] Men will always be false to you unless they are compelled by necessity to be true.'

Machiavelli was himself not Machiavellian enough. He wrote *The*

Prince to curry favour with the Medici of Italy but as the historian J.R. Hale said, 'Statesmen had been functioning efficiently on Machiavellian lines for centuries and by begging them to be self-conscious about the motives for their actions Machiavelli was not aiding but embarrassing [them].' Machiavelli dedicated his book to Lorenzo, the Captain-General of the Florentines, on his twenty-first birthday. Rumour has it that the Captain-General was more interested in a pair of greyhounds which were presented to him at the same time. He was already a prince and possessed all the deceptive abilities required by the position; he had no need to study how to become one.

The difficulty that we and other primates have to face is that any social interaction is a fluid problem and is likely to alter depending on the conduct of the participants. Just as in Alice's game of croquet with the Queen in *Alice in Wonderland*, there are some rules, but they change, as does the game itself. The balls were live hedgehogs, the mallets flamingoes and the playing-card soldiers were the arches through which the hedgehogs had to be hit. Alice complained to the Cheshire cat, 'I don't think they play at all fairly [. . .] and they all quarrel so dreadfully – and they don't seem to have any rules in particular [. . .] You've no idea how confusing it is all the things being alive,' she adds as two of the hedgehogs have a fight and her flamingo tries to fly into a tree.

Human beings use Theory of Mind to predict the behaviour of others. Because, like us, primates are constantly surrounded by other members of their group and they appear to be good at manipulating one another socially, they are strong candidates for having Theory of Mind. If there are other species that can think like us, we are not alone: the way we think would no longer be uniquely our own, nor could we continue to assert our total superiority over other animals. In this book, we will examine the evidence for and against the idea that primates can mindread. In addition, we will briefly look at the behaviour of other so-called intelligent species, such as dolphins.

The litmus test for Theory of Mind is whether an individual can understand that another has a false belief, a belief about the world that is logical, but which does not correspond to reality. We will chart the route by which we achieve this ability. First we will begin with a basic understanding of how eye gaze functions. Where we look and what we look at determines what we desire. If you can follow another person's gaze and understand why they are pointing, are you on the road to understanding what they want? The next stepping-stone towards a full Theory of Mind is comprehending another person's desires and emotions, followed by an understanding of their beliefs. We will also examine deception and empathy, by-products of Theory of Mind, for without these skills you cannot love, lie, cheat or communicate. How dishonest, double-dealing, devious and deceptive can we really be? We will also explore the strange and sad world of those who suffer from Asperger's syndrome and ask what this disorder can teach us about the mind. The ninth chapter is devoted to artificial intelligence and robots. So far, no robot has been made which, following the Turing Test, can fool us into believing it is conscious. Devised by the computer scientist Alan Turing in 1950, the Turing Test examines a machine's ability to think. It requires a robot to fool a person so that he believes he is having a conversation with another human. The irony is that in a recent recreation of the Turing Test, a woman taking part was classed as a robot! A robot with Theory of Mind might deceive us all. But first, we will look at the philosophical background to the mind, at how philosophers have thought about the thoughts of animals and how one philosopher launched a thousand experiments from the safety of his armchair.

2

OUT OF THE ARMCHAIR

On the planet Earth, man had always assumed that he was more
intelligent than dolphins because he had achieved so much —
the wheel, New York, wars and so on — whilst all the dolphins
had ever done was muck about in the water having a good
time. But, conversely, the dolphins had always believed that they
were far more intelligent than man — for precisely the same
reasons.
        Douglas Adams, *The Hitchhiker's Guide to the Galaxy*

Aristotle, a Greek philosopher who lived in the fourth century BCE,
was the first person to recognise that dolphins are mammals and not
fish. One of the few philosophers who examined nature carefully
and at first hand, he could almost be called the grandfather of
modern biology. He showed that one species of shark gives birth to
live young, a fact not confirmed until the 1650s; he realised that
reptiles can sometimes grow new limbs; that hyaenas are not her-
maphrodite and male octupi use one of their arms to inseminate the
female.

In this chapter I want to examine the attitude that philosophers,
such as Aristotle, had towards animals and whether they thought
that animals could think. And, if they granted animals a 'reasoning
part of their soul', how closely did they consider animal cognition
might resemble human thought processes? Most philosophers merely
speculated on animal minds, but this chapter begins and ends with
two, Aristotle and Daniel Dennett, who observed animals at first
hand.

Aristotle was the son of the court physician to the King of

Macedon. He entered Plato's academy when he was seventeen and remained there for twenty years, first as Plato's protégé and then as a teacher in his own right, leaving only when Plato died. His acute observations and relatively sound knowledge of biology led him to the conclusion that there is a continuity in biology from the lowest form of life to the highest. Despite this, Aristotle disagreed with his mentor about animal intelligence. Plato granted animals 'a reasoning part of the soul'. In *The Republic*, Plato wrote that some animals could have beliefs and aspire to reflections about things 'being thus and so'. Aristotle, in contrast, made a sharp intellectual distinction between animals and humans. Animals, he said, are not capable of reason, although he did credit them with technical knowledge: dolphins can dive to great depths without suddenly running out of air midway down, but it is only *as if* dolphins calculate how big a breath they need before diving. This idea was elaborated on by Gilbert Ryle, an Oxford philosopher, who wrote in the mid-twentieth century that there was a distinction between knowing *how* and knowing *that*. This means animals may know *how* to perform complicated patterns of behaviour but they do not have the understanding *that* they are performing such actions.

Following Aristotle came the Stoics, founded by the philosopher Zeno in 300 BCE. They dedicated themselves to the study of Reason and natural philosophy. They believed that Reason was the goal of human existence; therefore, it is of little surprise that they said animals had no Reason. They recognised that people could be irrational, but that was simply Reason malfunctioning. According to the Stoics, animals are born with an instinctive affection for themselves which allows them to seek out the type of food, shelter, mate and so on that accords with their nature. People too share this same self-affection, but tempered by Reason, which means that we can determine what is appropriate. One of the Stoics' more bizarre beliefs was that the earth was an intelligent being.

Rather more generous in his philosophical dealings with animals was St Thomas Aquinas. Born in CE 1225 in the town after which he was named, Aquino in Italy, he was originally schooled by the

Benedictine monks of Monte Cassino. To the consternation of his parents, he left home at the age of nineteen and went to join the Dominican Order of begging friars, who took him to Paris, where he studied philosophy and theology. One of his earliest contributions to philosophy was to make Aristotle's works known and acceptable to Western Christians, who'd regarded the ancient Greek as some kind of pagan.

Thomas Aquinas agreed with the Aristotelian belief that there is a 'continuum of souls' from plants to God. He considered that, in general, animals have a more sensitive soul than plants because they perceive the world through their senses and hold their sensory impressions in the imagination before storing them in the memory. This so-called 'sensitivity' is consciousness. People are superior to animals because we have a higher sensitive capacity and can reason, deliberate and be self-reflective:

> As regards sensible forms there is little difference between men and animals, for they are similarly worked on by external sense-objects. But there is a difference as regards the implications of the sense situation. For while animals perceive these purposes by a kind of natural instinct, men need to make comparisons [. . .] as regards memory, man does not merely have the sudden recognition of the past, as in the sense-memory of animals, but also the power of reminiscence . . .

Therefore animals can think by making direct reference to similar situations in the past, but they cannot make complex judgements and reach reasoned conclusions about future events. Aquinas further differentiated between people and animals by concluding that although animals may take pleasure in objects, they can do so only if these objects are related to food or sex, whereas we can appreciate beauty for its own sake. This capacity of 'sense-judgement' allows us to see objects in terms unrelated to us, although for animals, he thought, this was not so: 'A ewe knows this lamb, not as being a lamb, but as something to be suckled, and this grass, not as grass, but as something to be eaten.'

In addition, we have the power of committing an action of our own volition. Aquinas says that there is a two-fold knowledge of an end: imperfect and perfect.

Imperfect knowledge is merely perceiving a goal without understanding of purpose as such or of the adaptation of means to ends; animals enjoy that kind of knowledge through their senses. Perfect knowledge requires more, namely, understanding of the meaning of purpose and of the relation of means to end; it is proper to an intelligence. Hence the complete character of voluntary activity, endowed with deliberation and freedom, is found in rational nature alone. From imperfect appreciation of purpose there follows incomplete voluntary activity, the apprehension and spontaneous desire without deliberation which is typical of animals.

Under the philosophical jurisdiction of Aquinas, animals were granted souls, yet by the seventeenth century they had been relegated to the level of machines and René Descartes was responsible. Descartes (1596–1650), considered to be the father of modern philosophy, was perhaps a little too fond of royalty for his own good. He dedicated *Principles* to his young student, Princess Elizabeth of Palatine, and wrote *Passions of the Soul* in response to her criticism of his work. At the height of his success he took up an appointment as tutor to Queen Christina of Sweden. This was somewhat foolish since he had done the best part of his thinking in a large oven; in the middle of winter, during his early morning discussions with the Queen, he caught a chill which proved fatal.

In his *Discourse on Method* Descartes wrote that, as theological errors go, 'There is none more powerful in leading feeble minds astray from the straight path of virtue than the supposition that the soul of a brute is of the same nature with our own.' Feeble minds beware!

All this talk of souls may seem confusing or even irrelevant to us now, but to medieval and contemporary scholastics alike it was important. If an animal had a soul, it meant that even creatures such as ants would be allowed through the pearly gates and onwards to immortality. It was felt that those who needed to be kept on the straight and narrow by the enticement of the afterlife would somehow see heaven diminished if ants and earwigs were also to have their souls weighed.

In Descartes's opinion, the soul was the seat of consciousness, capable of thinking, doubting and feeling. Descartes believed so firmly that animals lacked souls that he dissected some animals while they were still alive. However, his dissections only served to show how similar we are to animals both physiologically and anatomically. Despite this empirical evidence, he concluded that only humans are conscious and rational, thus his only possible escape from this self-inflicted tautology was to continue to claim that we have a soul and animals do not.

Descartes also argued that animals have no soul using the following analogy: if the mechanical canaries fashionable at the time could be created by human industry, then surely God in his wisdom could do a better job? A real canary would be flawless compared to human replicas yet it would still be no more than an upmarket machine. He reasoned that if a mechanical ape and a mechanical person were constructed, one would not be able to tell the difference between the animal and the machine, but there would be a difference between a person and the machine. The android would fail two tests: it would react to knowledge on the basis of its design and without showing any creative reasoning and it would not be able to sustain a conversation with a person. Descartes was thus the real progenitor of the Turing Test.

Finally, Descartes believed animals were soulless because they couldn't speak and converse properly with people. In spite of this, he didn't deny that extraterrestrial life might prove to be conscious: 'I do not [. . .] infer that there are intelligent creatures in the stars or elsewhere; but I do not see that there are any grounds on which one could prove that there are not.'

Descartes left a two-pronged legacy: the first part was his definition of animals as automatons; the second, his famous division of mind and matter into two separate entities. The damage which Descartes wrought ought not to be underestimated. For nearly 300 years Western philosophers and scientists have struggled to unify bodies and brains and exorcise the ghost of Descartes. Furthermore, his theory on animal capabilities ultimately paved the way for the behaviourists, who treated animals as if they were machines.

This is not to say that Descartes had no contemporary critics. Fellow philosopher Hobbes accused Descartes of publishing 'old stuff' and in reply to the oft-quoted dictum, 'I think therefore I am', Thomas Hobbes replied,

> It seems not to be a valid argument to say, 'I am conscious therefore I am consciousness', or 'I am intelligent, therefore I am an intellect'. For I might as well say, 'I am walking, therefore I am a walk'.

Philosophers after Descartes tended to pay less attention to physiology and more attention to the mind, though few were willing to treat animals as thinking, rational beings. The philosopher, John Locke (1632–1704), is perhaps best remembered in psychology for his concept of a *tabula rasa* (literally, a smooth or blank tablet). The minds of animals and humans were compared by Locke to blank boards upon which their mental life could be written. He believed that knowledge was determined by the accumulation of experience rather than by innately determined rules. It all depended on the quality of your sense organs: quality goods allowed you to accumulate greater knowledge. For instance, cockles and oysters have little in the way of sense organs, therefore, according to Locke, they must be dull. He went on to add that as people aged and their sense organs deteriorated, there was nothing to distinguish them from a cockle.

Locke also allowed animals perception, sense and a modicum of reason. 'Brutes have memory,' he said. But what distinguished people from animals was the capacity for abstract thought. 'Brutes abstract not,' he maintained. A piece of chalk does not conjure up in animals associated ideas of white objects, such as cliffs, cheese and the moon.

A contemporary of Locke, Gottfried Wilhelm Leibniz (1646–1716), lost heart in his own work when Locke died. Leibniz had been on the verge of publishing, but ceased work on the manuscript after Locke's death for he said that his main purpose had been to elicit a response from Locke and it was cowardly to publish criticism when the dead man could not defend himself. *New Essays on Human Understanding* did not appear in print until half a century after his own death.

Leibniz disagreed with Locke: he thought that animals were not able to reason.

> The sequences of beasts are only a shadow of reasoning, that is, they are nothing but a connection in the imagination – a passage from one image to another; for when a new situation appears similar to its predecessor, it is expected to have the same concomitant features as before, as though things were linked in reality, just because their images are linked in the memory. It is true, moreover, that reason counsels us to expect ordinarily that what we find in the future will conform to long experience of the past; but even so, this is no necessary and infallible truth, and it can fail us when we least expect it to.

Guided only by their senses, animals were able to feel simple emotions such as anger because a 'violent effort to rid oneself of evil' was an intense emotion that needed no thought. Animals, according to Leibniz, could not think because thinking required an ability to reflect; animals only perceived events. Leibniz said that even if animals could speak, they would not have language; language was what gave us our reason by allowing us the capacity to reflect. Without language, we would be no more than beasts. Leibniz's idea that animals link one image with another is a good analogy for learning by conditioning. So, for example, when a man raises a stick above a dog, the dog anticipates that he will be beaten because he has been hit before. 'The tracks followed by repeated movements of the animal's spirits "are worn into a smooth path",' says Locke, describing the way an animal's thoughts follow the same route in its mind between image and event. Quite possibly this 'smooth path' may also be the series of neural connections an electronic impulse will follow when triggered by the sight of a stick.

The last of the so-called Rationalists was born in 1711 in Edinburgh and was a disappointment to his family who wanted their son, David Hume, to become a lawyer. Three months of this pursuit were enough to make the young man quit. He left for France determined to live frugally so that he could realise his dream of becoming a philosopher. By the time he was twenty-six he'd already published his most famous work, *A Treatise of Human Nature*. It sank almost without trace, but did slightly better when he republished it as *An Inquiry Concerning Human Understanding*.

Hume divided human knowledge into two categories: Relations of Ideas, and Matters of Fact. Some knowledge can be grasped simply by thinking, but most falls into the Matters of Fact category and is based on what Hume termed 'cause and effect'. By this he meant all instances where one deduced something from an experience. Almost all knowledge is derived from our past experiences: 'All inferences from experience, therefore, are effects of custom, not of reasoning [. . .] Without the influence of custom, we should be entirely ignorant of every matter of fact beyond what is immediately present to the memory and senses.'

If our knowledge is based on experience, this considerably reduces the gap between humans and animals. Hume said, 'No truth appears to me more evident than that beasts are endow'd with thought and reason as well as men.' However, although he believed that animals had a richer mental life than Locke or Leibniz granted them, he was not prepared to allow animals a large capacity to reason.

Hume maintained that the understanding of human mental capacity would be considerably strengthened if similar phenomena were studied in animals, so foreshadowing the burgeoning field of animal psychology.

First, it seems evident that animals as well as men learn many things from experience and infer that the same events will always follow the same causes [. . .] This is still more evident from the effects of discipline and education on animals, who, by the proper application of rewards and punishments, may be taught any course of action and most contrary to their natural instincts and propensities [. . .] The animal infers some fact beyond what immediately strikes his sense and this inference is altogether founded on past experience.

According to Hume, reason plays little part in animal or child cognition, nor in most people's everyday life for that matter. He did allow that instinct could govern much of animal and, indeed, some human knowledge, but he was quite adamant about the relation between human and animal thought. It was, he said, based on the same mechanisms and thus human superiorities were merely a matter of degree. In *A Treatise of Human Nature* he argued that pride, humility, love, hatred, fear, anger, courage, grief, envy, malice and 'other affections' exist in animals and that 'the causes of these passions are likewise much the same in the beast as in us'. This is a strong claim for a common biological basis underlying both human and animal behaviour, though he added that emotions such as pity, envy and malice are rarely found in animals because these require a greater effort of thought and imagination.

Another philosopher whose ideas are relevant to current scientific practice is Arthur Schopenhauer (1788–1860). He coined the word 'motivation', which is now applied with increasing frequency to robots (see chapter nine). He believed that one could arrive at a complete knowledge of the consciousness of animals by selecting a limited set of characteristics which would highlight the major differences between the human and animal mind. Schopenhauer, somewhat unoriginally, postulated that the main difference between us and other animals was language: 'It is by the help of language alone that reason accomplishes its most important achievements.' Another major difference between the human and animal mind was the ability to think in abstract terms. According to Schopenhauer, animals live in the present and are incapable of reflecting on past and future events. As Ludwig Wittgenstein said, 'We say a dog is afraid his master will beat him; but not he is afraid his master will beat him tomorrow.' Schopenhauer did think, however, that primates, poodles and elephants were capable of some degree of intelligence. His poodle, World-Soul, appeared to have a memory of past events. Schopenhauer recounted his pet's perplexity when

27

the philosopher bought a new pair of curtains that opened by pulling a cord. The poodle sat and watched the curtains as if wondering how they opened.

Schopenhauer was particularly fond of elephants, perhaps because of his erroneous belief that they lived to be 200 and so had sufficient time to exercise their mind. Schopenhauer was delighted to find that elephants did indeed never forget. A report from Morpeth in the *Spectator* on 27 August 1830 described how zoo-keeper Baptist Bernhard had been seized and crushed by an elephant for an offence against the elephant committed two years previously.

Karl Raimund Popper (1902–1994) was the first philosopher to put forward a theory approximating to modern cognitive science, albeit unintentionally. Although he believed, like Descartes, that something over and above brain activity is necessary for thought, he postulated a psychological category, outside the realm of human thought, which is potentially open to animals. He divided the world into three: world one is the brain; world two is subjective consciousness; and world three contains ideas derived from physical products of human societies. Hence an idea can be found in a book in world three and can live independently of any human mind perceiving that idea. He allowed animals to attain level two and have rudimentary mental events, but denied them entrance to world three. For all we know, he might have been too hasty since chimpanzees might have mental representations of the tools they use to crack nuts, fish for termites and those they employ to soak up water and act as napkins. They also leave their tools where they can find them the next day. The philosopher John Searle's distinction between 'brute' and 'institutional' facts may be of some relevance here. Searle (1936–), a philosopher from the University of California, Berkeley, maintained that brute facts are physical or mental data or relationships that do not depend on social rules, whereas institutional facts are rules embedded within a social context. For instance, a brute fact about a honey-bee is that a bee with a stomach full of two molar sucrose recruited seventy-seven of her sisters by a waggle dance ninety degrees to the vertical. This makes no sense unless one knows the social rules that provide a framework within which these actions become meaningful: the dances are a way of recruiting bees and each step of the dance tells the other bees where to find nectar and how plentiful it is. These social behaviours are, in a sense, ideas derived from the physical world. Furthermore, animals may not leave behind books, televisions and cigarette butts, but chimpanzee tools, bower birds' nests and beehives can live on independently of any individual animal mind.

So, after St Thomas Aquinas, things had taken a turn for the worse for animals. Soulful and sensitive, they had became little more than automatons. Descartes had granted them nothing, and the Aristotelian and medieval scholastic tradition had viewed reason as the boundary between human and animal thought. David Hume thought there was a continuity between us and other animals, a difference in degree and not of kind, but other contemporary philosophers saw a huge gap between animals and humans simply because animals could not speak. In the new science, psychology, the behaviourist Burrhus Frederic Skinner (1904–90) treated animals as if they were machines. He also thought that people clung to illusions of free-will when their destiny was merely controlled by the environment and their past life.

It was not until the 1970s and 1980s that it became acceptable once more to speak about animal consciousness. Two of the main exponents whom we are going to look at are a biologist who became philosophical, Donald Griffen (his original claim to fame was as the discoverer of bat echolocation in 1958), and a philosopher, Thomas Nagel, who wanted to know what it felt like to be a bat.

Griffen believed that if an animal subjectively thinks about objects and events it is possible that it experiences a simple level of consciousness. Since an animal's body is a prominent feature in its own world and contributes enormously to sensory input, it seems likely that if animals are conscious, they are conscious of their own bodies and to this extent are self-aware. Many scientists require an animal to be self-reflective in order to say that it has self-awareness, in other words, to know that 'It is I who am smelling that food'. Griffen argued that we should leave this question aside until simpler levels of consciousness are proven. He said that,

If we allow a particular animal to be aware of a reasonably wide range of objects, events and relationships in the world around it, while denying the possibility of self-awareness, we run the danger of redefining self-awareness in a roundabout way as a sort of perceived hole in the universe.

He added that self-awareness is assumed to be a trait possessed only by our own species, but that direct evidence for this is almost non-existent.

According to strict behaviourists, it is safer to explain animal behaviour without postulating that animals have any mental experiences. Griffen has two arguments against this idea. The first is the argument from the point of view of physiology. Neurophysiology has so far discovered no fundamental differences between the structure or function of neurons or synapses in humans and other animals. Thus, unless one denies the reality of human mental experiences, Griffen believes that it is more logical to assume that mental events are as similar from species to species as the neurological processes are. This implies a continuity, though not an identity, of mental experiences among multicellular animals.

Griffen's second argument comes from his belief that to suggest that mental experiences are a unique attribute of a single species is not only an unlikely proposition, it is conceited.

The ability to think about the probable results of alternative actions and to choose the one most likely to achieve a desired result is especially valuable when animals face unpredictable problems in carrying out important activities such as obtaining food, avoiding predators or other hazards, seeking mates or raising young.

As Popper says, a foolish impulse can die in an animal's head rather than lead it to needless suicide.

To deal with Griffen's first point: he claims that because neurophysiology is basically similar throughout the animal kingdom, there is a continuity of mental experience. In essence, what matters most is our *reactions* to outside forces. We do not fully understand the neurological basis for the acquisition of knowledge, nor what structural similarities or differences in the brains of various species might entail. Even if we knew how a person would react when their brain was in state X, it does not necessarily follow that another animal whose same portion of the brain is in state X will either react in the same way or feel the same way.

Although it is likely that there is a continuity of mental experiences between us and mammals, this does not mean that this exists in other animals. This is not to say that a squid, for example, may not be highly intelligent or does not possess a form of consciousness, but the empathy we have for mammals derives from experiences that we know we share, such as mate bonding, social bonding, suckling of young and care of offspring, and because in many cases we inhabit a very similar environment. This is probably a failing – albeit a reasonable one – on our part: we can't imagine what it is like to be a squid. We do suffer from a failure of the imagination when it comes to mammals, such as dolphins and whales, which live in a radically different environment, but it is probably fair to say that we find it easier to identify with them than with creatures like the squid that are so radically different. Hence, I would argue that the mental experiences of animals that are very different from ourselves and which live in completely different environments are not going to be continuous with ours. I do not deny, though, that they may be as likely to have mental experiences as mammals are.

Finally, although we may have evolved from the same ancestral stock, there may not be a linear progression in mental continuity between us and other animals. In Griffen's defence, however, I would like to say that as a species, one of our limitations is in dealing with gradation: we like to see things in black and white with neat cut-off points, preferably between us and other animals. Should someone discover or recreate our recent ancestors, I think we would be faced with serious ethical problems precisely because of this general inability.

Griffen's second point is that it is unlikely that consciousness evolved only once. The brief response is: not necessarily and it depends on what is meant by consciousness. It is unclear whether and in how many species (other than in ourselves) a high level of self-reflective consciousness has evolved. The absence of animals as obviously intelligent as ourselves suggests that higher-level consciousness is not a definite possibility in evolution (unlike, say, limbs for locomotion in land-living animals) and that consciousness may be costly to run (our brains use a fifth of our total daily energy budget). However, what more open-minded research is now showing us is that there is a patchwork mosaic of higher consciousness in animals, with some birds, such as parrots, and mammals, such as primates, dolphins and whales, visibly demonstrating advanced levels of intelligence.

When the philosopher Thomas Nagel looked at the problem of what goes on in other minds, he decided to examine a bat. Nagel could have chosen any animal but he picked one close enough to us (a mammal) for us to empathise with it and distant enough for us to have very little conception of its subjective experience, since, for example, we have no idea how it feels to echolocate. Bats, like whales and dolphins, 'see' and communicate by making sounds and listening to the echo as the sound bounces back from objects and other animals. In his paper written in 1974 and entitled, 'What is it like to be a bat?', he asks us to imagine just that. He does not ask what is it like for us to imagine what it is like to be a bat, but rather, what is it like for the *bat* to be a bat. The somewhat depressing answer is that we can't imagine what it is like.

Nagel also points out a major flaw in what he termed 'reductionist euphoria'. Scientists and philosophers alike, when dealing with the experiences of people and animals, leave out the subjective quality of experience:

> . . . no matter how the form may vary, the fact that an organism has conscious experience *at all* means, basically, that there is something it is like to *be* that organism [. . .] We may call this the subjective character of experience.

He adds that even though we cannot accommodate a detailed description of a bat's experience, or even an alien's, this does not mean that we can claim that bats and aliens do not have experiences as rich as our own. Using a reductionist and objective criterion, by definition, something is left out and this is the subjective character of experience. It is precisely this quality that we cannot afford to lose since it is the subjectivity of mental states that makes them what they are. Nagel does not, as one might at first expect, refute this 'reductionist euphoria'; instead he hopes the dilemma will be solved by creating an objective classification of subjectivity.

In the Nagel sense, we never can know what it is like to be a bat. We cannot even know what it is like to be another human, especially someone who has very different experiences from ourselves, such as a blind person. We can never be another person and the workings of someone else's mind will always remain opaque to us. Whilst we can appreciate the philosophical intractability of this problem, at the same time, we do know what other people think, particularly those close to us. Human society could not function if all we could do was speculate wildly on other people's thoughts and feelings. Instead we use folk psychology to determine other people's thoughts on a day-to-day basis.

Folk psychology is the common sense yet immensely rich structure of laws and generalisations which explain pain, belief and desire. To understand another person we tend to describe them in psychological terms; we give them beliefs and desires depending on their background and what we know of their personality and from this we predict how they would react given the circumstances they find themselves in and the mental states we have attributed to them. Because beliefs and desires are the main psychological components of a rational being, folk psychology is often dubbed belief-desire psychology, but it is different from Theory of Mind. Theory of Mind refers to mental states which are intensely personal and private; folk psychology explains the physical behaviour people display by referring to what we believe is going on inside their head. The names of and motivations for mental states will differ between cultures according to folk psychology, but these words describe pre-existing categories of behaviour which occur in most humans, and which may also be seen in animals. Folk psychology, therefore, enables us to determine, to a certain extent, what is going on in the minds of animals, provided we also take into consideration the specific nature of the species in question.

Folk psychology follows what is known as soft functionalism. This is the belief that brain states produce mental states, but, using an analogy from computer terminology, the underlying hardware need not be the same as the resultant software. My friend and I might both have the same desire to go for a walk, but this does not mean that our brains are in identical states; similarly, if I play chess with a computer, the computer and I might both 'believe' that if it moves its king, the outcome will be checkmate. However, my brain and the computer's silicon chip will not be in the same state. Nor do I think that the advent of optical programming or 'wet-ware' will change this state of affairs.

Folk psychology does have critics, in particular Pat Churchland from the University of California, San Diego, who would rather see the mind explained purely in neural terminology. She believes this cannot yet be done, but wishes research to be directed towards this end. There are two main arguments against this. The first is Nagel's point: neuroscience, even if sufficiently advanced, can never truly comprehend what it is like to have a sensation, for that requires the ability to have the sensation. Second, when we interpret another person, we do so using our knowledge of their psychology and their outward behaviour. We do not interpret their actions using neurological terminology. A person can get angry, but a brain can't. Emotions are personal not neurological. Studying the mind simply in terms of neurology is analogous to the human genome project. Whatever the rights or wrongs of spending many years and large sums of money on mapping the 'average' person's genes, the results are unlikely to tell us, as some would claim, what that person is like, nor will they reveal what it is to be human.

One tool we can use to pry open both the minds of animals and people, and which is an inherent part of folk psychology, is that of intentionality, a theory first put forward by Daniel Dennett. Dennett's ideas were initially formulated in the 1970s and dealt with 'intentional systems' – thinking, believing, desiring, goal-orientated creatures. In the previous chapter we discussed Dennett's levels of intentionality and how they form the backbone of Theory of Mind. Dennett didn't realise it, but his work was going to become hugely influential in the study of psychology and would immensely further our understanding of our own species as well as expand our knowledge of the animal mind.

Ten years after publication of his first paper about intentionality, Dennett read an account in a scientific journal written by primatologists Robert Seyfarth and Dorothy Cheney and bird song expert, Peter Marler, about an African monkey.

Vervet monkeys give different alarm calls to different predators. Recordings of the alarms played back when predators were absent caused the monkeys to run into the trees for leopard alarms, look up for eagle alarms, and look down for snake alarms.

Dennett found this tantalising. Were the vervets using language? Did they mean what they said? Were they more intelligent than other species because of their 'linguistic' talents? What was going on in their heads? He believed that the everyday language of belief and desire could be used as a precise mechanism for uncovering the vervets' intellectual abilities, their Theory of Mind. In chapter five we will discuss the vervets and their natural language more thoroughly.

Suffice to say, Dennett was sufficiently motivated to get out of the armchair and into the African bush. While he was in Kenya with Cheney and Seyfarth they studied what they called the MIO – Moving Into the Open – grunt. Shortly before a monkey moves out from under cover, he or she gives the MIO and as often as not, it will be repeated by others. The second monkey may remain behind for a further five to ten minutes before repeating the MIO and moving cautiously into the open. What does it mean? The team thought it might be a request for permission:

May I go, please?

Yes, you have my permission.

But then higher-ranking monkeys usually give the grunt first and move out and they don't need permission from anyone. Dennett then thought it might be a command:

Follow me!

Aye, aye, Cap'n.

Dorothy Cheney didn't think this was very plausible.

The philosopher, wandering around under the baking African sun, in an unfamiliar environment, surrounded by an unfamiliar species, dealing with an unfamiliar field of science, said, 'I found myself tempted to indulge in a fantasy: "If only I were small enough to dress up in a vervet suit, or if only we could introduce a trained vervet, or a robot or a puppet vervet who could . . ." and slowly it dawned on me that this recurring escape from reality had a point: there is really no substitute [. . .] for going in and talking with the natives.'

In this book we are going to talk with the natives. Dennett wrote at the time,

> As a philosopher, an outsider with only a cursory introduction to the field of ethology, I find that the new ethologists, having cast off the strait-jacket of behaviourism and kicked off its weighted overshoes, are looking about somewhat insecurely for something presentable to wear.

Dennett's new suit is that of intentionality, and this is the tool we will use to ask the natives what they think and know and, by speaking to them wordlessly, we will decipher what is going on in the minds of new-born infants, young children, people suffering from autism and, ultimately, animals.

3

WINDOWS TO THE SOUL

. . . and in thy voice I catch
The language of my former heart, and read
My former pleasures in the shooting lights
Of thy wild eyes.
      William Wordsworth, 'Tintern Abbey'

Ralph Waldo Emerson, a nineteenth-century essayist, wrote in his book, *Conduct of Life*, 'The eyes of men converse as much as their tongues, with the advantage that the ocular dialect needs no dictionary, but is understood the world over [. . .] An eye can threaten like a loaded and levelled gun, or can insult like hissing or kicking: or in its altered mood, by beams of kindness, it can make the heart dance with joy.'

Eyes are terribly important, they convey a wealth of emotion. Think of the old silent films: even without words they are easily understood. Charlie Chaplin was one of the first people to use close-ups in cinema. He deliberately decided to employ this novel camera technique because he wanted people to see the emotion in his face and knew that they could understand what he was thinking by seeing his expression. Bizarrely enough, cinema goers were horrified. They thought that because the film had shown a shot of the whole of Charlie from his head to his toes and then cut to a close-up of his face, he'd suddenly turned into a giant.

But there is something that is even more basic to understanding someone's mind than seeing the expression on his or her face and, without this ability, we would never be able to understand silent films, let alone 'talkies', nor be able to look at cartoons, read books, or even – and most importantly – know how to interact with each other. Before we look at how we begin to understand the mind through the language of the eyes, we need to turn to this very basic skill. It's known as ID (pronounced like the Freudian one). Short for Intentionality Detector, it's a concept first described by child psychologist Simon Baron-Cohen of Cambridge University. ID is primitive. It is activated whenever we see something with a self-propelled motion. We, as do other animals, instantly interpret a moving object as if it were motivated by a rational goal. No matter what the object — be it a person, a dog, an amoeba, a triangle or a billiard ball — if it moves by itself, we treat it as if it is an animate agent with its own set of goals.

You might find it difficult to believe that we could treat a billiard ball as if it were rational, but think about how human society operates. We constantly refer to objects as if they have thoughts, beliefs and desires. Many of our religious systems operate by bestowing human-like properties on to objects. The Hindus of Java believe that Brahma created the world and that he dwells in the heart of a volcano: Mount Bromo. Every year, lest he should over-whelm the island with legions of fire gods in his anger at his subjects' forgetfulness, they worship him by throwing food into the crater. A slight shift in the earth's crust and Mount Bromo would erupt in fiery lava — and the molten rock would be interpreted as Brahma's wrath. As children, we have nightmares because the shadow on the ceiling looks, not like an innocuous black shape, but like a monster who will come and get us while we sleep. We also treat pets as if they understand us and we understand them, as in the Gary Larson cartoon, 'What we say to dogs'. The cartoon shows the dog's owner talking to his dog. Underneath the picture we read 'What the dog hears': meaningless noise and in the middle of this verbal nonsense, the word 'Ginger'.

Because ID is so basic and because anything that moves of its own accord could be treated like a rational agent, it means that there is a danger of over-attribution: as very young children we might think that clouds want to get from one side of the sky to the other until we learn better. But it is precisely this over-generalisation of ID that is its strength. If you are a gazelle, it is better to take note of a moving black shape at the corner of the waterhole: if it turns out to be a shadow, well and good, but if the shape is a crouching cheetah, ignoring it could mean the difference between life and death.

As long ago as 1944, two scientists, Fritz Heider and Marianne Simmel, then at the Smith Institute in America, conducted an experiment where they showed a silent film to people. In the film, geometric shapes moved around and the scientists asked the onlookers to describe what they saw. Most of the people interpreted what amounted to two triangles and a circle in a rectangle as if the shapes had motivation and rational goals. A typical viewer began by saying, 'A man has planned to meet a girl and the girl comes along with another man. The first man tells the second to go . . . he shakes his head. The two men have a fight, and the girl starts to go into the room to get out of the way . . .' However, one person described the whole thing in geometric terms: 'A large triangle is shown entering a rectangle. It enters and comes out of this rectangle and each time the corner and one-half of one of the sides of the rectangle form an opening . . .' and so on in a rather dull fashion. Most people find it easier to treat self-propelled objects *as if* they have goals and to talk about them using terms that describe their motivation, such as 'tells', 'plans', 'leaves', 'wants'. This is not to say that people really believe that the triangle truly harbours lust in its pointed breast for the smooth curve of the circle, but ascribing motivation to moving objects is a skill so basic we may be born with it, or at least the ability to develop ID at a very early age.

Gyorgy Gergely, a psychologist from the Hungarian Academy of Sciences in Budapest, proved that children as young as a year old have this same skill. The infants interpreted geometric shapes as if they were rational agents with goals and the children had an expectation about how these simple shapes were supposed to obtain their goal. Gergely used an elegant and deceptively simple experimental procedure. He showed the babies geometric shapes following certain sequences of actions on a computer screen until the infants were habituated (until they were so bored by seeing the same thing over and over again that they took no more notice and no longer looked at the computer screen). The infants were shown a large circle and a small one with a rectangle in between the two. The large circle expanded and contracted, then the small circle expanded and contracted, and so on, the two circles taking it in turns to change their size. The small circle then moved towards the big circle, jumped over the rectangle that was between them, continued to approach the big circle, touched it and they began their expansion-contraction routine again.

Adults who watched this sequence typically interpreted it in the following way: the large circle, the mother, is calling her baby, the small circle, to come to her. The baby responds and starts running towards her mother, but stops when she sees an obstacle. She retreats, but this time jumps over the obstacle and when she finally reaches her mother they hug and kiss happily. This way of explaining the sequence also makes it easier for most people to visualise what is going on.

Once the young infants had seen this sequence, they were divided into two groups and shown the same set of events, but with a slight variation. Both groups saw a small circle and a large circle on either side of the screen, but this time the rectangle was behind the small circle instead of between the circles. One group of infants watched the small circle head straight towards the large circle – which is logical, if the goal of the small circle is to be by the big circle and there is no obstacle in the way. But the second group of infants were shown the small circle make exactly the same movements as those the infants were shown first. The small circle jumped before it approached the large circle, even though there was nothing to jump over. The infants who were watching this were more surprised by the second type of behaviour – for what is the point of jumping when all the small circle has to do is go straight towards the large circle? – and they dishabituated (they started to look at the screen again). What is more, the babies looked for longer at this version of events than at the logical sequence. Now, the 'logical' sequence is only logical if you think these shapes have motives and goals. Since the shapes have no goals and motives of their own, it would make perfect sense for either of these scenarios to take place – for the small circle to get from one side of the screen to the other by heading straight towards its destination or by leaping once. The fact that the babies were surprised at the 'behaviour' of the shapes indicates that at this very young age they already have an awareness of moving objects as beings that have goals and which 'want' to achieve their goals in a rational manner.

ID is basic, yet it is also a crucial skill. Without it we would treat people as if they were objects lacking rational goals and desires. ID is linked to another very primitive function: causality. Causality is understanding that one thing causes another and, like ID, is a necessary first step towards acquiring a Theory of Mind. In the physical world, causality is the ability to understand that your action causes an effect, that if you push a vase of flowers, they will fall over.

The Scottish philosopher, David Hume, believed that we understood causality by applying our past experiences. After we've watched several causal sequences, we learn to recognise them. For example, after seeing a ball hit a bottle and knock it over on a number of occasions, we would understand that balls were capable of causing other objects to fall. The famous Swiss child psychologist Jean Piaget argued that we understand cause and effect by knocking over bottles with balls ourselves rather than watching it happen. In the sixties, scientist Albert Michotte disagreed with both men. He argued that understanding causality was not something you had to learn, it was an understanding you were born with. However, it was not until the 1980s that anyone got out of their armchair to test these ideas. Alan Leslie, a psychologist from Rutgers University, Piscataway, showed that babies do have the ability to understand causality and that this skill is in place in seven-month-old infants. His experiments proved that both Piaget and Hume were wrong, since babies of such a tender age will have had very little experience of watching causal events or of making them happen for themselves.

Leslie constructed an experiment which was very similar to the one that Gergely used but instead of showing children computer animations of geometric shapes, he played them film clips which were on a continuous loop, so the children saw the same clip over and over again until they became bored and looked away. They were then shown a similar clip on a continuous loop and timed to see how long it would take for them to become bored again. One film clip was of a Russian doll sitting on a table. A hand appeared, picked up the doll and removed it from the field of view. The hand *causes* the doll to move. The next sequence showed the doll and a hand appearing at the top of the screen to pick it up as before, but this time both doll and hand disappeared without the hand touching the doll. Here there is no *cause*, the doll moves as if by magic (in reality, of course, there was a cause: Alan Leslie tugging a piece of thread wrapped round the doll).

The children, no longer interested by the hand picking up the doll, found this floating doll rather more surprising and suddenly started watching intently. Of course, this could mean that the babies were reacting to the novelty of the new film clip. Leslie got round this problem by dividing the children into two groups. He showed one half of the children the doll-and-hand sequence first and the other half the floating-doll sequence first. Both groups were then shown the film they had not already watched. The infants who were shown the odd sequence first, the floating-doll, took a long time to habituate to it, which implies that they thought there was something strange about it. When these babies were shown the second sequence, the doll-and-hand version, they very quickly became accustomed to it, as if they recognised that there was nothing unusual about this sequence. However, the children who saw this doll-and-hand sequence first got used to it very quickly, but took a long time to habituate to the strange sequence. This shows that very young babies recognise that one thing causes another and they find it odd to see things happening without any apparent cause.

I repeated this experiment with chimpanzees, bonobos (pygmy chimpanzees) and spider monkeys, but I used a banana instead of a doll. The chimpanzees and bonobos reacted in exactly the same way as the children. They looked for longer when they were shown the strange sequence with the banana floating into space after a disembodied hand. The animals that had seen this version of the film first hardly looked at the proper sequence where the hand grasped the banana, as if these events were banal because this was what they had expected to happen. However, the spider monkeys looked for the same amount of time no matter which film clip they were shown and it did not seem to matter in what order the films were presented to them. In fact, few of the monkeys looked at the television screen for more than a few seconds and most would not watch it at all.

I tried another experiment along the same lines, which did not work, but for a rather interesting reason. This film – the causal sequence – showed chimps hunting colobus monkeys and then capturing and killing one of the monkeys. The 'odd' version which had no cause showed the same film clip played in reverse, so that the dismembered colobus monkey reassembled and ran off backwards into the forest. The chimps watched both versions for an equally long time and were far more engrossed in them than they had been in the banana film. The likely explanation is that they found watching other chimps hunting so inherently fascinating that either version was equally interesting to them and, indeed, many of the male chimps became exceptionally worked up: their hair stood on end, they swayed from side to side and they gave 'panthoots' – typical hunting and fighting calls.

A discussion of causality may seem like a sidetrack, but it is not. In the physical world, an object touching another object will cause an effect in the second object, be it to smash that object, make it fall, make it stick, and so on. As we have seen, this understanding of causality seems to be present in our cousins the chimpanzees and in very young children. Causality also operates in the mental world. Here we are not dealing with causes that derive from physical force, but causes that are based on the transmission of information. Knowing what another person knows will lead one to predict how that information might cause him or her to react. This is an ability which young children and possibly most animals do possess and we shall deal with this in chapter five. However, without an initial understanding of cause and effect in the physical domain, it is unlikely that this more complex type of understanding could develop.

These two abilities, ID (reacting as if objects, animals and people have goals that they strive to obtain) and causality (understanding that a person's or an object's action can affect another object or a person) are the first and most basic steps towards understanding what goes on in other people's minds. However, having either of these abilities does not mean that you automatically understand other minds, rather ID and causality are the foundation stones of Theory of Mind. Whilst these abilities are special, it is likely that they are innate; in other words, babies and chimpanzees are born with the ability to develop these skills without any understanding of why they react in this way. This ability probably shows no more conscious understanding in animals and young children than does a reflex action (a reflex action is an involuntary movement, such as rapidly withdrawing your hand if you touch a hot stove).

The next stage in the development of Theory of Mind is under-standing the language of the eyes. The old saying 'Eyes are windows to the soul' is not far from the truth. When someone stares directly into your eyes, your heart rate increases as does the electrical activity in your brain. The effect of direct eye contact is so intense that we normally only stare directly at a person who is staring back at us in one of two situations: either when we're incredibly angry, or when we're in love. As Shakespeare said in *Love's Labour's Lost*, 'A lover's eyes will gaze an eagle blind'.

We are often acutely aware when someone is looking at us. Imagine that you are in a café having coffee on your own, when you suddenly feel strange. You look up quickly and, sure enough, someone is staring at you, but as soon as you look at them, they turn away and usually both of you are left feeling uncomfortable. It is such a common experience it has even been written about in novels. 'Mr Phunky, blushing to the very whites of his eyes, tried to look as if he didn't know that everybody was gazing at him, a thing which no man ever succeeded in doing yet or, in all reasonable probability, ever will,' wrote Charles Dickens in *The Pickwick Papers*.

There are very good reasons why we should be able to tell where other people are looking. It is an old phenomenon and one which evolved millions of years before humans appeared on earth. Reptiles, the oldest living creatures in the world, are well aware of eyes. There haven't been too many studies on detection of eye gaze in reptiles, but snakes are supposed to be particularly sensitive to eye direction. If you stare at a hog-nosed snake from a distance of about a metre, it will feign death. The death-feigning behaviour only occurs if you are actually staring at the snake, standing quietly and looking away is a little worrying to the snake, but doesn't cause it enough anxiety to make it play dead. The idea is that a predator will not want to eat a dead creature. Even butterflies, which evolved forty million years ago, have adapted their wing patterns to fool predators. Many butterflies, such as the owl butterfly – which has wings patterned like an owl's face – flash wing spots shaped like eyes. The eyes are often very large and trick the predator into thinking that the butterfly is a much larger and more frightening creature than it really is. If this doesn't work, then, at the very least, the predator will attempt to grab the tip of the wings, thinking that is the head region. A butterfly can survive with nicked wings, but not with its head bitten off.

Some animals show tonic immobility. Like the Medusa effect, a stare freezes them and they cannot move until the intruder has stopped gazing at them. Lizards, chickens, blue crabs and ducks, amongst other animals, adopt this frozen posture when they're stared at. It's a bit like playing grandmother's footsteps – if they hold still, they blend into the background – but as soon as they move, they're out and eaten.

In primates, a direct gaze is a threat. Macaque monkeys look less at slides of faces where the eyes are staring at them than ones where the eyes are looking away. Infant macaques are more disturbed when they see pictures of a full face staring at them than when the face is in profile with the eyes averted.

Monkeys and apes know all about rank: their societies are the embodiment of the proverbial pecking order. One individual is usually the most dominant and all the others descend in a scale of dominance and subordination from him. The most dominant animal normally is a male, although macaques are unusual because the females are more dominant. Baby macaques adopt their mother's rank, so if its mother is high-ranking, the new-born will automatically rank higher than another older monkey whose mother is subordinate, or lower-ranking, to the baby's mother. Incidentally, it was the Japanese who first figured out monkey hierarchies, aided, no doubt, by the fact that in Japanese society at the time rank was of overriding importance.

In a monkey show-down, both aggressors will stare directly into the eyes of their opponent until one backs down by looking away. When a dominant individual looks at a monkey who is subordinate to him, and the subordinate does not want to challenge the dominant individual, he or she will usually make appeasement gestures: in macaques this consists of smacking their lips together and chattering their teeth.

In the late sixties, primatologist Michael Chance noticed that eyes were the key to understanding this social network in monkeys and apes. Every individual monitors other individuals, but in a specific way. The most important thing that Chance noted was that primates pay more attention to those animals who rank slightly above them than to those who are lower down the scale. 'The chain of attention [acts] within the group, each individual is linked to the one above in his status class by the attention he pays to him [. . .] focused via intermediate links to the dominant male.' The only way to become more dominant in monkey society is to take over the position in the hierarchy directly above you, but at the same time, until you are ready for a confrontation, it is best to stay out of trouble. Gaze therefore plays a vital role in primate groups, and we too are primates.

Imagine the following scenario: Alex is a newcomer to the scene, but he would very much like to make Thalia's acquaintance.

Alex stared at Thalia until she turned and almost caught him looking at her. He glanced away immediately and then she stared at him until his head began to turn towards her. She [looked at the ground], but as soon as Alex looked away, her gaze returned to him. They went on like this for more than fifteen minutes, always with split-second timing. Finally, Alex managed to catch

Thalia looking at him [. . .] Thalia froze and for a second she looked into his eyes.

Six years after this initial encounter, these two were still firm friends. It might sound like two people in a singles bar, but Alex and Thalia are olive baboons, which live a hundred miles north of Nairobi along the Great Rift Valley and this encounter took place while they were being watched by primatologist, Barbera Smuts, from the University of Michigan.

The evolutionary reason why you should take very good care to detect eye gaze is because when another animal is looking at you it can mean one of the three 'F's. Either that animal wants to fight you, feed on you, or mate with you. This ability to concentrate intensely on the eyes has led to what Simon Baron-Cohen terms EDD – Eye-Direction Detector. This is a mechanism in the brain that allows animals to do three things: first, detect the presence of eyes (or what look like eyes, such as the butterfly's wing spots); second, detect eye movements (whether the eyes are directed towards the watching animal or towards something else); and, finally, to interpret gaze as seeing. This last point seems very obvious, but it isn't. It is one thing to feel that someone is looking at you from across a crowded café; it is quite another to know consciously that what they are seeing is you and to imagine what the room and you yourself look like from their perspective. We will return to this a little later.

The first thing that EDD does is to detect eye gaze. We know that animals are capable of this: the death-feigning hog-nosed snake and the blue crab frozen in a game of grandmother's footsteps, where survival is the prize, show their ability to detect a suspected predator's gaze. Babies as young as two months old pay more attention to the eyes than to any other feature in their mother's face. They may be attuned to their mother's eyes because it is innate behaviour, but eyes must seem very salient to them. A mother breast-feeding will quite unconsciously stare at her child for over half a minute at a time.

The second thing that EDD does is allow an animal to determine whether another animal is looking at them or not. Six-month-old infants spend two to three times as long looking at a face that is looking at them, than at one which is looking away. Simon Baron-Cohen and his colleague Pippa Cross have shown that three year olds can easily point to a picture of a child that is looking at them. The pictures they were shown were of children who were facing them and so the only clue was the eye direction.

Because of the dual role that eyes play – at the very basic level they show a love-hate relationship, for the starer is either angry or friendly – eye gaze has to be used in moderation. Too much staring makes young infants cry and too little upsets them because they are not getting enough attention or stimulation. This may be why people play peekaboo with infants which, as everyone knows, is all about hiding the eyes and then revealing them.

The final skill with which EDD equips us is the ability to interpret gaze as seeing. So far, all we have postulated is that an animal can tell eyes from things that aren't eyes and that animals and infants can determine whether they are being looked at or not. Interpreting that eyes are what you see with and that others can see, too, requires something a little more complex. The great apes seem to understand that you see with your eyes and they quite often play games. One of the chimpanzees that I studied, Flynn, used to walk upright across the equivalent of a tightrope strung across his cage with his hands over his eyes. Two young bonobos, Kichele and Jasongo, would swing from branch to branch of the trees in their enclosure with a paper bag over their heads – but they peeked every so often, just to get their bearings. Juan Carlos Gómez, a psychologist based at Stirling University, worked with a young gorilla in Madrid for a while. Muni would often play games with her sight: she put clothes over her head, or else held biscuit tins with shiny, reflective surfaces against her face so that she was completely dazzled. She would then try to run round her room. Gómez tries to explain the great apes' behaviour by saying, 'It is a game that has an understanding of vision; if they understand something about seeing, they can play with it.'

Great apes clearly understand something about vision, but do they have the ability to interpret gaze as seeing? This more complex aspect of visual behaviour is often called joint attention because it involves two people or two animals, both of whom need to understand what the other one is looking at. Babies can orientate themselves roughly in the direction in which an adult is staring by the time they are about six months old. It is not until two to three months later that they can easily turn their head and look in the same direction as the adult and not until they are about a year old that they can follow where another person is looking using that person's eye movements alone.

I conducted an experiment on chimpanzees, bonobos and spider monkeys to find out if they were able to do what these young infants could do – detect the direction of my gaze. I stood in front of each animal and looked into its eyes until it was staring at me and then very deliberately looked away to another object. I looked back to see if the animals were able to follow the movement of my eyes and determine what I was looking at. The bonobos and chimpanzees were able to do this, but none of the monkeys could. One of the bonobos was so curious about what I was looking at that he would walk down his cage in the direction I was staring and press himself flat against the glass in an attempt to get a better view.

A similar experiment was conducted by Daniel Povinelli and Timothy Eddy at the New Iberia Research Centre in South-West Louisiana. He used seven five- to six-year-old chimps. The chimps had to come in to the test area where they were separated from a human experimenter by a clear plexiglass panel with a hole cut out of it. The chimps had to go up to the glass and put one hand through (this up-turned palm gesture is typically used by chimpanzees when they want to beg food from other members of their group). The experimenter then gave them a biscuit. Once the chimps had got used to that, the experimenter would stare at the chimp as he came into the room and then would look either to the left or right of the chimp. The chimps would turn to see what the experimenter was looking at. This is complex behaviour because the chimp has to look over his shoulder to space that is not apparent by just looking straight in front of him. This is something that human infants can't do until they are about a year and a half old. For babies younger than this, it is as if the only part of the world that exists for them is what is right in front of their nose.

The next part of the experiment was more complicated. Half of the clear glass window was blocked off with a piece of wood so neither experimenter nor chimp could see through that section. A sticker was put on the glass in front of the wood on the side where the experimenter sat. When the chimp came in and begged for his biscuit, the experimenter looked at the sticker. The eye movement of the experimenter was still the same as it had been in the previous trials, only this time her gaze was blocked by the wooden panel so that she couldn't look into the chimp's cage behind the wooden partition. From the chimp's side, the sticker was not visible. Daniel Povinelli and Timothy Eddy thought that this gaze tracking behaviour shown by the chimps in the earlier part of the experiment was innate; in other words, it was such an automatic behaviour that they would unconsciously turn to see what a person or another chimp was looking at. This is important behaviour as we have said, because if a predator is approaching, there's some tasty food nearby or a dominant individual is heading for you, by monitoring where others are looking, you will get advance warning. But what the primatologists argued was that the chimpanzees had no under-standing of what they were doing. They were automatically looking, but they wouldn't understand that if a person or an animal looks in a certain direction, they are actually watching something. For them, there was no necessary connection between the two processes. So what they expected was that the chimps would turn to look behind them, as they always had, to see what the experimenter was looking at, without thinking that the experimenter could not see behind the chimps because her gaze was occluded by the wooden panel.

None of the chimpanzees showed their usual tracking behaviour. Not only did they not look over their shoulder, but, like the bonobos I studied, they came up to the partition and tried to squint along it to see what the experimenter could see that they could not.

The fact that children as young as nine months to a year and a half can understand that eyes are a real clue to what is going on has been shown by Simon Baron-Cohen and his colleagues Wendy Phillips and Mike Rutter. They demonstrated either an ambiguous or an unambiguous action for each child. In one ambiguous action, an adult cupped her hands over the child's hands whilst the child was playing with toys; in a second, the adult offered a toy to the child, but withdrew it just as the child began to reach for it. The unambiguous action was simply to give or to present an object to a child. On most trials, the infants immediately looked at the experimenter's eyes when faced with the ambiguous action, but few glanced up if the action was unambiguous. This suggests that when the goal of an action is uncertain, the first place young children look is at a person's eyes.

As we said earlier, joint attention is a complex piece of visual behaviour where two people or animals focus on what each one is attending to. It is divided into two types: dyadic and triadic joint attention. Detecting eye movement and where eyes are looking leads to dyadic representations. For example, my-sister-is-looking-at-me; the-lion-is-looking-at-a-tree. A representation, as we said in the introduction, is a mental picture of what is going on. The kind of representation that is happening in dyadic joint attention when a mother sits in front of her child and looks at a toy is either mother-looks-at-toy or child-looks-at-toy.

Triadic representations are mentally more complex. In this scenario, again, there are two individuals and an object. One individual – say, the father – looks at a toy gorilla lying on the floor and then over to his young son. The young boy sees that his father is looking at something, he looks down and he too sees the toy gorilla, then he looks back up to check that his father really was looking at the gorilla and that his father has seen him looking at the toy. This kind of checking behaviour, from the eyes of one individual and over to the object that individual is looking at, is crucial to triadic joint attention. Mentally, the child has a representation which is triadic or triangular because it involves the child himself, the toy gorilla and his father. The child thinks: I-see-that-Daddy-sees-the-gorilla; or: Daddy-sees-that-I-see-the-gorilla. Embedded within this mental picture the child has built up is the simpler dyadic representation:

(I-see-)Daddy-sees-the-gorilla. Simon Baron-Cohen was the first person to formulate joint attention in this way. As he says, 'A piece of knowledge about the eyes that young normal children possess is that people use their eyes to *communicate* their interest in something.'

Children are capable of this kind of checking behaviour (to see who is looking at what) by the time they are a year and a half old. This may be the kind of representation that the chimpanzees were using in Daniel Povinelli's experiment where the experimenter looked at the sticker and also when I looked into the distance and the chimps followed where I was looking. I conducted an observational study on the spider monkeys, chimpanzees and bonobos at Twycross Zoo to see how much of this kind of joint attention they used with one another. All three species showed dyadic attention. The problem was that, for the following reason, I could not show that they understood what was going on in each other's mind: if two animals are looking at an object and they are not looking back up to each other's eyes to check what the other one is looking at, then it is impossible to tell whether they are thinking. For example, Dee and her father Spike are spider monkeys who are both staring at the same piece of fruit. Dee and Spike might be looking at the food completely independently of each other; if Dee does not check to see where Spike is looking, it is impossible to know whether she is aware that Spike is also looking at the fruit.

Triadic joint attention, the more mentally complex behaviour, was seen in the chimpanzees and bonobos, but no monkeys showed it. The immediate conclusion is that chimps and bonobos can do what young children do, namely, look at toys, food and members of their group at the same time as other individuals and know what these individuals are looking at. This is a hasty conclusion for two reasons. The first is that, as I said earlier, monkeys perceive gaze as a threat. Whilst I was watching the spider monkeys they would sometimes grow uncomfortable with me staring at them and the male would come over and threaten me. He would press himself against the glass in a cruciform shape and stare directly into my eyes. Spider monkeys have black fur which is as spiky as a Gothic punk, pink faces and bright blue, rather human-like eyes. The effect was mesmerising. He would then raise his eyebrows and bare his sharp, pointy canines. So, naturally, the spider monkeys would not do this checking behaviour and stare at each other for prolonged periods. This could mean that they do not show joint attention, or it could mean that they use peripheral vision to see what is going on. If you stare straight in front of you and stretch your arms out to the side and wiggle your fingers, you should just be able to see them. Our peripheral vision stretches to almost a half circle in front of us and although it hasn't been tested, monkey sight ought to be at least as good as that.

Daniel Povinelli argues that just because bonobos and chimps can show triadic joint attention, it does not mean that they are able to understand the mental component behind it. It is true that the number of times the chimpanzees and bonobos showed joint attention levels was low and, although this kind of naturalist study has not been conducted on humans, I suspect that there would be far more meaningful gazes in human subjects. However, there is little that is novel in a zoo and if people were kept in a zoo, I'm sure that their joint attention levels would go down too.

Some evidence against Povinelli's argument comes from Muni, the gorilla Juan Carlos Gomez studied. Muni had a problem. She was rather inconveniently locked into her cage which had a door and a bolt right at the top. For the first year of her life she tried to get out by pushing boxes towards the door and climbing on top of them. For the next six months, she used a human as a box by dragging Gomez over to the door. Gomez was rather better than a box because he is taller and Muni was able to manœuvre him around and climb over him. Once she was older than a year and a half, she adopted a more subtle approach. She would lead him to the door and stand looking from his eyes to the latch and back again, while waiting for him to open it for her. In most cases, she would also lift his hand in the direction of the latch, but then stop halfway and again alternate her gaze between the latch and his eyes. Muni had progressed from treating him as a physical object to requesting that he go to the door and open it for her. Gomez argues that this shows an understanding of mind. He says prelinguistic one year olds and gorillas have a rudimentary understanding of what people see when they look at objects and that looking at an object can lead to someone doing something about it for you. What both infants and great apes may be able to understand is that a person's or an animal's behaviour depends on what they are paying attention to. But other intelligent animals might be able to understand attention as well.

Irene Pepperberg, from the University of Arizona in Tucson, taught Alex, a grey parrot, to speak. In rigorous tests she demonstrated that he actually understood the words he was using and was not merely mimicking her. More recently, she and Mary McLaughlin showed that parrots understand joint attention and that without joint attention they cannot learn how to speak. She and McLaughlin tried to teach two juvenile grey parrots, Alo and Kyaaro, how to talk using two different techniques. One was the standard method Pepperberg had used to coach Alex. She would 'teach' McLaughlin a word by holding an object and pointing to it whilst engaging her colleague with her eyes and repeating the name of the object. McLaughlin was rewarded for speaking the word properly and, if she said the word incorrectly, Pepperberg removed the object as a punishment. McLaughlin was also rivalling the parrot for Pepperberg's attention, part of the reason, they say, why the parrot wanted to join in with this new game. The other technique involved no eye contact and the object was simply suspended from the ceiling on a string in front of McLaughlin. Both the parrots learnt the words for objects taught using triadic joint attention, but none of the words when their trainers did not engage in eye contact.

Dolphins also show triadic joint attention when they are dealing with humans. Biologists John Gory and Mark Xitco have been training dolphins to use symbol language at the Epcot Centre in Florida. When the dolphins needed to use an object as a symbol to complete their sentence, or when there were toys in the pool that the trainers had not seen, the dolphins used eye gaze to attract their attention. Typically, they would make their whole body rigid and point with the rostrum (the long beak-like protuberance) at the object and then swing their head from the object back to the trainer, whilst alternating their gaze at the same time. 'Their behaviour implies that they understand joint attention,' says Xitco, 'because it emerged fully formed and not gradually as if they had learnt it.' Even though dolphins communicate with each other by echolocation, Xitco thinks vision is also important: when dolphins are swimming together they flash subtly different coloured areas of their body at one another.

If someone is not paying attention to whatever it is you want them to look at or do, one way to get their attention is to use eye gaze as Muni did, but pointing is more effective whether it's with your hand or your rostrum. Pointing gestures have been given two rather cumbersome titles: protoimperative pointing and protodeclarative pointing. The pointing is called 'proto' because it arises before imperative or declarative speech. At its most basic, a protoimperative is a gesture which has the equivalent function of an imperative in the English language. For example, when you point at an apple, it means the same as saying, 'Give me the apple' or 'I want the apple'. A protodeclarative is more airy. It means the equivalent of 'Look at that star!' You are not pointing at the star because you want to put it in your back pocket, you are pointing at it in order to remark on the star to your companion.

Young children are able to follow the direction in which someone is pointing by the time they are nine to fourteen months old, and they start pointing at about a year to a year and four months, although pointing can sometimes appear as early as nine months old. Usually babies look up after they have pointed, but at about sixteen months old they look up *before* they have pointed. It is as if they are making sure they have the attention of whoever is with them – the visual equivalent of a nudge, or an exclamation – before they point out something. This is rather sophisticated behaviour because in essence it means that babies of this age have learnt or understood what makes a successful point: I must have the attention of my mum because, if she does not see me, she cannot follow me pointing, and if she cannot see what I am pointing at, she cannot bring it to me; she won't see that I am looking at that man with the funny umbrella.

So what about primates? When I conducted experiments in which chimpanzees, bonobos and spider monkeys were shown toys, but could not reach them, the two species of chimpanzee showed an increase in triadic joint attention and, in addition, they made proto-imperative gestures as if they were requesting me to give them the toy. None of the spider monkeys made any gestures that could have been interpreted as 'asking' for the toy. I also saw one example of a protodeclarative. One of the chimps, Flynn, was playing with a toy when Molly Badham, the director of the zoo, walked past. Flynn is not always the most well behaved of chimps and whenever he gets the opportunity to spit, throw sawdust (and other nastier substances) or to pee on people, he usually takes it, as I have found to my cost. However, Molly brought him up and he has always treated her nicely. She had not seen the toy he was playing with (it was one I had given him) and he rushed over and held up the toy for her to look at.

Molly has looked after Flynn since he was a baby and there is some evidence to show that chimpanzees and bonobos become more human-like the longer they are kept with people. Malinda Carpenter and Michael Tomasello, from the Yerkes Regional Primate Centre at Emory University, Atlanta, wanted to test this and find out whether joint attention differed between chimps and children and what the effect was of what they called 'enculturation', a term which, although it sounds like growing yoghurt, refers to a prolonged period of contact with humans. They elicited the help of Sue Savage-Rumbaugh, from the Department of Biology and the Language Research Centre at Georgia State University, who 'donated' four bonobos and two chimpanzees. Two of the bonobos and one of the chimps had been brought up by their mothers and the other three had been reared at the Language Centre by people. They all had participated in a lot of other experiments and had been taught to use a keyboard so they had a language of symbols and could understand some spoken English. Savage-Rumbaugh played with toys in front of the chimps and demonstrated tasks to them to see if they would copy her actions. The same thing was done with six eighteen-month-old children. They found that the chimps that had spent most time with people were much more like the young children than the ones that had been reared by their mothers. The human-reared chimps used more triadic joint attention than the other chimps, looking from the experimenter to the toy and back again. The mother-reared chimps used more imperative gestures than either the other chimps or the children. This indicates that they were interested only in grabbing the toys and did not care what the experimenter was doing or looking at.

Autistic people can understand dyadic joint attention. If an autistic child sits in a room full of toys with an experimenter and the experimenter looks at a toy by moving her eyes only and not her head, the autistic child is usually able to say what the experimenter is looking at. However, they do not spontaneously monitor other people's gaze and yet they can, with a higher degree of accuracy than normal children, pinpoint very slight degrees of change in the orientation of someone's gaze. People with autism know what is sometimes termed the 'facts of vision'. They know that you have to have your eyes open to see and that objects that are not occluded by any other objects and which stand along an imaginary line from the person's eye – the line of sight – will be visible. They also know that what one person does or does not see has no bearing on what another person can see. They are able to hide dolls so that other people cannot see them. If they're given a doll and a coloured cube and the doll is moved to a different position from them, they can say which side of the cube the doll is staring at. Those autistic people who do have problems with these kinds of experiments tend to have a low mental age. Their mistakes are thus more to do with their general level of intelligence than because they suffer from autism. Simon Baron-Cohen concludes, 'Autistic people can understand the geometry of gaze – they can work out the angles of sight, but not the mentalistic relevance of gaze.'

Some people with autism can also understand protoimperative pointing – they understand that if you point at a piece of cake it is because you want them to pass you the cake, not because you want to remark on how nicely decorated it is. And they can also point to the cake themselves if they want to be given it. However, many autistic people have trouble with pointing and more often than not will look at the tip of your finger instead of what you are pointing

57

to. Even more oddly, they do not seem to be able to understand protodeclarative pointing, which in this case would be pointing at a cake because you want to comment on the amount of cream it is smothered in. Neither do they point in a protodeclarative fashion themselves.

This inability to understand what it means when people look at objects and point is linked to ID. Autistic people do not treat others as if they have motives and goals. At the beginning of the chapter we discussed a film in which triangles moved around; one adult described the whole sequence in geometric terms with no reference to motivation. This is a typically autistic trait, yet for most animals and young children ID is a very basic ability. The link between joint attention and ID was shown by Gomez's gorilla, Muni, when she tried to get out of her cage. First she treated Gomez as if he were an object, but gradually she started to treat him as a person who could (she hoped) be made to release her. She noticed where he was looking and tried to direct his attention. Muni seemed to understand the connection between her goal, Gomez's behaviour and what she considered he should be paying attention to.

Muni's behaviour inspired Gomez to design an experiment for children in which they had to enlist the help of an adult in order to get a toy that was out of reach. Most normal young children used the strategy finally embarked upon by Muni: gestures combined with eye contact. In his experiment, autistic children did not treat the adult as an object, but they used objects to try to reach the toy far more than the other children did. They also showed a deficit in triadic joint attention. Gomez and his co-workers think that this experiment shows that autistic people have a problem with imperative gestures as well as protodeclarative pointing, or at least they use this type of pointing in a different way from other children.

So what does it all mean? We said that protoimperative pointing is simple and that no understanding of the mind is required. By pointing you want to change the physical world: you want the world to change from seeing a piece of cake in the middle of the table to a world where that cake is on your plate and you are tucking into it. Protodeclaratives are a means of commenting or remarking on the world and that is a way of trying to change somebody else's mental world. If you are walking along through the Basilica di San Marco in Venice with your companion who is looking at the people and you point to the ceiling and she looks up, her mental world changes: the ceiling is covered with two acres of gold. This mental change means that you understand what she is thinking (her thoughts prior to your pointing have no comprehension of gold on the ceiling) and that if you point to the ceiling she will look at the gold and her thoughts will change to knowledge of the gold and amazement at it. You don't consciously have to think about what other people are thinking or how you are altering their thoughts, it is something that happens subconsciously. Nevertheless, it is a complex piece of mental behaviour and it is quite possible that protoimperatives are deceptively complicated, too.

However, before we leap too far ahead of ourselves, a note of caution. Because we know that babies develop into children who can tell us how they feel and what they think, we risk assuming a more complex understanding in young children than they often deserve to be credited with. What is likely to be the case is that although children will eventually have Theory of Mind, along the route to a full blown Theory of Mind children will only have developed the intermediate steps. At a certain point they are capable of understanding what other people are thinking when they, for example, point to a sunset or a crocodile, but before they have reached this stage the same behaviour is not linked to any comprehension of what is going on in another person's mind. It is simply that young infants are born with the ability to develop skills such as looking at other people's eyes or following where they are pointing. They quickly learn how to respond to others and are rewarded by the response from that person. What babies and young children may be doing when they point is trying to change your state of attention. Their behaviour may be the same as our own, but what they gain by pointing is a response: you will smile or frown at what you see when you look at what they are pointing to.

When an older child points, although her behaviour is outwardly similar to a young child's, internally a more complex process is taking place. She points because she wants you to attend to what she is looking at. This is the first step along the road to picturing other people's thoughts and beliefs in your mind. Simon Baron-Cohen says, 'I think that long before kids are interested in trying to manipulate your attention or follow your direction of attention they are fascinated by the eyes. A lot of their behaviour may not be mentalistic.' Once a child is able to understand that other people can think and that they have minds, even a gesture as simple as protoimperative pointing can take on a more complex hue. If you are able to reach a cake, you could just take it, but apart from the social convention that this is rude, you sometimes point to an object because you *want* the other person to *know* that you want it.

We treat animals somewhat differently from young children when we try to infer what is going on in their head. We are unable to talk to them and so we cannot and do not assume that they have Theory of Mind. Therefore, a particular behaviour seen in animals is interpreted differently from the same behaviour seen in young children. We tend to treat animals' behaviour much more sceptically. But, as Roger Fouts, from the Primate Institute Centre at Ellensburg, Washington, says, 'If you can define a behaviour, then when it is observed in two different species it should be viewed as a similar behaviour. If you observe deception in humans and define it as deception then you must also define it as deception in chimpanzees if it is observed there as well. Otherwise you are using a "rubber ruler".'

However, sometimes there is a good reason for treating animals differently. Even if they show the same kinds of behaviour as we do, they do not necessarily feel or think in the same way. We are, after all, different species and each species has its own particular 'nature'. Chimpanzees, for example, rarely share toys or food in the wild. The fact that we do not see this behaviour does not mean that we should assume that a chimpanzee cannot understand that another chimp would like to take some of her food or play with her toys. Nor should we assume, if we do see two animals sharing food or toys, that they understand each other's desires.

Joint attention is a very special skill. We have already said that we should not presume that being able to show these gestures means that the child or the animal has a full understanding of what they are doing, but we know that in children at least this comprehension will develop. Chimpanzees and bonobos are capable of using joint attention and will hone this skill when they are brought up in close contact with humans. Other evidence which indicates that joint attention is crucial to developing Theory of Mind comes from autistic children who, as we have said, are not able to show or understand triadic joint attention or protodeclarative pointing and even sometimes have trouble with protoimperatives.

That there is something very peculiarly wrong with autistic people who can understand the 'facts of vision' yet do not use sight to help them comprehend other people is perhaps best illustrated by the blind. It might sound strange, but blind people can understand seeing. Just as we check visually from an object back to the person who is looking at it, blind people do this by touch. They take you over to an object and put your hand on it. They also direct people to look at something by saying 'look' and 'see'. Blind children can also respond accurately to requests such as 'Let Mummy see the car' by taking the car and pressing it into their mother's hand. This suggests that although they could never have a normal sense of what it means to see an object visually, they have a good idea of what see means – to explore an object. One blind adult, when asked to give a definition of 'gaze' said, 'To look at something intensely. An equivalent would be to listen to something very hard.'

If joint attention is something that we can do using senses other than vision (although vision is what we normally use) then it stems from something deeper: the beginnings of understanding someone's mind by sharing their attention and their perspective. As Baron-Cohen says, 'When we make eye contact, we usually also feel able to judge whether we have really "connected" with the other person. My guess is that what we are doing here is detecting if the other's attention is squarely on us or slightly away. This may be one of the most powerful forms of behavioural evidence that we have achieved a "Meeting of Minds".' He adds that autistic children cannot establish joint attention either visually or aurally: 'I suspect that normal children modulate their intonation to make their speech interesting and audible to the listener and that children with autism do not because they lack a concept of the other person as an interested listener.' Some autistic people have actually complained that they are unable to understand how people talk to each other with their eyes, or what they are silently saying to one another. Others say that they cannot make eye contact because they can't stand the way people's eyes move about all the time.

Eye contact, as we have discussed in this chapter, is a way of establishing what another person is attending to, or is interested in, and their interest is a function of their goals and motives. In short, eye contact is an indication of another's desires and how a person or an animal will act to achieve that desire. It is to the comprehension of desires that we will turn in the next chapter.

4

HEART'S DESIRE

Which of us is happy in this world? Which of us has his desire? or, having it, is satisfied?

William Makepeace Thackeray, *Vanity Fair*

Charles Darwin had a deep and abiding fascination with facial expressions. Plagued by illness for much of his life, he was not able to observe foreign faces at first hand. Instead, he painstakingly collated reports on the facial expressions of different races. Some reports were more reliable than others; Darwin singled out Mr J. Scott, a curator of the Botanic Gardens in Calcutta, for special praise: 'The habit of accurate observation gained by his botanical studies has been brought to bear on our present subject.' In 1872, using these reports and observations based on his own prodigious brood (Darwin had nine children, seven of whom survived), he wrote *The Expressions of Emotions in Man and Animals*. His conclusion was that facial expressions throughout the world are remarkably similar.

Once children have grasped the concept of joint attention, understanding the desires of others is the next step towards a full Theory of Mind. Everybody has desires, they are fundamental to human and animal nature. At the most basic level, we desire food, warmth, shelter and sex. Many human desires are, however, rather more complex. Comprehending what another person wants involves two main cognitive skills: an understanding of how attention is linked to goals and an understanding of emotions. In the previous chapter we saw how young children and apes understand that knowing what another person or animal is focusing their attention on can lead to comprehending what that person or animal wants. When Muni the gorilla wanted to be let out of her cage (her *goal*), she used eye gaze

63

to indicate that her *attention* was directed towards the lock. In this chapter we are going to look at how we understand emotions before discussing whether – and how – children, animals and people with autism know what others desire.

'That the chief expressive actions exhibited by man and by the lower animals are now innate or inherited – that is, have not been learnt by the individual – is admitted by everyone,' wrote Darwin. 'So little has learning or imitation to do with several of them that they are from the earliest days and throughout life quite beyond our control.' Darwin's evidence was anecdotal (he once gave a cebus monkey a pinch of snuff to see if it would weep), and it was not until the 1970s that anyone seriously tried to test his ideas. Paul Ekman, from the University of California, at San Francisco, and Wallace Friesen travelled to New Guinea to study the Fore, a group of people living in the south-east Highlands. They chose those members of the tribe who neither spoke nor understood English or Pidgin and who had not had any contact with Caucasians. Ekman and his colleague felt that it was important to pick people from New Guinea who had not met Westerners in case they'd learnt to interpret different, non-indigenous facial expressions. The researchers told the Fore stories and then showed them pictures of Westerners with various facial expressions: happiness, sadness, anger, disgust, surprise and fear. The Fore had to pick the correct expression. For example, one story was about a woman sitting alone in her house in the village. A wild pig runs into the village and stands at the doorway. She has no weapon of any kind in her house and she thinks the pig may charge and bite her. The correct emotional expression was obviously fear.

Both adults and children were able to choose the right response for five of the emotions. They were less well able to determine when surprise should be chosen and although they could easily distinguish fear from disgust, anger and sadness, they found it very hard to tell surprise from fear when the two expressions were presented at the same time. Ekman and Friesen also took photographs of the Fore posing with various facial expressions. Back in the US, Americans were correctly able to interpret their expressions. As

Darwin had said a hundred years earlier, 'It has often struck me as a curious fact that so many shades of expression are instantly recognised without any conscious process of analysis on our part. No one, I believe, can clearly describe a sullen or a sly expression; yet many observers are unanimous that these expressions can be recognised in the various races of man.'

More recently Simon Baron-Cohen and colleagues presented Japanese, British and Spanish adults with portraits by the Spanish artist, Diego Rodríguez de Silva y Velázquez, and the contemporary British artist, David Hockney, which showed a range of more complex and subtle emotions, such as regret, astonishment, distrust, contempt and surprise. All three cultures showed a good agreement in their choice of which emotion the artists had depicted. Baron-Cohen points out that Velázquez was painting over three centuries ago, yet he is still as readily understood today as he was in his era and culture. He adds that the expressions in the sparse line-drawings of portraits such as *Gregory*, and *Celia in Black Dress with Red Stockings* by Hockney are actually easier to understand than the information-ally rich oils by the Spanish artist.

It does seem likely that emotional expressions are universally understood and conveyed. Recent research shows that Darwin was correct: the ability to recognise simple emotions is a skill we are born with. If new-born babies are given a sweet or a bitter substance for their very first feed, it's possible to tell from the babies' expressions what kind of liquid they were given and, from the intensity of their expression, whether it was mild or concentrated. Babies under twelve months also show expressions for anger, distress and happiness.

Darwin believed that young infants could recognise emotions. He describes an incident between his nurse and his six-month-old son. 'His nurse pretended to cry and I saw that his face instantly assumed a melancholy expression, with the corners of the mouth strongly depressed; now this child could rarely have seen any other child crying and never a grown-up person crying and I doubt whether at so early an age he could have reasoned on the subject.'

As well as showing recognisable emotions, babies as young as four to seven months old can tell the difference between happy and surprised faces. The babies were given four pictures, each portraying a different woman, but all four had the same expression. Once the infants were bored with the photos, they were shown new pictures of the same women but with a different expression. The older babies started to pay attention again, as if they realised that the photos were not exactly the same and that the women were expressing another emotion.

Babies as young as ten weeks old are sensitive to their mother's expressions. When mothers were asked to hold their babies on their laps and talk to them showing happiness, sadness and then anger, the babies looked happy when their mother did and angry when she was angry. Babies at this age don't seem able to mimic sadness though; when their mother looked sad, they stayed still, or chewed and sucked on their hands and toys and looked away from her more often.

Being able to recognise emotions is crucial for young children. In a dangerous, uncertain and unpredictable world, the emotions adults display act as a guide to how infants should behave. James Sorce and Robert Emde, from the University of Colorado, and Joseph Campos and Mary Klinnert, from the University of Denver, gave twelve-month-old infants 'The Visual Cliff Test'. The visual cliff is a drop covered with clear glass. In this experiment, the researchers used a hollow table with a plexiglass surface. One half of the table was shallow – the glass was balanced above a short drop; the other half of the table was scooped away so that the drop was half a metre deep. A child crawling on the plexiglass surface was perfectly safe, but it's not something babies particularly like to do. The babies were happy to crawl around above the shallow drop. They rarely looked at their mothers, and if they caught sight of her giving a fearful expression, they showed a slight hesitancy, but continued to crawl. When a child started to crawl towards the deep end, the mother, who was sitting at the far end, had to signal to her child with either a happy, an interested, a sad, a fearful or an angry expression. Happy or interested mothers were able to encourage their babies to cross, fearful or angry ones could rarely persuade their children that the table was safe, and mothers who looked sad had intermediate success. The researchers concluded that adults' facial expressions regulate behaviour in young children, especially when the children are nervous or uncertain. Learning how to react to situations by looking at adults has survival value and is a trait shared with other animals. Young rhesus monkeys are not afraid of snakes, but if they see their parents reacting to a snake with intense fear, the youngsters also become afraid of snakes.

Many higher monkeys and apes have hairless faces and elaborate facial musculature, which allows them to make and recognise a wide variety of expressions and, as one would expect, facial expressions play a key role in close-up communication. One particularly dramatic expression is the fear grin given by chimpanzees. It is given in response to frightening stimuli and in complete silence. Jane Goodall, who has spent the past three decades studying chimpanzees at Gombe in Tanzania, says, 'When the expression suddenly appears, it is as though the whole face has been split by a gash of white teeth set in bright pink gums.' It is usually used to convey danger at a time when making a noise would be detrimental to the chimps' safety. The first chimp in space grinned frantically. The newspapers claimed he was loving his space trip; in fact, he was probably terrified. Goodall gives an example of how even very young infants closely monitor their companions' expressions. 'I watched one infant male, Goblin, as he reached very, very cautiously towards a banana peel that lay beside a feeding adult, who had dropped it; throughout the whole successful manoeuvre he scarcely took his eyes off the other's face.'

A study by Simon Baron-Cohen showed that children, once they can speak, are capable of identifying what emotions other children in photographs are displaying. However, although children with autism could distinguish happiness from sadness, they could not usually tell when someone was looking surprised. Sometimes they said that the child in the photo was yawning.

The key to detecting emotions are the eyes and the mouth. In 1964 Tapio Nummenmaa published a monograph, *The Language of the Face.* He cut out pictures of people's eyes and mouth as they expressed various emotions and asked people to guess what the emotion was. He discovered that simple emotions, such as sadness and happiness, could be recognised from either the mouth or the eyes, but complex emotions – surprise, cruelty, and surprise and anger combined – required information from the region around the eyes. More recently, Baron-Cohen and Jessica Hammer stopped people in the streets of Cambridge and asked them to identify emotions from pictures of eyes only. They found that women were better at this than men – the difference was slight but statistically significant. Culture and upbringing could have something to do with this difference. 'Girls get more socialisation and play to do with relationships than boys, so they might become more sensitive to expressions,' says Baron-Cohen. People with autism performed even more poorly on this task than men and to Baron-Cohen this could be significant. 'Obviously, my interest with autism is linked to the fact that it is mainly a male disorder, and there might be something in the idea that autism is an extreme form of the male brain.' Baron-Cohen's argument, that the ability to understand emotions is biologically rather than culturally driven, will be explored more thoroughly in chapter eight.

Eyes, as we have seen in the previous chapter, are very important. They help us understand not only how someone is feeling, but, through the direction of their gaze, what they want. Baron-Cohen and his colleagues have demonstrated this in a delightfully simple experiment. They drew a face – little more than a circle with a nose, a mouth and two eyes – on some card. Around the picture of 'Charlie' they stuck four sweet wrappers. Charlie's eyes were angled (by the direction of the iris) towards one of the sweet wrappers. When Baron-Cohen and his colleagues asked 'Which one does Charlie want?', children between the ages of three and four years old had no difficulty with the answer. The researchers tried to confuse the children by pointing a big black arrow at one of the other chocolates, but this had no effect on the children's ability to choose the sweet that Charlie was looking at and therefore 'wanted'.

Children start to use words that indicate their desires and those of other people when they are about two years old. 'Want' is the most prevalent word, as any parent knows; ones that are used less often for emotional states are words like 'happy'. A large number of children's first words are to do with pleasure and pain ('Me fall down. Me cry.' 'You sad Mommy. What Daddy do?') and with pleasant or unpleasant physiological states such as being hot, cold, warm, tired, thirsty and so on.

Henry Wellman and his colleague Karen Bartsch, from the University of Michigan at Ann Arbor, looked through a database containing nearly 400,000 examples of childish speech. Words that indicated desire were: want, wish, afraid, care; belief terms were: think, know, expect, wonder, believe, understand. Approximately three per cent of the children's speech included one or more of these terms, so the sample was reduced to 10,000 child utterances. The researchers were careful to use words that they thought referred to a mental understanding of desire or belief. For instance, saying 'I *want* that toy' is a request and not the same as a more genuine reference to desire, such as 'I *wish* I have a kite'. Similarly, '*Know* what I mean?' doesn't refer to what the child knows or thinks another child knows. A genuine reference to belief was seen in some of the quotes the researchers collected: 'Some people don't like hawks. They *think* they are slimy.' 'Can I put my head in the mail box so the mailman can *know* where I are?' Wellman and Bartsch showed that a genuine reference to desire was well-established by the age of two and that reference to belief begins at about the age of three. Desire references always preceded belief references.

Wellman's work indicates that children talk about themselves and what they want and feel more than they do about others. But some children do have a sophisticated grasp of the difference between their own desires and another person's. One child who was not even three observed his younger sibling playing with a balloon and said, 'He going to pop it in a minute. And he'll cry . . . I like the pop.'

However, even though young children are using words that refer to mental states, it is difficult to know whether they actually understand the meaning of the words; they may simply be copying how their parents and siblings use words. Young children may be able to express their own current desires, but that doesn't mean that they have any understanding that they or anyone else has a desire. Experimental evidence is what is needed to understand more fully what is going on inside a child's head.

The first pioneering study in this area was conducted by Helen Borke from Carnegie-Mellon University, Pittsburgh. She told children short stories in which something happened to the main character – she went to a birthday party, for example, or got lost in the woods. The children then had to choose from a selection of pictures which face best expressed what that character's emotional reaction would be. When the main character was in a situation where she would feel happy, just over half of the three year olds were able to pick the happy face. Children older than three and a half were increasingly more accurate at this task. Three year olds were able to predict when the heroine would feel sad, but both they and four year olds were less adept at deciphering when she would feel anger or fear: their responses were usually random. Contrary to the idea that girls are better at deciphering emotions than boys, no gender difference was seen.

Overall, as Borke points out, young children are best able to distinguish generalised unpleasant from generalised pleasant responses. They find more complex emotions harder and do not develop an understanding of them until they're older. It is the comprehension of these more complex emotions that is the foundation stone for the ability to show empathy. This is a skill which takes some years to develop and which we will discuss more fully in chapter six. On a more simplistic level, young children can work out how someone would feel if they were in a certain situation and they can also work backwards from the person's emotion to the kind of situation that person might be in. For example, if three- to four-year-old children are given words for emotions, such as happy, excited, surprised, sad, angry and scared, about three-quarters of the time they can make up an appropriate story to explain how the character had got to feel that way.

Paul Harris, a lecturer in experimental psychology at Oxford University, says there is nothing complex in this ability. The children could simply be learning links between situations and emotions. For example, they feel happy when they get a present, or sad when they lose a toy. Having learnt what situations amuse or upset them, they are able to generalise this knowledge and predict how another person would feel. Learning links between behaviour and emotions in this way would restrict children to answering only those questions that related to their own experiences but it wouldn't necessarily prevent them from knowing what other people desired. Simon Baron-Cohen, who had just given me a cup of coffee, explained it this way: 'Children might be able to understand desire in a simple way, so if you say you want coffee, I could learn the notion of "want", so that whenever I hear "Sanjida wants coffee" I would associate Sanjida with coffee and then I could predict that she'll choose coffee and not tea if given a choice.'

I have already said that two key abilities are crucial in understanding another person's desire: knowing that the focus of their attention can tell you what they want, and recognising and comprehending emotions. Young children are able to do the former and at three to four years old they can understand expressions and determine how people might feel in certain situations when simple emotions are involved. The question is, is young children's understanding of emotions simply rote learning, linking situations to desires, or are children capable of recognising that when a person has a desire, their desire is a mental representation? In order to find the answer, we need to look more closely at the nature of children's desires.

Desires can mediate actions. Our actions lead to an outcome and this leads to a reaction which is dependent on our initial desire. For example, today I went to the gym. Why? Because I wanted to use the pool. My desire to go swimming leads me to take action – to go to the gym. When I get there, I'm sad because the pool is full of people doing aqua-aerobics and there's no room for me to swim. My action, going to the gym, led to my reaction and my reaction is dependent on my initial desire – wanting to swim. If I hadn't wanted to swim, but was going to keep a friend happy, I might secretly be quite pleased that the pool is full of splashing people, kicking their legs about.

Henry Wellman and his colleague, Jacqui Woolley, showed that children as young as two understand that actions are mediated by desires. They told children stories using a doll as the central character. The doll was looking for something in one of two locations. There were three scenarios: in one the doll found what she was looking for; in the second, she didn't find what she was looking for, but she did find something else equally attractive; and in the final situation, she didn't find anything. The children were asked how the doll would feel and what she would do next – would she carry on searching or would she stop? The correct answers were that when the doll found what she was looking for, or the substitute item, she would be happy, but she'd be sad when she found nothing. She would carry on looking in the Finds-Substitute and Finds-Nothing scenarios. Two year olds were able to choose the correct answers, thus showing that they had an understanding of simple desires and how they could affect a person's actions.

But what children of this age lack is what psychologists term the 'causal nature of intention'. 'Intention' in this sense is a state of mind which mediates between desires and actions. Janet Astington, a child psychologist from the Ontario Institute for Studies in Education, Toronto, explains, 'When I desire something I form an intention to obtain it, which causes me to act in a way that will fulfil the desire . . . If I want someone to be dead, my desire will be satisfied no matter how he dies. If I *intend* to kill someone, my intention will not be carried out unless I act on that intention and murder him; my intention will not be carried out if I accidentally run over him, or if he dies of a heart attack.'

Three year olds can distinguish between intentional and unintentional actions (such as dropping a drink on purpose, as opposed to spilling it by accident), but young chimpanzees do not seem to be capable of making this distinction. Daniel Povinelli and his colleague, Helen Perilloux, trained four- and five-year-old chimps to point to a human experimenter who would hand their trainer a cup of fruit juice. The trainer gave the drink to the chimps. One experimenter then started to hand the fruit juice to the trainer, but accidentally dropped it; another experimenter deliberately spilled the juice; and the third aggressively threw the drink on the floor. When the chimps had a choice of which experimenter to point to in order to get their juice, they did not show any preference for the person who accidentally spilled their juice as opposed to the ones who deliberately spilled it. However, they did prefer experimenters who spilled their drink quietly, rather than picking the angry person who tossed the fruit juice around!

To return to young children, although they can tell the difference between accidental and intentional outcomes, they don't appear to have a sophisticated mental concept of intention. What three year olds do is link a person's goal to the actual outcome. If a person's goal and the outcome in the real world don't match, three year olds think the action must have been unintentional and will not be pleasurable. Children of this age think that if you meant to do something, you'll always enjoy it – and we know that this is often not the case.

Janet Astington and Alison Gopnik, from the University of California, at Berkeley, demonstrated young children's lack of understanding of intentions. They gave children pairs of pictures showing a child doing something and another child who was intending to do something: for instance, a child on a slide and another picture of a child starting to climb up the steps of the slide. The researchers asked 'Which boy is sliding?' and 'Which boy is about to slide?' Three year olds chose the child actively doing something – sliding – as a response to both questions, whereas older children were able to distinguish between the two sets of events. Astington says that at four to five years old, children begin to separate intention from desire and understand that 'we act to achieve our goals, or we don't act and we don't achieve our goals. However, sometimes we do perform the intended action but fail to achieve the desired goal, or sometimes we may not act and the desired goal comes about anyway.'

Interestingly, children are less good at remembering when their desires have not been fulfilled than when they were granted what they wished for. Astington and Gopnik offered children a choice of two toys and asked them which one they wanted to play with. Once the children had chosen, the toys were put in a bag and they had to pull one out. Unbeknownst to them, the researchers were able to manipulate which toy the children received. Once they'd got their toy, the researchers asked them whether they'd got the toy they wanted. Three and four year olds were correctly able to say when they'd got the toy they'd chosen, but when they received the toy they hadn't chosen (an unfulfilled desire) fewer children could remember that less than a minute previously they had not asked for that toy. Neither could these children report a false belief of theirs. The researchers showed each child individually a box of crayons and asked what was inside. The children were then shown that the box contained sweets. The box was sealed up and the children were asked what they had thought was inside before the box was opened. Very few gave the correct answer: that they had originally thought the box was full of crayons. Four year olds, even if they can remember their past fulfilled desire, cannot recall either an unfulfilled desire or a false belief.

An experiment I carried out on young children aged between three and six years old showed that they were even worse at understanding other people's unfulfilled desires than Astington and Gopnik had thought. As well as giving the children a standard false belief test (like the crayon one above), I gave them two tests to see if they understood another person's desire. The first was a verbal desire test, the second a non-verbal task I had designed. Because there are so few non-verbal tests, children need to do both kinds of test at the same time; if the results from both tests are the same, one can argue that the non-verbal task is testing the same skill as the verbal one.

In the non-verbal task, each child had to choose one of a pair of picture cards. Each pair of cards had a picture of a child wanting something on one card and on the other the same scenario but without the child wanting anything. For instance, one card showed a child looking at and reaching for a sweet, the other had the same child and a sweet but the child was neither looking at the sweet nor about to pick it up. The 'correct' picture was the one showing a child desiring an object. Of course, at first the children did not know which card was the correct one, but every time they chose the right card, they were given a sweet and they very quickly learnt which one to pick. Once they were able reliably to identify the correct pictures from two pairs of cards, they proceeded to the test phase of the task. This was essentially the same: they were presented with two pairs of cards, one after the other, but this time they were allowed only one attempt to choose the right card in each pair. The idea was that the children should have learnt why they were picking one card and not the other: if they chose the correct cards in the experimental part of the task, I thought this would show that they understood that the correct pictures were illustrations of another child's desire. In the test phase, one pair of cards showed the child about to obtain the object she wanted, as in the learning phase of the experiment, but the other pair showed an unfulfilled desire – the child in the picture could quite clearly not reach the teddy bear she was trying to get.

The results showed that all the children from the age of three upwards were able to understand another person's fulfilled desire when they were given a narrative-style test. The younger children were not able to report a false belief, although by the time they were five years old they were able to do this. As for the non-verbal desire test, all the children scored highly on the fulfilled desire part. In other words, they understood that the correct card to pick was one showing a person desiring an object. However, only sixty per cent of all the children – regardless of their age – were able to make the correct choice when they were shown the last pair of cards in which a child was unable to reach her teddy. In other words, they could not understand an unfulfilled desire.

I think that all the desire tests described in this chapter show that at around the age of three, children do start to understand desires, but they have far more difficulty reporting unfulfilled desires and understand even less when they are asked about their own false beliefs. This same distinction is seen in children's use of words: desire words are used well before words referring to beliefs. Children also initially assume that other people's desires will be like their own; they find other people's mental states as difficult or as easy to understand as their own thoughts. As Oscar Wilde once said, 'To know everything about oneself one must know all about others.'

Why should this be so? We think that we have access to our minds and that it is only the minds of others that are opaque.

Imagine living in the fantasy world created by Hermann Hesse in *The Glass Bead Game*. In the city of Castilia several centuries into the future, society is run by an intellectual élite who play the Glass Bead Game. Education is 'pure and keen' and every child longs to become a Glass Bead Player. The game is a synthesis of intellectual pursuits from philology to philosophy, unified by maths and music. The citizens of Castilia do not think in terms of equations, crotchets and quavers, but in the power of music and the force of mathematical ideas. In order to imagine a move, the players of the Glass Bead Game don't torturously run through all the concepts, equations, facts and fictions at their disposal, rather they meditate on each symbol and listen to the harmony of the music that flows from their game.

Our knowledge of our ordinary psychological states in this world might be like playing the Glass Bead Game. Our understanding of other minds is great, and our knowledge and expertise about our own minds is even greater. Because of the force and pervasiveness of our knowledge, we think that our beliefs about our psychological states are direct, when, in fact, they might easily be indirect. We have to learn how to know *what* we think, just as we have to learn how to know what others think, yet we cannot ever remember a time when we did not know these things.

For the intellectual élite of Castilia, it might not even be possible to elucidate how they arrived at a particular move, whether that move arose from instinct born of long years of immersion in the game, or whether they had been taught how to respond. The discrepancy would only be highlighted by a young player who might have learnt enough to think that he can play but not enough to play well. His perception of how to play the game may be quite different from the way in which the game is actually being played; he may hear the music and feel the maths and think he is in harmony, but when the game starts to fall apart he will realise his error. In the same way we can see that children's minds are not like ours. Because we know what is going on in our own heads, we believe that children know their own minds too. Only by giving children psychological tests do we discover that their thought processes are opaque to themselves and strangely different from our own.

The verbal desire test that I was using was adapted from an experiment which Paul Harris and his colleagues had devised. He had seen that children are able to work out how someone will feel in a certain situation and that they are able to report on desires they'd held previously which were fulfilled. What he wanted to find out was whether children can *mentally* picture another person's desire. As Harris says, 'If young children can project themselves into the mental world of another person by imagining what that individual wants, they should readily acknowledge that different people might bring different desires and emotional reactions to a given situation.'

The story he and his colleagues devised to test this involved Ellie, a toy elephant, and a mischievous monkey called Mickey. Ellie really likes milk but hates coke. She has bought a carton of milk, and leaves it with Mickey while she takes a stroll round the zoo. When she's away, Mickey empties out her milk and fills the carton up with coke. She comes back, hot and thirsty from her walk, and takes a big slurp from the carton. The researchers then asked the children how Ellie would feel? Most four year olds could correctly answer this. In other words, they could understand another creature's thwarted desire. The researchers then asked the children to describe how Ellie feels *before* she takes a drink? To get this one right, the children have to remember that there is coke and not milk in the carton and that Ellie likes milk and not coke (which is easy and relies on a fully functioning memory: simple questions show that there is nothing wrong with most children's ability to remember details of a story). What is hard about this question is that the children have to understand that Ellie *thinks* there is milk in the carton, although they *know* it contains coke. Only the six year olds were able to answer correctly. Although the question is about Ellie's desire, the children have to understand that she has a false belief about her drink. Again, this test highlights the difficulty young children have understanding others' beliefs; even understanding someone's desires is hard for them if a belief is involved. As George

77

Bernard Shaw wrote in *Man and Superman*, 'There are two tragedies in life. One is not to get your heart's desire. The other is to get it.' Obtaining your heart's desire and not being happy is all to do with your belief about your desire prior to fulfilling your desire.

The film *Jagged Edge*, a tense and rather brutal psychological thriller, is about the interplay between belief and desire. Teddy Barnes (played by Glenn Close) is a prosecuting lawyer. She successfully prosecuted a man called Henry Styles, only to discover later that her prosecuting partner, Thomas Kresny (Peter Coyote), withheld information from her which would have proved his innocence. Styles hanged himself in jail. Teddy Barnes abandoned criminal law until her firm asked her to defend Jack Forrestor (Jeff Bridges) who is accused of the savage murder of his wife and maid. Barnes says she will only defend Forrestor if she believes he is innocent. He convinces her that he is and gradually she starts to fall in love with him. Her desires — for him and to defend him — rest on her belief that he is innocent and, in part, on her guilty conscience because of her previous false belief about Henry Styles. The film swings between portraying Forrestor as the bereaved and grieving husband and insinuating that he is guilty. Barnes's desire for him treads this same rocky road between passion, fear and disgust as she alternates between believing and doubting his innocence. Finally, his guilt is proven without a shadow of doubt and Teddy Barnes is overcome with horror and revulsion.

In a rather less grisly way, Janet Astington has demonstrated how much desires depend on beliefs. She showed children a large and a small Smarties box and asked them which one they would pick. Most of the children naturally chose the large box. She then opened the boxes and let them see that there were almost no Smarties in the larger box, but that the small one was full. She closed up the boxes and asked the children which box they had wanted when they'd first seen them and which box their friend (who hadn't seen any of the boxes) would pick? Almost no three year olds could report that they had wanted the large box and even fewer said that another child would initially want the large box.

When a similar experiment was given to a chimp with the simple rule: the first pile of sweets you pick goes to another chimp, the animals were incapable of pointing to the smaller pile first and time and time again became frustrated as they were left with fewer sweets than their companion. As soon as the piles of sweets were replaced by numbers, the chimps were capable of picking the lower number first. That chimps can understand written numbers and the amounts the numerals symbolise is amazing in itself; alternating the trials between numbers and actual sweets caused the chimps' performance to fluctuate accordingly. It seems that the rational thought processes of both chimps and children are completely overwhelmed when they are faced with a pile of Smarties!

Despite this caveat, this experiment succinctly captures the idea that both beliefs and desires are involved in actions and that desires depend on beliefs. As Alison Gopnik says, 'If the chocolate cake I am intent on obtaining turns out to be made of carob and tofu, I will be frustrated. My desire was less for this piece of cake, than for this piece of cake as I first thought of it, full of sin and cholesterol.'

Other researchers, such as Wellman, have also consistently shown that when beliefs are involved, young children are unable to answer questions about desires correctly. But even adults and older children will explain slightly ambiguous stories in terms of desires – an easier mental concept – unless they are prompted. For instance, if told that Jane is looking for her kitten, which is hiding under a chair but she is looking under her piano, most people will say she's looking there because she *wants* to find her cat. Only after prompting will all adults, most four year olds and about three-quarters of three year olds give an explanation that takes into account Jane's belief about where her kitten might be.

But why are desires so much easier to understand than beliefs? According to Simon Baron-Cohen it is because when you have a desire you want the world to change to fulfil your desire; when you have a belief you change your mental state to fit the way you perceive the world.

People's desires differ from each other because they are *mental* constructs: they are representations of their desire rather than the object of desire itself. But do young children realise this? In

Wellman's experiment with the doll who was looking for something, in one scenario, the doll found another item that was as attractive as the one she was searching for. Alison Gopnik wondered what would happen if the objects were not equally attractive. She devised an alternative experiment which involved showing children two books. One was an adult's and one was a child's. They were asked which one they would choose for themselves, for another child, and for an adult. Three year olds chose the book they liked best for everyone, but four and five year olds were less likely to make that mistake and did not think adults would love to read *Peter and Jane go to the seaside*. Gopnik says, 'Three year olds assume that other people's desires will be like their own desires, just as they assume that the beliefs of others will be like their own beliefs. Or to put it a better way, they assume that desirability is an objective feature of the world and is not a function of representations.'

If young children are not treating desires as if they are mental representations but objective features of the world, it is likely that they will not appreciate that a person's desire can change. Before we deal with this issue, we will first turn to studies on people with autism, for their abilities and deficits in comprehending desires may shed light on this matter.

One telling shortcoming is autistic children's inability to use words that refer to mental states. Even when autistic children have a vocabulary that is as extensive as a four year old's and can refer to desires and emotions, unlike normal children, or mentally retarded children such as those with Down's syndrome, autistic children very rarely use words that refer to mental states, such as 'believe', 'know', 'imagine', 'dream', 'remember'. The emotional words they are capable of using are ones such as 'hug', 'kiss' and 'smile'. Even when they are using emotion words, they always link the emotion to a situation or someone's behaviour and not what that person might think. Autistic children almost never use words such as 'surprise'. This makes sense because 'surprise' is actually a complex emotion, for you need to understand what someone believed and how their belief differed from the real world in order to see why they would be surprised. As I mentioned earlier, autistic people say that photos of someone looking surprised actually show them yawning. And even though autistic children can refer to how they perceive the world, they never speak about paying attention to what anyone else is looking at or talking about. As we said in the previous chapter, people with autism can understand the basic facts about vision, but they cannot understand the concept of joint attention. To a greater degree than other children, they also tend to talk about how they feel and what they want far more than they refer to anyone else's emotions and desires.

Peter Hobson, from the Tavistock Clinic, London, has shown the difficulty that autistic children have in understanding emotions. He designed a series of experiments that involved showing children video clips of a person displaying some kind of emotion. He then asked the children to choose a picture of a person with an emotion that matched the actor's. The video clips showed a person with a mask over his face, acting out an emotion and giving the correct gestures, such as shaking his fist to indicate that he was angry. The children then saw a blank television screen but could hear the actor making sounds, growling with anger, or humming to indicate that he was happy, for example. Finally, they were shown the actor enacting a situation in which he might feel an emotion – tripping and hurting his knee; being given a birthday cake. In addition, the children watched videos of objects – trains, cars, birds, dogs and so on – and, whilst watching a blank screen, heard the sounds these objects made and saw the context in which they occurred: for example, they were shown clips of an empty railway station or an empty dog basket.

The autistic children were able to pick out the pictures of things that matched the objects on video, even when they were only listening to the sounds the objects made or looking at the context in which they occurred – they could correctly choose a dog to go in the dog basket, for instance. However, they were unable to choose the correct emotion to match either the actor's gestures, his sounds, or the context in which the emotion might occur. The autistic children were consistently worse than either normal children or those with Down's syndrome. Neither were they able to choose a picture of someone making the appropriate gesture to match either a film of someone's facial expression or the sound they might make if they were happy, sad, angry and so on. They could not label the emotion the actor was expressing either by looking at his face or by listening to him. This reveals a huge lacuna in their ability to understand other people or to react normally in society, for we are intensely emotional creatures. It is little wonder that Leo Kanner, who first coined the term autism, said that they 'have come into the world with innate inability to form the usual, biologically provided contact with people', but they have 'a good relation to objects'.

Simon Baron-Cohen adapted the tests that Paul Harris had used on normal children (the one with Ellie who liked milk but not coke, and the mischievous monkey, Mickey) for autistic children. He first asked whether they could understand what situations would give rise to what kind of desires and then gave them two tests to see how well they could understand someone else's desire. Finally, he tested them to see if they could understand that knowing someone's belief was crucial to knowing what they desired.

The situation tests were fairly simple: how will Jane feel if it's her birthday and her mother bakes her a cake, and so on. The other tests revolve around Jane who is eating her breakfast. She likes Rice Crispies, but doesn't like Coco Pops. The children were asked how Jane would feel depending on which box of cereal she was given to eat — a situation familiar to all parents and children. This tests whether children can understand that desires cause emotions and if they can understand fulfilled desires (Jane is given Rice Crispies) as opposed to unfulfilled desires (she's given Coco Pops). Jane is then given the Rice Crispies box but finds it empty. She opens the Coco Pops box and discovers that it is full of Rice Crispies. This is the same kind of test, but the circumstances are a little more complex, since the actual content of the boxes is different from their apparent content.

In the belief test, the same mix-up has occurred, but Jane doesn't know — she's gone for a walk and meanwhile the children have peeked in the boxes. They were asked how Jane would feel when she came back from her walk and was given the Rice Crispies box.

The answer is that she'll feel happy, because she doesn't know the box is empty.

Normal children aged between four and seven were able to complete both desire tests correctly and most could understand the belief test. Just over half of the autistic children could pass the desire tests, but extremely few could do the belief test. In other words, they couldn't work out how Jane would feel when she was given the Rice Crispies, thinking the box is full, although in reality there is no cereal inside at all.

It seems that some autistic children can understand other people's desires and that in a certain situation they know how another person will feel. On face value, this seems strange since Peter Hobson showed the extensive difficulties autistic people have understanding emotions. What Baron-Cohen suggests is that these children have learnt some social rules governing which situations give rise to different emotions in other people, so that birthdays are seen as happy events, even though many children with autism don't enjoy social situations such as birthdays. This doesn't mean that they are any better at recognising emotions, even though they can use some simple emotion and desire words. The autistic people who can understand desires are able to do so because simple emotions such as happiness and sadness do not require metarepresentation. As we said in the introduction, mental entities are representational, they refer to something: in this case, metarepresentation is the capacity to represent mentally an image of someone else's desire.

We have seen that desires can be understood not as intentional, mental states, but as simple internal drives that guide a person towards certain objects and away from others. Hence understanding someone else's desire does not always require metarepresentation. Young normal children initially treat desires simply as relations to desired situations and only later understand them as mental representations of situations. Desires, therefore, do not always require metarepresentational capacity. The idea that young children can understand and express desires and speak of the desires of others, but cannot yet represent mental events, and thus cannot understand another person's belief, is backed up by much of Henry Wellman's work. He adds, 'The reason these young children cannot yet under-stand beliefs is because the child must consider (and conceive of) two sets of contents: the contents of the world and also the (representational) contents of the mind – the contents of the person's beliefs.'

This inability to think about the contents of someone's head is reflected in the difficulties children have distinguishing between real objects and imagined objects. Young children find it difficult to realise that you can't touch or see mental images; for instance, they think that their dreams can be visible to others. Brenda Mallon, a counsellor and therapist, once received a letter from a worried mother saying that her son had been having nightmares about a man with no face who slashed at him with his fingers and cut him. She said, 'The man is very real to him' and that both his teacher and doctor had no idea what might be wrong with the child. Mallon later started to research a book on children's dreaming and was inundated with childish nightmares on the same theme: 'I dreamt that when I was sleeping he came to me. His nails were big sharp blades [. . .] he ripped my tummy open and ripped out my eyes.' Freddy Krueger, a faceless subhuman monster with razorblades instead of fingers, is the 'Nightmare on Elm Street', and at the time had come to haunt the dreams of hundreds of children who, certainly in their dreams and often when they were awake, felt that he was as terrifying in reality as on celluloid.

Wellman says, 'If children believe ideas are literally physical things [. . .] then they could be acquired in the same way that physical things are acquired. That is, we might collect them [. . .] or they might seek us out and attach themselves to us like stray dogs.' He and his colleagues have conducted a whole barrage of experiments to determine whether children can distinguish between mental and physical entities. There are three criteria that can be used to distin-guish between mental and physical objects. First, you can use your senses to investigate physical objects. You can sit on a chair, burn it, break it, but you can't do this to a thought of a chair. Second, physical things have a public existence. No one else can see my dream chair, but you can, of course, see my real chair. Third, physical objects are consistent. My chair will always look the same, but my image of a chair can change.

To find out whether children used these criteria to distinguish between mental and physical objects, Wellman asked children about a 'thought cookie'. He wanted to know if they could see their cookie, whether it could be seen by someone else, and if they could change it? Children older than three could answer appropriately, but the interesting thing was that they didn't understand that 'thinking about a cookie' specified a mental event. They changed this concept into the idea that a child thinking about a biscuit didn't actually have one, thus translating the mental image into a real but absent object.

In a similar vein, when the children were asked why they couldn't touch a thought about a dog, although some used mental terms such as mind, dream, imagination and so on to explain why you couldn't, others said that the reason they were unable to touch the dog was because it had run away, or even, 'My mom won't let me' or 'You can't touch it because you'll get dirty'. Wellman concluded that 'Ideas and dreams may indeed be conceived of as special, seemingly insubstantial physical things, perhaps equivalent [. . .] to such real substances as smoke or shadows or air.' In other words, young children don't think that all objects are physical, or that objects in dreams and thoughts have the same properties as their physical counterparts in the real world, but they have a third category for dreamt and thought-of objects which share some of the real object's physical properties.

Many children can tell the difference between mental items and 'close imposters' – objects that you can't touch but which aren't imaginary, such as used-up toothpaste or smoke. Over half of the children Wellman tested agreed that you couldn't feel the close impostors and did not use mental terms to explain this. So, for instance, when they were asked why you can't hide used-up toothpaste, one child said, 'Cause when it's gone, you can't see it.' Others believed that you can't touch a lion in a picture but 'you *can* touch the *picture*'. Three year olds, whilst they were able to do this test, were not as consistent as five year olds. All too often they used explanations of the 'you can't touch it because you'll get told off, or you'll get dirty' type. Wellman thinks that when the children made mistakes, it was because they were talking about the object itself and not about the *thought* of the object.

He went on to study children's understanding of their own mental images. He told them to make a picture in their head of a balloon and asked the usual questions to see if they could distinguish their balloon from a real balloon: Can you see your balloon? Can you touch it? Can someone else see it? Just by thinking, can you make your balloon long and skinny? The children did act as if the image in their head was different from a real balloon, or even a real but hidden balloon (remember, in early experiments, Wellman showed that children sometimes thought that mental objects were real but absent). Initially, all the children thought that they couldn't alter the balloon in their head, but, after prompting, realised they could think of the balloon as long and skinny. Three year olds and even some four year olds still thought that they could touch their mental image of a balloon and that others could see it. Again, Wellman said it sounded as if they were talking about a real balloon. One three year old, typically for his age, said, 'Yes, I could touch it because it's right over there on the floor where you put it.'

Wellman's next idea was that if young children confuse mental with physical objects, they would be likely to confuse a mental picture and a photograph, especially as we often talk about 'pictures in our head'. He asked the children to answer questions about an imaginary object and a photograph of the same object. Both the photograph and the mental image are representations in that they depict something else and the object that is being represented cannot be touched. He referred to the objects as 'the picture in your head' and 'the picture in the box' (the photograph). The children were able to distinguish between the two, but at first many children spoke about their mental image as if they could touch it. Only with prompting, and when the contrast between the photograph and their 'picture in their head' was pointed out, did they correct themselves.

It does seem that children who are older than four can readily distinguish between mental images and real ones, but that younger children are confused by 'pictures in the head'. Wellman says, summing up his work,

> I think children are clear, in principle, about the basic distinction between mental and physical entities, but at least two deep issues confront and perplex them. One concerns how to place single experiences into those categories. When waking from a compelling dream, its phenomenal qualities may be so vivid that a young child does not know that *that* experience was mental not real (while still knowing the distinction and even knowing in general, perhaps, that dreams are mental). A second confusion concerns what we mean by saying something is real. This is a very complex issue. To paraphrase the philosopher Austin, a not-real duck might be not real because it's a picture, it's a fake-decoy, or it's dead. It's really (biologically speaking) a different type of bird (though commonly called a duck): it's an imaginary mental duck. Knowing the distinction between a real duck and a thought about a duck, still leaves room for confusion and thinking about these other distinctions. Young children have lots to wrestle with on that front, and thus are more confused about these things than older kids and adults, while still knowing the basic distinction – and indeed, these confusions and struggles are tricky, complex and imperfect even for adults.

Autistic children are not able to make the distinction between mental and physical objects – they think that a person who is thinking of a lollipop is equally likely to be able to eat it as someone who is holding a real lollipop. Since autistic children and children younger than three confuse real and mental objects, yet young children and roughly forty per cent of autistic people can understand questions about desires, it appears that initially their understanding of desires does not rely on understanding other people's mental states. Desires are thus understood as a person's drive towards some objects and away from others and certain situations are seen to be conducive of particular emotions, so that, for example, in our society, it is usual to feel happy when we are given a present. It is only as children develop and understand more fully the difference between mental imagery and real objects that they realise that desires are mental representations of situations.

Can animals understand desire? Anyone who has ever kept a dog or a cat, seen a caged animal in a zoo and watched animals at play will have no doubts that animals do feel happy or sad and have desires for food, affection, warmth and freedom. I think the emotional capacity of animals cannot be disputed; the question is, Can an animal understand another animal's desire? Sue Savage-Rumbaugh has taught the chimpanzees and bonobos in her care a language that relies on pressing or pointing to symbols. Before she embarked on this programme she studied bonobos both in the wild and in captivity. Bonobos are renowned for their love of sex: they often trade sexual favours for food. Savage-Rumbaugh, commenting on two of the bonobos in the group she was studying, remarked that, 'On some occasions, Matata would take food out of Bosondjo's mouth in mid-copulation.' Bonobos are happy to have sex with each other in every possible combination – males with males, males with females, females with females, in groups and with youngsters – and in every possible position. The females indulge in what is known as G-G rubbing, where they rub their large, pink clitorises against one another. Savage-Rumbaugh says, 'The more I observed copulatory bouts between bonobo couples, the more it became clear that the positions they assumed were not achieved passively. One or other of the couple had a clear notion of the preferred position and used a series of gestures to indicate what was required.'

The bonobos used three different types of gestures to get their partner into the position they wanted them. The most simple was placing a hand on their partner's body and deliberately moving that part of their body. The second type was more sophisticated and involved touch and gestures indicating movement. One bonobo would touch the part of his partner's body he wanted her to move and would then make a gesture indicating the direction in which he wanted her to go. The last type of gesture involved a bonobo standing up bipedally and raising his arms with the palm face down.

With her colleague, Beverly Wilkerson, Savage-Rumbaugh used a slow-motion video camera to capture these gestures. It soon became apparent that they were not random and that there was always a correlation between the gesture of one individual and the subsequent movement by their partner. Savage-Rumbaugh says that hand gestures require a high degree of cognitive sophistication since any species which uses gestures to communicate needs a clear concept of self and other. Moreover, these animals must realise that their personal desires can be communicated to another individual. She sees their gestures as a primitive language.

In the wild she observed branch dragging. Here the gestures of one bonobo are writ large for the whole group to see. An individual can spend up to half an hour searching for the right branch, using some impenetrable criteria to reject branches that are not quite right along the way. Once the male (it usually is a male) has found a branch, he runs through the forest dragging the branch behind him and making a noise to attract the group's attention. When all eyes are on him, he runs back and forth, which encourages the group to set off into the forest in the direction from which he has dragged the branch. If the male wants the group to change direction at some point, he will again start dragging his branch. Mon, an adult male, used this activity to wake up his friend, Ika, who was nesting in a nearby tree. Mon had seen a fruit tree and he dragged the branch between the nesting tree and the fruit tree. Eventually, Ika woke up. Mon stopped dragging, squeaked excitedly and jumped around. Ika, still sleepy, disappeared back into his nest. Mon resumed his dragging and after about five minutes Ika reappeared and the two set off for the fruit tree.

At the lowest level of desire comprehension, young children can understand what desire or emotion a person will feel in a given situation. This seems to be what chimpanzees are capable of. Chimpanzees have their own code of conduct and one unwritten rule is that when a female is in season she ought to disappear off into the jungle with a male. Females usually aren't so keen on the idea, but for a male the situation is perfect. A female on heat is an object of desire and all the males will compete to mate with her. Dragging her off on her own means the male can mate with her at his leisure without worrying that other males will nip in and fertilise her behind his back. Jane Goodall describes one incident involving a male, Evered, and a female, Winkle, who was less than enamoured at the whole prospect of 'honeymooning' with Evered.

For about twenty minutes Evered shook branches violently at Winkle to try to get her to follow him. 'It was obvious that his patience was wearing thin and finally it gave out altogether. With hair bristling, lips compressed, he leapt on to Winkle, pounding and dragging her until she pulled free and ran off screaming.' He followed her and again she refused to obey him. He waited for about half an hour and then eventually disciplined her. 'Now, at last, when he stopped his pounding and summoned her to approach she responded instantly. Hastening to crouch before him, with nervous panting-grunts, she pressed her mouth to his thigh, kissing him. And then, as is the way of male chimpanzees after aggression, Evered reassured her, grooming her until she relaxed under the gentle caress of his fingers. Once punishment has been handed out, then it is time to make amends, to restore social harmony.'

Perhaps a male chimpanzee understands how his partner will feel having been beaten and knows that he needs to reassure and comfort her (while not letting these feelings get in the way of what he wanted in the first place). Nevertheless, this behaviour need involve no mental understanding: a male may have learnt how his behaviour will change the behaviour of a female in a way that is advantageous for him.

Weaning is another emotional time in a chimpanzee's life. Goodall watched the weaning of Frodo who was thrown into despair when his mother Fifi tried to stop breast-feeding him. He threw violent tantrums, screamed, tore his hair and flung himself on the ground. 'Always Fifi reached out to him, trying to draw him close. If, as was so often the case, he had then hurled himself to the ground, pulling away from her conciliatory gesture, she had usually taken him into her arms and held him there. And however violent had been his rage, Frodo had always calmed after a while, perhaps intuitively understanding his mother's message: "You can't have milk (or ride on my back) but I still love you, anyway." '

There have been almost no experiments specifically designed to test an animal's comprehension of another animal's desire. A pioneering experiment on a sign language-using chimpanzee, Sarah, by David Premack, indicates that this chimpanzee, at least, might understand what another person wants. Sarah was shown a video in which one of her trainers was in some predicament and then she was asked to choose a picture with the solution. For example, in one video clip, he was locked in a cage; the correct picture showed him unlocking his cage. Another video clip showed the trainer trying to reach a bunch of bananas hanging from the ceiling and the solution was a picture of the trainer standing on a chair to reach the fruit. Sarah correctly chose the right card for each of the situations her trainer found himself in. Moreover, when she was given photos of her favourite trainer and others of a trainer whom she disliked, she continued to chose the correct option for her trainer, but chose photographs that showed the trainer she didn't like still locked up in his cage, or unable to reach the bananas. David Premack says, 'That the actor is not merely jumping up and down, but "wants" the bananas and is "trying" to get them is an interpretation of the actor's behaviour, one that depends on assigning certain states of mind to the actor – for a problem is nothing so much as an individual who is seen as having certain states of mind that are unfulfilled.' Three-and-a-half-year-old children were unable to choose the correct solution. 'They sometimes chose a yellow flower because it matched the yellow of the bananas,' says Premack. Even when the tasks were translated into suburban locations, such as a person trying to reach a chocolate chip cookie on top of a fridge, the children did no better.

However, I think that Sarah's actions, whilst incredibly clever, do not indicate that she understands what someone would feel in a given situation. Sarah might have been thinking about what *she* would want in the situations she was presented with. Because she chose nasty options for the trainer she didn't like, this explanation is more likely to be correct. It is impossible from this experiment alone to say whether Sarah had a mental representation of her trainer's desire. Still, it does seem that chimpanzees have some concept of desires, probably very similar to that of young children, which involves little or no mental representation. Although we will deal with animals' abilities to deceive each other in chapter seven, one example of a deceptive 'arms race' witnessed by primatologist Emil Menzel who was then at the Delta Regional Primate Centre, Covington, Louisiana, does illustrate desire comprehension in two chimpanzees.

Belle, a young chimp, watched while Menzel hid food in the middle of a large open enclosure. The rest of the group was kept indoors and could not see what he was doing. Once Menzel had finished hiding the food, Belle and the other chimpanzees were allowed into the enclosure. Belle always led them straight to where the food had been hidden. Shortly after Menzel had adopted this procedure, a larger chimp, Rock, began to take all the food and refused to share it with any of the others. Belle stopped uncovering the food if Rock was nearby. Instead, she would sit on top of the food. Rock soon learnt this and if she sat in one place for more than a few seconds, he would push her aside and dig up the food. Belle then started sitting a little distance away from the food but Rock countered this by looking in the area surrounding her. She sat further and further away from the food, and would wait until Rock was looking in the opposite direction before she'd dash over and unearth it. Rock started to amble around the enclosure looking uninterested, but as soon as Belle was about to uncover the food, he would run back. He often found food that was hidden thirty feet away from Belle and would adjust his search by looking at her. She gave the game away by an increased nervousness whenever he got near to the hiding place. Belle then led the whole group away from the food and when Rock was busy looking for the cache, she would double back. Menzel fuelled this arms race by hiding smaller bits of food in addition to the larger hoard. Belle immediately led Rock to one of these and tried to rush back to the bulk of the food. When Rock began to ignore these small bits of food and pointedly waited for Belle to uncover the large stash, Belle, at her wits' end, had temper tantrums.

The last example I am going to give of desire comprehension was witnessed by Sue Savage-Rumbaugh. This time, Kanzi, her symbol-using bonobo, understood Savage-Rumbaugh's desire and communicated it to another bonobo. Savage-Rumbaugh was playing with a bonobo called Matata and her daughter Tamuli, who knows no language. Tamuli asked for Savage-Rumbaugh's keys by pointing to them and looking at her face with a questioning expression. The scientist gave her the keys, which the young animal played with until she became bored. When Savage-Rumbaugh left the room, she forgot to take the keys with her. It was only when Kanzi asked if he could visit Matata that she realised she'd left them behind and could no longer get back into the cage with Matata and Tamuli. She asked Tamuli to look for them, thinking the bonobo would not understand her command. To her surprise, Tamuli immediately went and found the keys, but instead of handing them back, she started playing with them. For about a quarter of an hour, Savage-Rumbaugh coaxed, cajoled and bribed the young bonobo, all to no avail. Eventually, she turned to Kanzi and said she couldn't open the door because Tamuli had the keys. She said, 'Please tell Tamuli to give me my keys.' In Savage-Rumbaugh's words, this is what happened next:

> Kanzi climbed to the top of his room where the wire mesh separated his area from Tamuli and looked at her while making a small noise. Tamuli approached Kanzi, looking directly at him. Kanzi made several multisyllabic sounds to Tamuli. Tamuli listened, then to my amazement quietly walked over and handed the keys back.
>
> Did Kanzi tell her to give me my keys? Did she understand him and comply? It certainly seemed so. If such an event were to occur between human siblings, we would call it language, even if it were in a tongue we could not yet recognise or catalogue.

5

TRUE BELIEF

'There's no use trying,' she said: 'one *can't* believe impossible things.'
'I dare say you haven't had much practice,' said the Queen.
'When I was your age, I always did it for half an hour a day. Why,
sometimes I've believed six impossible things before breakfast.'
Lewis Carroll, *Alice Through the Looking-Glass*

'Within a month,/Ere yet the salt of most unrighteous tears/Had
left the flushing in her gallèd eyes,/She married – O, most wicked
speed! To post/With such dexterity to incestuous sheets!' moans
Hamlet about the speedy marriage of his mother to his uncle Clau-
dius, who Hamlet correctly suspects has killed his father. Hamlet's
former love, Ophelia, has been sent to discover the source of
Hamlet's apparent madness. Neither knows that the King and his
counsellor, Polonius, are listening, but halfway through their conversation Hamlet becomes suspicious. He mistakenly believes his
mother is eavesdropping, and so, for her benefit, he maligns Ophelia
and denounces her sex as a way of hurting the Queen.

> I have heard of your paintings well enough. God hath given you
> one face and you make yourselves another. You jig and amble,
> and you lisp, you nick-name God's creatures, and make your
> wantonness your ignorance. Go to, I'll no more on't, it hath made
> me mad. I say we will have no more marriage. Those that are
> married already – all but one – shall live.

However, Hamlet is wrong; it is the King who is listening and
who benefits from Hamlet's false belief (that it is Hamlet's mother
who is listening), as he realises that Hamlet plans to murder him to

revenge his father's death. How and when we begin to understand another person's false beliefs are to be the topic of this chapter.

In chapter three, we saw how young children and animals first begin to understand the language of the eyes, initially by detecting the direction in which a person is looking and by the realisation that looking at another's eyes can be informative. In chapter four we saw how eyes act as a salient clue when guessing someone's emotions and how an understanding of what someone is paying attention to can lead to an understanding of their desire. In this chapter, I want to draw these two strands together, first by returning to the eyes and showing how, in older children, 'seeing' becomes a much more complex activity. By understanding what someone else can see, it is possible to understand what they know: this first glimmer of another person's thoughts filters through a child's consciousness at the age of three. Second, we will discover how and when beliefs are understood and, finally, decipher the litmus test of Theory of Mind: comprehending another being's false belief about the world.

We all take the process of seeing so much for granted that we are no longer consciously aware that looking at an object leads to acquiring information about it. Yet children younger than three or four and most autistic people do not have this insight. A very simple test is enough to prove this. Imagine that two people are standing next to a cupboard, one is leaning against the cupboard and the other has opened the door and is looking inside. Surprisingly, neither young children nor autistics can tell you which person knows what is in the cupboard. In order to know about our environment, we have to have information about it, and to do this we need to see it. It is this link between knowing and seeing that is not understood by small children or those with autism.

Young children, people with autism and animals can link gaze to a person's or an animal's actions, but they don't necessarily *mentally* connect gaze with actions. The fact that an organism can appreciate the properties of seeing, as I outlined in chapter three, does not mean that it understands the mental consequences of perception. This comprehension usually appears in young children between the ages of three and four. Prior to this, children conflate the idea that seeing will lead to knowing with their burgeoning comprehension of other people's desires; for example, they think you must know all about an event or a situation if you are interested in it. In the cupboard example, if the person leaning against the cupboard and unable to see inside acts enthusiastically, a two year old will think that this person knows more about the cupboard's contents than the person who is actually looking inside but is not particularly excited about the left-over can of beans that she can see.

Although young children cannot understand that seeing leads to knowing, they can grasp the fact that eating leads to satiation or that starving leads to hunger. At first, this distinction, made by Josef Perner, from Salzburg University in Austria, and Jane Ogden, from the University of Sussex, seems fatuous, but hunger and knowledge have much in common. Both are internal states which cannot be seen, both rely on internal organs (the stomach and the brain), both are 'fed' with external products (food and information) and their state can be inferred from the situation a person is in and how he is behaving. For instance, if we see a boy peer into a cupboard which contains his football and we find out he wants to play football, we assume that he knows where his ball is and will fetch it. Similarly, if someone is prevented from eating dinner, we assume that he or she is going to be hungry. There are degrees of hunger and knowledge: a person who has just eaten two tubs of ice-cream is less hungry than someone who has only eaten a Mars bar; a child who looked through a box thoroughly will have a greater knowledge of what's inside than her friend who has only given the box a cursory glance.

The major difference between these two internal states is that eating leads to satiation and can be physically felt. We never seem to get full of knowledge – there's always room for another fact – and, unlike the phrenologists, we cannot point to our right temple and say, 'There, that's the place where I hold the knowledge that Aunt Martha is hungry.' Three year olds understand perfectly that if Dad won't let you have any tea, you'll be hungry, but fail to comprehend that because Jasmine saw the ball in the garden, that's where she'll look for it. This is not because they do not understand the interaction between observable events and internal states, but for quite another reason. Josef Perner thinks children can't understand knowledge because they can't represent mental states. We saw in the previous chapter that young children have difficulty comprehending desires and that it is only later that they develop a more explicit mental understanding. Until this time their responses consist of attitudes towards situations. This still allows young children to have a rich and complex mental repertoire: they understand their own behaviour and other people's in terms of their goals, fears, dislikes, wishes and so on, and can imagine various scenarios, provided they are linked to concrete situations.

Although children younger than three can tell you what's going on in their head, they are incapable of justifying why they do or do not know a fact. Children of this age think adults know more than they do, indeed, more than adults could possibly know, and they think other children know less than they could know. Neither do they realise that if they are told a secret, they possess unique know-ledge. They act, instead, as if everyone knows, as many a parent has found out to his embarrassment. It is not that they are completely egocentric, it's just that they don't understand the conditions under which knowledge is acquired or that misleading information leads to false beliefs.

Autistic children have even more of a problem with understanding knowledge; about fifty per cent of autistic children will fail a simple, limited knowledge task. The test, devised by Alan Leslie and Uta Frith, went as follows: one person and the child watched whilst an experimenter hid an object – a yellow counter – in full view of both of them. The person who was watching then left the room. The experimenter produced an identical counter and asked the child to hide it. The child was asked if the person who had left the room knew where the counter was that the child had hidden and, if that person came back, where she would look for the counter. Obviously the answer is that she doesn't know where the second counter is because she didn't see it being hidden, and she'll look for the counter she saw the experimenter hiding, yet autistic children are unable to answer these questions.

Between the ages of four and eight, children's understanding of what other people know when they see objects changes drastically. Husband and wife team, John and Eleanor Flavell, and their colleague, Frances Green, are all from Stanford University, California. They've shown that at four years old, children show little comprehension that a person who is preoccupied with some visual task, such as staring intently at a photograph to work out if they know anyone pictured in it, will not be paying attention to other inconspicuous or obviously irrelevant objects that happen to be in that person's visual field. So, for instance, the children would say the woman staring at the photograph is also paying close attention to the gilt-edged picture frame and the piano in the corner of the room. By the age of eight, children have a sophisticated grasp of how seeing can determine what someone is paying attention to and the process of thinking itself. Eight year olds understand that the picture frame is not of *no* interest, but perhaps fragmentary attention will be paid to it while the woman focuses most of her attention on the photograph. While their friend is thinking about what movie she went to last week, she might appear to be *looking* at the piano, but she is not *attending* to it. Six year olds were bang in the middle: they are better than four year olds at this test but not as confident as eight year olds. The Flavells put it this way: 'Four year olds may implicitly conceive of the mind as more like a lamp than a flashlight, that is, a device that can radiate attention and thought in all directions at once rather than in only one direction at a time.' Four year olds don't assume that people are paying attention to everything in the room, it is just that they haven't figured out how attention and perception work. They overestimate people's attentional capacity in the same way that they overestimate brain power; they often exaggerate how many things they can remember at one go and it is only later that they realise how depressingly few things one can memorise. This lack of understanding of perception parallels unfamiliarity with the process of acquiring knowledge and their incomprehension when faced with information that is false or misleading.

It is only after the age of five that children can refer to the brain as an organ for thinking and talk about its mental functions, such as dreaming, remembering and imagining. Autistic children have no idea that the brain is used for thinking. To them it is an organ like any other. When asked what the brain does, they say things such as, 'It makes you move.' Uta Frith once conducted an experiment on reading with some autistic children. When one child did particularly well, she asked, quite by accident, 'Oh, how did you know that?' He replied, 'By telepathy.'

It's almost impossible to determine whether animals think and actively know that they are thinking. The only animals you can ask are ones that will answer. Sue Savage-Rumbaugh was driving through the woods with Kanzi's sister, Panbanisha, when she noticed that the bonobo appeared to be very quiet and pensive. 'I was moved to ask her what she was thinking – a question I generally avoid since I have no means of validating the answer, nor even if an ape understands the question. However, at this moment Panbanisha looked literally lost in thought, so I dared. She seemed to reflect upon the question for a few seconds and then answered "Kanzi". I was very surprised as she almost never uses Kanzi's name.'

We have looked at how understanding vision leads to understanding knowledge and explored children's mental understanding of attention. Can animals understand that seeing leads to knowing? Daniel Povinelli and Timothy Eddy wanted to find out whether young chimpanzees aged between four and five could understand that vision shows what a person or another chimp is paying attention to: could the chimps interpret visual perception as a device that connects them to others and to events and objects in the world? Would they gesture only to those people who could see their gesture? If chimps cannot understand that when a person looks at them, they are paying attention to them, they should gesture to anyone, regardless of whether they are looking at them or not. Povinelli and Eddy trained the young chimps to beg for food from a trainer. They then gave them a choice of two trainers, one of whom could see the chimps and one whose vision was restricted. The simplest way the trainer was prevented from looking at the chimps was by standing with her back to them. Other ways that Povinelli restricted the trainer's vision was to get her to cover her eyes with her hands or a blindfold or to put a bucket or a paper bag over her head. The two trainers swapped roles so that the one who could not see the chimps was not always the same person.

The young chimps showed no immediate disposition to gesture to the person who was looking at them, although they rapidly learnt from whom to beg for food. Towards the end of the study they were correctly able to ask for food from the person who was able to see them from the very first trial. These results could be interpreted in several ways. Because the chimps learnt rapidly, they may have understood that a person is only mentally connected to you if they can see you, but, because of their youth and the fact that it was a rather alien experimental set-up, it took them a few attempts to work out what was being asked of them. Another hypothesis is that chimpanzees develop mentally much more slowly than human children; it is possible that chimps of this age still had not reached the same level as three-year-old humans. Indeed, in other experiments on older chimpanzees, Povinelli seems to have shown that chimps are capable of a far more sophisticated approach to seeing and knowing.

An alternative explanation is that the chimpanzees rapidly learnt a rule, such as, 'gesture to the person *holding* a bucket, not the person with a bucket *over* their head'. This rule may then have become generalised: 'Gesture to person whose eyes are *not* covered.' Since they were rewarded with food each time they gestured to the correct person, these rules were likely to be picked up quickly. But when Povinelli gave this test to three-year-old children, from their first attempt they had no problems indicating which person was looking at them in order to get their sweet reward. That the chimps had learnt a set of rules very quickly now seems the most likely explanation, for, two years later, Povinelli repeated the same experiment on the same chimpanzees. Although they could immediately choose the person facing them as opposed to the person who had her back to them, on any other combination of seeing and not-seeing they were right back at chance levels – yet in the intervening two years these chimpanzees had all participated in experiments that were connected to gaze-following and attention. 'I was stunned, to be honest,' says Povinelli. 'If they had a mentalistic understanding of attention, why on earth do they fall apart when they're tested again? They had to learn all the rules again – it's exactly as if the apes became primed to rapidly learn what the relevant cues were.' He adds that he doesn't think their joint attention behaviour is mentalistic. 'It's not that they don't explore body posture and gaze, they clearly do – they're very sensitive to gaze direction. But they learn rules, their gaze-following is not a window into the mind.'

Andrew Whiten, from the University of St Andrews in Scotland, disagrees. Whiten worked with Sue Savage-Rumbaugh's chimps to find out whether they understood that attention was like a 'psychological spotlight'. The experiment was simple. Normally, when researchers want the symbol-using chimps to name an object, a researcher will hold up an object and ask the chimp to name it. Whiten sat next to a chimp surrounded by everyday objects. He obtained eye contact with the chimp and then looked at one of the objects and said, 'What's that?' The chimps spontaneously named the object in a rather eerie fashion.

Whiten tried other scenarios, such as looking at objects placed behind the chimp or sitting with his back to the objects so that the chimp had to guess what Whiten was looking at using only the back of his head. The only thing the chimps weren't good at was determining what Whiten was looking at when he moved his eyes but not his head. This ties in with Povinelli's work which suggested that for chimpanzees the eyes alone were not indicators of attention. This may be because chimps will naturally turn their head to look at objects rather than only move their eyes and, in addition, the white sclerota that surrounds the iris cannot normally be seen. When we glance to one side, it is very easy to see what we are looking at, but it's harder when a chimpanzee does this, since the whole surface area of their eyes is dark. Whiten was able to train the chimps to respond to eye gaze alone, but they seemed to interpret this as something quite separate from the 'mentalistic understanding of attention' they were using to name the objects Whiten was attending to.

A few years before Whiten's experiments, Povinelli conducted some rather more sophisticated tests on chimps (albeit older ones) which were designed to test whether they could understand that seeing leads to knowing and that not-seeing leads to ignorance – in other words, if you haven't seen an event, but pretend to know, will chimps understand that you are merely guessing? One person hid food in one of four cups, whilst a second waited outside the room. Both people then pointed to a cup. The person who had hidden the food was the Knower – he had seen where the food was and consequently pointed to the correct cup. The Guesser, who had been outside the room whilst the food was hidden, pointed to any cup at random. If a chimp gestured towards the Knower, the Knower would share the hidden food reward with the chimp. The two people playing the Knower and the Guesser swapped roles so that a chimp watching would have to understand the connection between seeing and not-seeing, rather than learning that one person would always point to the cup with food in it.

The chimpanzees Povinelli tested were aged between seven and twenty-eight and they quickly learnt to point to the Knower. They seemed to have grasped the complex mental difference between the state of mind of a person who knows and one who is ignorant: when a third trainer hid the food whilst the Knower watched and the Guesser remained in the room, but with a bag over his head so he couldn't see, the chimps still chose the Knower. However, the chimps could have rapidly learnt a rule that enabled them to choose the right person, just as they did in the seeing-knowing experiment.

Povinelli and his colleagues also tried this same test on rhesus macaques but none of them was able to gesture to the Knower. Their inability certainly did not stem from lack of trying on Povinelli's part: most of the monkeys had over 600 goes at this experiment and one, a male called Tuck, had more than 800. Povinelli then made the trainer who played the role of Knower wear a pink glove and the monkeys were able to indicate correctly who 'knew' where the food was. All that they were doing, in fact, was using the pink glove as a clue to discriminate between the right person to pick and the incorrect one. The monkeys had learnt a simple rule: to get food, point to the person wearing the pink glove. Any rules the chimps might have learnt were far more sophisticated and complex since they were not provided with any salient and consistent cue such as the pink glove.

Although the term 'Theory of Mind' was coined by psychologist David Premack following observation of a chimp, Sarah (who, incidentally, was the twenty-eight-year-old subject of Povinelli's experiment), thereafter, the bulk of experiments have been conducted on children and most of the tests carried out on animals have been adapted from ones previously done on children. Povinelli works in the opposite way. He usually conducts his experiments on chimps first and then on children. He found that all the children he tested who were older than three were able to point to the Knower. However, none of the three year olds — but most of the four year olds — was able to tell him *how* they knew who was the right person to point to. Indeed, one child said she knew where the sweet was because her mother fed her lots of carrots so she could see very well! Povinelli concludes that even though three-year-old children have been pointing and responding to pointing for nearly two years, they do not appear to be aware of how this gesture functions to create knowledge in themselves and others. Children of this age have yet to understand the link between perception and knowledge: they still don't fully understand that seeing leads to knowing.

Even more unusually, other psychologists picked up on Povinelli's experiment with primates and tried it out on adults. Joseph Gagliardi, Mark Blumberg and colleagues from the University of Iowa, in Iowa City, conducted the experiment on 'thirty-seven undergraduate students (*Homo sapiens*) enrolled in introductory psychology courses'. Unsurprisingly, the adults quickly, within a couple of trials, correctly chose the Knower.

The same skill — understanding someone else's state of knowledge — has been demonstrated by Sue Savage-Rumbaugh and two of her symbol-using chimpanzees, Austin and Sherman. On the first trial, Austin followed Savage-Rumbaugh to the fridge where she put some banana slices in an opaque container and put the lid on. She led the chimp with the closed container over to a colleague, Sarah Boysen, who had not seen the transaction. Boysen asked Austin to identify what was in the container. He pressed the symbol for 'banana'. Sherman, who had watched Austin disappear into the kitchen and return with the container, quickly also lit up 'banana' on his keyboard. Savage-Rumbaugh says, 'While we had no reason to believe Austin recognised on the first trial that he was telling Sherman what was in the container, Sherman seemed to believe that Austin was describing the container's contents [. . .] The singular fact that the chimp who did not know what was in the container nearly always waited and watched until the other one revealed its contents was sufficient to show that the chimp recognised differing states of knowledge, based on observing or not observing the baiting process.'

Although the chimp that hadn't seen the food being hidden seemed to understand that the other one knew what was in the container, the 'knower' did not act as if he understood that he needed to tell his companion what was in the container. In any case, it didn't matter to him whether the other chimp knew or not – they both got the goodies in the end. Savage-Rumbaugh imposed the constraint that both chimps had to signal correctly what was in the container before it was opened and the food was shared. This meant that the 'informer' needed to ensure that the other chimp was paying attention. It took the chimps a few attempts before they realised what was being requested of them. On one occasion, Sherman, who had seen the container being baited, pressed the key for 'apple'. Austin, who prefers bananas, perhaps out of wishful thinking, pressed 'banana'. The container was opened, and Austin immediately tried to correct his mistake to 'apple'. After that, Sherman monitored Austin very closely and if ever he looked hesitant, Sherman would quickly repeat what the food was. But again, Sherman and Austin could have learnt a complex set of rules, motivated by the fruit.

On another occasion, the researchers put a banana in a cardboard tube with covered ends and left it in a cage. A chimp called Mercury discovered the fruit. The next day he was again let into the cage on his own. He raced across to the tube expecting another treat. What he found made him practically jump out of his skin with fright. A live iguana was curled up inside. Mercury gave 'waa-waa barks', his hair stood on end and he rushed back to Panzee, Lana and Sherman. They reacted by barking anxiously. When they entered the cage that Mercury had been in, they were extremely cautious and approached the cardboard tube with some trepidation. The researchers assumed that Mercury had 'told' the others about the iguana, understanding that they did not know about the scare awaiting them in the next room. However, Mercury's fear may simply have frightened the other chimps. They, in their heightened state of fear, were expecting to see something awful in the next cage.

We've seen that children only from the age of four onwards can understand that seeing leads to knowing and are able to grasp the concept of knowledge as a mental state. Chimpanzees over the age of six might also be able to understand that if you are visually connected to a situation, you are paying attention, and that seeing leads to knowing, whereas not seeing leaves a person in ignorance. However, it is not clear whether chimps are using a complex set of rules or whether they do have a full mental awareness. In the previous chapter, we saw how children younger than four cannot understand beliefs and hence, even though they can normally understand another person's desire, they cannot predict a character's desires when that character's belief is involved. At around the time when they are beginning to grasp what it means to know something, young children also start to understand a fundamental mental concept: simple beliefs. For example, given a story such as 'Sam wants to find his puppy, but the puppy is lost. It might be hiding in the garage or under the porch. Sam *thinks* his puppy is under the porch,' children of three to four are able to predict where Sam will look for this missing puppy. Sam's belief is correct, the puppy is under the porch. However, at this age, children still have problems with *false* beliefs.

A false belief is where a character's belief differs from the situation in the real world and consequently affects their actions. At around the age of four and a half, children are able to answer a simple false belief task where the child is explicitly told that the central character holds a belief that is wrong. In the case of Sam and his puppy, the child would be told that although Sam *thinks* the puppy is under the porch, it's *really* in the garage.

Heinz Wimmer and Josef Perner were the first psychologists to show that children under the age of between four and five cannot understand false beliefs. They devised a task now called the Sally-Ann test. Children were told a story about two dolls, Sally and Ann. Sally has a basket and Ann has a box. Sally places her marble in her basket and goes out. While she's out, naughty Ann moves Sally's marble from the basket to her own box, then she goes out. Sally comes back in.

The children were asked where Sally would look for her marble. Of course, Sally will look for it where she thinks the marble is – in her basket. Sally has a false belief about the marble's location. Children are not able to give the correct answer to this question until they are older than four or five. This understanding of false beliefs is what truly opens the gates to a full comprehension of other people. False beliefs are a hallmark of Theory of Mind because in order to understand another person's false belief it is necessary to comprehend their internal, invisible mental world rather than referring to the situations in the real world. It is a skill understood the world over, from North America to Japan, and even amongst preliterate people living an ancient hunter-gatherer life-style. Jeremy Avis and Paul Harris, from Oxford University, have shown that the Baka pygmies who live in the rain forests of south-eastern Cameroon can understand beliefs and desires. The children normally play in a miniature village, Ndabala, behind the main camp, where they practise hut-building, spear-shaping and fire-making. One child was summoned from there to a star-shaped fire. The two experimenters, Mopfana and Mobissa, cooked wild mango kernels, a favourite delicacy. Mopfana put his kernels in one of the cooking pots and covered them with a lid. He then went to *mbanjo*, the male meeting place, to smoke. Mobissa and the child hid the kernels in a different pot. Mobissa asked the child where Mopfana would look for his mango kernels when he came back and, 'After he lifts the lid, will his heart feel good or bad?' The children were able to answer both questions correctly, the first about Mopfana's false belief, and the second on his desire – at the same age as Western children. 'The fact that belief-desire reasoning emerges at approximately the same age in such diverse settings strengthens the claim that this mode of reasoning is a universal feature of normal human development,' says Avis.

But although children with Down's syndrome can pass this task, the majority of autistic children cannot. Simon Baron-Cohen, Uta Frith and Alan Leslie gave a non-verbal version of this test to autistic children by telling children a story in pictures and asking them to arrange it in the right order. 'I was looking for ways to test what Daniel Dennett calls the intentional stance,' says Baron-Cohen. 'Imagine you're trying to make sense of a social interaction frame by frame: without the intentional stance, without the notion that someone wants something, you wouldn't see the links, you'd just see slices of behaviour.'

The stories showed a causal sequence where a girl trips and hurts her knee; a desire scenario, where one child wants the other child's ice-cream; and a false belief picture sequence, in which one child steals another's teddy when she's not looking. 'The autistic kids were okay at the physical causal stories, but they had a lot of difficulty trying to find a meaningful sequence for the mentalistic stories,' says Baron-Cohen. 'They never knew where to put the final picture in the false belief story. The child is surprised that her teddy has disappeared but the autistic children said she was tired, or she was yawning.'

The Sally-Ann test is essentially the same as the Smarties task, where the child is asked what is inside the tube, only to discover that it does not contain sweets, but is full of pencils or birthday cake candles. As Janet Astington and Alison Gopnik discovered, children younger than five can neither understand someone else's false belief, nor report their own false belief. The very instant the lid is snapped off that Smarties tube and its true contents are revealed, small children are unable to report their own false belief. This seems an extraordinary finding. In Western philosophy, we've always treated the mind as if it were private and as if we, alone, had access to our thoughts. As we said in the previous chapter, it runs contrary to our own belief system to discover that children do not know their own minds.

Perner says that it's because children of this age cannot metarepresent: in other words, they are unable to hold a representation about a representation in their heads. He thinks that because young children react to the world as if it were composed of situations, they cannot hold two conflicting views of the world – one must be right! Thus in a child's mind there is no hierarchy between different versions of the truth. When they are asked to search their memory for a belief, they look for a description of a situation and run into two conflicting situations – one in which they did not know what was in the Smarties tube and one in which they did. Unable to deal with two different modes of reality, they fall back on what is currently true – they know what is in the Smarties tube *now.*

Children have a similar problem distinguishing between an object's appearance and what it really is when they are younger than four. For instance, if you show a child a sponge which looks like a rock, only a five year old will be able to say, 'I thought it was a rock until I touched it; now I know it is a sponge, but it still looks like a rock.' A particularly striking example of young children confusing appearance and reality is seen if you give a child a white flower and place a blue filter above it. Children now think the flower really is blue. Whilst the flower is under the filter, one of its petals is removed and pulled out from underneath the filter. Another petal, a blue one, is placed next to the white petal. If children are asked which petal came from the flower, they point to the blue one. Again, they are battling with two different modes of reality and they can't hold them both in their mind at the same time.

Autistic people are unable to make the distinction between appearance and reality: to them the sponge looks like a rock, therefore, it must be a rock, regardless of the fact that they can scrub themselves in the bath with it. Simon Baron-Cohen says, 'If, as appears to be the case, most children with autism really are unaware of the appearance-reality distinction, as well as being blind to their own past thoughts and to other people's possibly different thoughts, their world must be largely dominated by current perceptions and sensations.'

Norman Freeman and Hazel Lacohée, from Bristol University,

wanted to find out whether children's own false beliefs were lost and gone for ever, or whether they were buried in their brains and could be accessed. As they point out, the beauty of the Smarties test is that a handful of Smarties is a vivid reminder of their earlier belief. 'It would be a tribute to "amnesia" if children would, through a mouthful of Smarties, say that they had thought that the Smarties box contained pencils all along,' says Freeman sardonically.

What Freeman and Lacohée discovered was that children as young as three were able to remember their own false belief about the Smarties, but only during certain conditions. If they were given a handful of Smarties to eat when they first saw the Smarties tube and the experimenter had a brief conversation with them about the sweets and then, when they were shown the real contents of the tube, they were asked, 'When you were eating those sweets I gave you, what did you think was in this tube?' the children were able to access their past false belief. As Freeman says, 'Giving the children Smarties to put in their mouths can be categorised as getting the children literally to test a sample of reality.' Simply stuffing a few Smarties at the children and asking them what they thought was in the tube without any elaborate prompting did not work.

Giving the children a picture of whatever they thought was in the Smarties tube or in an egg box and asking them to post the picture through a slit in a shoe box also helped. The children were much better at recalling their past beliefs when they were given a picture of the object rather than the actual object to post into the shoe box. Presumably, this is because the picture reminds them of the egg that will be in the egg box, whereas, if they post an egg they are confused as, in their minds, the egg cannot now be in the egg box. These tests don't suddenly turn three year olds into the mental equivalent of a four or five year old. Children of this age can compute a false belief, but can't deal with two seemingly conflicting versions of the truth without clues to help them recall what they'd previously thought.

Even at the tender age of three, children are beginning to see glimmerings of the mental cogs whirring away in other people. Alan Leslie and Daniel Roth, from the University of Tel Aviv, tried to make the Sally-Ann test easier for young children by framing the story as a great deception. Sally has been given a bar of chocolate which Ann hides in her box when Sally goes out of the room. When Sally returns and cannot find the chocolate, she asks Ann where she's put it. Ann tells a lie and says it's in the dog's kennel. The children were asked where Ann thinks the chocolate is and then where Sally thinks it is. Although the three year olds still couldn't understand a false belief (where Sally thinks the chocolate is), they could say that Sally would think that Ann was lying about the whereabouts of the chocolate. This, Leslie and Roth say, indicates that three year olds have some inkling of the characters' mental states. Autistic children, however, always answered without recourse to mental states.

In fact, children as young as two years and eleven months old have an implicit understanding of false beliefs, even though they cannot verbally answer questions about a person's false belief until they are nearly five. Josef Perner, along with Wendy Clements, who is based at Sussex University, built an underground mouse house which had two exits on ground level. At each exit there was a coloured box, one blue, the other red. The two puppet mice protagonists were called Katie and Sam and Sam had a piece of cheese. The experiment was essentially the same as the Sally-Ann task, except that the children were filmed. Sam hides his cheese in one box, and when he's not looking Katie moves it to the other box. When the children were asked where Sam will look for his cheese, they correctly *looked* at the box where Sam had hidden it, but until they were four years and five months old, they always *said* that he would look in the box where Katie had hidden the cheese. The onset of an implicit understanding of Theory of Mind is very abrupt, as is the onset of an explicit and hence communicable Theory of Mind.

Understanding a false belief is quite different from understanding that the world has altered. This was aptly demonstrated by Alan Leslie and Laila Thaiss, currently at McGill University in Montreal, who showed normal four-year-old children and twelve-year-old autistic children how to use a Polaroid camera. They took a photo of a toy cat sitting on a chair, then laid the photograph on the table, face down and removed the cat. Leslie asked the children, 'In the photo, where is the cat?' This ingenious experiment is the equivalent of the false belief task: the Polaroid is 'out-of-date', just as Sally has an 'out-of-date' belief. Strikingly, all the autistic children were able to do this test, yet four year olds could not, even those who could pass false belief tasks. The reason may be simple, though: autistic children who are given psychology tests tend to be older than four and so they may be better at the test because they have more experience with cameras and are more familiar with the concept of pictures mismatching reality.

Leslie recognised this problem, so he repeated the experiment, but this time he made a map of the toy room and placed a sticker on it where the toy was before removing the toy from the room. The map is now 'out of date'. All the children found this task more difficult, but the results stayed the same: the autistic children who passed the map task were still unable to answer a false belief test properly and the normal children who passed the false belief test could not do the map task. Leslie says, 'Autistic children can pass photograph and map tasks because they have a good command over the general cognitive processing demands of the tasks and over the concepts of "photographs" and "maps". However, these children tend to fail false belief tasks because they do not have easy access to the concept "belief". Three year olds and some four year olds tend to fail both sets of tasks because they cannot meet the general processing demands made by both sets of task (false belief and photographs). Older four year olds pass both sets of tasks because they have access to all the required concepts and enough of the processing resources required.' This still does not explain why four and five year olds who can pass a false belief task sometimes fail the photo test. Leslie explains, 'They have greater access to the concept "belief" than they do to the concepts "photograph" and "map". This is so despite the fact that beliefs are private, unobservable and thoroughly "theoretical", while photos are public and observable entities. Beliefs ought to be much harder to learn about. For this reason, I don't think the normal mechanisms of learning will account for these findings. I'd argue that normally developing children possess a sort of "instinct" for attending to the invisible mental states of other people – a special intelligence.' Thus we are born with the potential to understand mental interactions well before we can understand concepts from the 'real' world.

John Swettenham, from the University of London, tried to see if he could teach children to pass false belief tasks. He designed a computer game based on the Sally-Ann test. In the program, Sally puts her ball in either a red box or a blue box. Sally leaves and Ann hides the ball. She then asks the child where Sally thinks her ball is. If the child correctly indicates where Sally thinks her ball is, music plays, and a flashing message, which changes colour, appears saying, 'Yes, well done!' Sally then searches for her ball and says, 'The ball is not there any more,' and waves her arms and stamps her feet in disappointment – this acts as a reinforcement, showing that the child has understood that the ball is not where Sally left it. If the child chooses incorrectly, Sally tells her the answer by saying, 'I think the ball is in the blue box where I left it.'

Normal three-year-old children, children with Down's syndrome and autistic children were then given the non-electronic version of the Sally-Ann task and three other belief tasks such as the Smarties test. Both the three year olds and the children with Down's syndrome were able to pass these other tests. Swettenham says, 'I think at three years normal children are pretty close to passing false belief tasks and the cognitive mechanisms for passing are there. Perhaps they just need the input – repeated examples and explanations – in order to get things working.' However, even though the autistics were almost eleven years old, they could pass only the Sally-Ann task they had practised and none of the other tests. Swettenham says they were probably using a rule of thumb, such as 'Pick the box where the ball isn't', so they were completely floored by the other tests. When he visited their school three months later they recited the entire text of the computer game out loud and from memory!

Since autistic children are good at learning rules, Swettenham wondered whether he could come up with a rule that he could explicitly teach children to help them solve all false belief tasks.

Initially, he thought about using the analogy of the computer as a person with its own mind and teaching the children that computers make decisions on the basis of the information they have, thus using the computer to bridge the gap for the children. In this way, the children could learn about the concepts required for Theory of Mind so that they could use them to understand people. Eventually, he, Simon Baron-Cohen and colleagues decided to capitalise on the idea of a photo in the head, which, he thought, was visually easier to grasp than the idea of a computer as a person. He said to the autistic children that the eye is like a camera and people have something similar to pictures in their heads: just as pressing the shutter on a camera captures an image, looking at a scene and blinking is a way of imprinting a picture on your mind. As Baron-Cohen says about autistic children, 'They understand about cameras so we've already got to first base.'

It is unlikely that normal children use a photo-in-the-head model for mental states (we've already seen how difficult it is for them to understand an out-of-date photograph), but for adults photos serve as a reasonable metaphor for what beliefs are – they're about things and they endure even when reality changes. Swettenham says, 'For children with autism, they may be the closest approximation to what beliefs are *actually* like, if they cannot conceive of beliefs themselves.' For an hour a day for five days, the children were taught a Theory of the Mind-as-a-camera. They and the experimenter took Polaroid photographs of Sally's 'beliefs'. The photo was slotted into a mani-kin's head, so that Sally, the manikin, literally had a picture in her head. The children were then taught to predict where Sally would look for her ball on the basis of the picture in her head.

After the training, the autistic children could not spontaneously use photos to understand false beliefs, nor explicitly link mental states to photos, but they could connect the photos to the character's actions. Before the teaching exercise, they all failed false belief tasks and did not understand that seeing leads to knowing. After their training, most of them passed both the Sally-Ann test and a seeing-knowing test and about a third of them could do the Smarties task. Despite this explicit coaching, the children were still not using the photos to infer mental states, they were operating on a behaviouristic principle. 'I don't think they understood any more about mental states,' says Swettenham. 'But that's okay. We're saying, "Let's teach them some behavioural rules or strategies to help them solve social situations – at least be able to predict people's actions a little better – with their own picture-based theory of mind." ' He thinks that the results are promising and that a larger scale and more intensive study could prove fruitful. Baron-Cohen, pointing out that each child was only taught for five hours, says, 'You could argue that there should be a special curriculum for mindreading!' This does not mean that the autistic children would eventually become like normal ones, Swettenham cautions. 'I doubt they would eventually recognise mental states in the same way that we do, but I think they would develop their own way of explaining and understanding other people's behaviour using this strategy.'

Normal children don't need this special teaching, but, as Norman Freeman and John Swettenham have both shown, they can be helped to understand false beliefs. Freeman and a colleague, Charlie Lewis, told false belief stories to children, but did not read to the end of the stories. They then asked the children to retell the stories in their own words. They then read the same stories, but in full, and the children were tested for their understanding of the characters' false beliefs. 'The kids cracked it,' says Freeman, 'even young three year olds. They'd got an understanding of false beliefs but they needed to consolidate the episode in their minds before they were able to switch to a mental framework.'

Freeman argues that these three crucial experiments – his and Charlie Lewis's where children rehearsed part of the narrative of the test, John Swettenham's study in which children were taught how to do a false belief test using a computer game, and the Perner and Clements experiment indicating that young children had an implicit understanding of false beliefs – all point in one direction. 'These three tasks show that three year olds have the computational base for understanding false beliefs, but they don't know *when* to use it. They can understand false beliefs if they are prompted whereas autistic people have to be taught.'

Although Theory of Mind is universal, the age at which children are able to pass a false belief test varies. Henry Wellman says, 'The main thing is not the exact age at which children pass or fail but the sequence of acquisitions and it's the sequences and patterns with age that are most important.' Children begin by understanding joint attention, then comprehending fulfilled desires, followed by unfulfilled desires. They then develop an understanding of other people's beliefs before finally comprehending false beliefs. However, a number of factors affect the age at which an individual child will acquire the various skills that constitute Theory of Mind. High verbal IQ, a large number of siblings and, most importantly, a great deal of co-operation and affection between the children and good maternal verbal fluency help a child acquire a Theory of Mind at an earlier age. Family discourse allows children to enquire, argue and reflect on why people behave in the ways they do. For instance, parents often sort out disagreements between siblings by explaining how the other child's mistaken beliefs governed his or her actions: 'He thought you had finished yours'; 'She didn't know I had promised it to you'; 'He thought it was his turn'. Girls usually acquire Theory of Mind slightly earlier than boys do.

As I have mentioned, there is some evidence that chimpanzees can understand the link between seeing and knowing and that they can tell the difference between mental states such as knowing and guessing. But can animals pass this crucial test for Theory of Mind? Can they understand the beliefs of others and, more importantly, can they understand false beliefs?

Dorothy Cheney and Robert Seyfarth, a husband and wife team from the University of Pennsylvania, spent eleven years looking at the social behaviour of East African vervet monkeys to find out how monkeys see the world and how much they know about what goes on in another monkey's head. They discovered that the monkeys have three different alarm calls which are related to specific predators. They give a barking alarm call in response to leopards and wild cats such as caracals; monkeys hearing this alarm call react by running into the trees. They also have an alarm call for crowned and martial eagles, which elicits a quick scan of the sky and a dash into the nearest bush; and a warning call for snakes, whereupon the monkeys stand on their hind legs and peer into the grass. The monkeys aren't simply acting like this because they have spotted the predator and are frightened, rather they react specifically to the alarm calls as Cheney and Seyfarth showed. They played back the calls of the monkeys to them, hiding loudspeakers in the bushes, and no matter whether they altered the calls so they were louder or softer, or longer or shorter than normal, the monkeys always responded appropriately.

The key question, as Cheney and Seyfarth say, is this: 'What do monkeys *mean* when they vocalise to each other? Can we actually define "leopard alarm", or "grunt to a dominant" in the same way we define words like anarchist, bordello, or sycophant?' The listening monkeys clearly treat the alarm calls as if they're conveying some kind of information, but do the calling monkeys *intend* the others to understand what they're saying?

Steven Pinker, author of *The Language Instinct*, says, 'Human communication is not just a transfer of information like two fax machines connected by a wire; it is a series of alternating displays of behaviour by sensitive, scheming, second-guessing social animals.' Genuine communication where symbols, words or vocalisations have a meaning only occurs when the speaker intends listeners to understand the meaning of the word as the speaker understands it. In *Through the Looking-Glass*, Humpty Dumpty says, 'When *I* use a word, it means just what I choose it to mean — neither more nor less.'

'The question is,' said Alice, 'whether you can make words mean different things.'

'The question is,' said Humpty Dumpty, 'which is to be master — that's all.'

In human society, there are conventions about what words mean, but they can mean several different things at the same time or have different meanings in differing circumstances.

Humpty Dumpty says, "Impenetrability." That's what *I* say!'

When Alice asks what he means, he replies, 'I meant that we've had enough of that subject and it would be just as well if you'd mention what you mean to do next, as I suppose you don't intend to stop here for the rest of your life.'

'That's a great deal to make one word mean,' Alice said in a thoughtful tone.

'When I make a word do a lot of work like that,' said Humpty Dumpty, 'I always pay it extra.'

Because autistic people cannot scheme or second-guess they don't understand the intention behind words. When one autistic child was asked, 'What should you do if you cut yourself?' the reply was, 'Bleed'; a standard response to a request to pass the salt would be, 'Yes'.

Daniel Dennett defined several levels of intentionality which I discussed in the introduction, and which we, because we know what we mean and we mean what we say, use unconsciously. In the film, *The Lion in Winter*, Peter O'Toole plays Henry II and Katharine Hepburn, his estranged wife, Eleanor of Aquitaine. The two of them are plotting against each other as to which of their three sons should inherit the throne. Henry says of Eleanor, 'She knows I want John on the throne and I know she wants Richard. We're very frank about it.' Which leaves the third son, Jeff, who is equally frank. In a brilliant exposition of levels of intentionality, Jeff says, 'I know. You know I know. I know you know I know. We know Henry knows and Henry knows we know it. We're a very knowledgeable family.' After Jeff has left the scene, Eleanor pithily sums him up, 'He'll sell us all you know. But only if he thinks we think he won't.'

To return to the vervets, what level of intentionality are they capable of understanding? If they are using zero order, then they are reacting because they are frightened and we have already established that that is not the case. If they are using first-order intentionality, the monkeys have beliefs and desires, but they have no beliefs about their beliefs. When a monkey calls, it is because he believes that there is a leopard nearby and he wants the other monkeys to run into the trees. He need have no conception of his audience's state of mind, nor does he need to recognise the distinction between his own and another animal's beliefs. If the vervets were capable of using second- or third-order intentionality, they would have some idea about another monkey's state of mind. A second-order communication would be one in which the caller wants the rest of the group to believe that there is a leopard in the vicinity. Using third-order intentionality, both the signaller's and the audience's state of mind are considered. A calling monkey would give a warning because he wanted the other monkeys to believe that he wanted them to run into the trees to escape from the leopard.

It is unlikely, though, that the monkeys have such a sophisticated understanding. Baby vervets give eagle alarm calls to pigeons and falling leaves, but the adults never correct them or 'praise' them when they call properly. As Cheney says, 'They learn by observation – those that don't, get eaten.' There is no vervet word for a larger category of meaning, such as 'danger' or 'family'. The adults don't give calls to warn baboons of danger, even when the predator poses no risk to themselves and when it is highly likely that the baboons' babies will be killed. They are, says Cheney, sublimely egoistic. Both she and her husband believe that 'Monkeys have a kind of laser beam intelligence – extraordinarily powerful when focused in a single domain, but much less well developed outside that narrow sphere. Although they solve social problems with little difficulty or training, they often flounder when confronted with the same problems outside the social domain. They do not always generalise their social abilities to other species or to inanimate objects and in this sense their skills seem relatively restricted. Apparently, the animals do not know what they know and cannot apply their knowledge to problems in other domains.'

For instance, the monkeys don't give alarm calls if they see a python's tracks disappearing into a bush, neither would they give a leopard call if they saw a carcass hanging in a tree – an indication that a leopard is almost certainly nearby. They don't react to alarm calls given by a starling or an impala and they don't act surprised to hear a hippo or a stilt's calls when the monkeys are nowhere near water.

The two researchers went on to study baboons. The females give contact calls to one another when they're travelling in a group through the woods. What they wanted to know was whether the females were deliberately calling to share information or to maintain contact if they were on the periphery of the group? Do baboons *intend* to communicate? Cheney and Seyfarth recorded contact calls and played them back to the group. They discovered that only females who were related would respond to calls. In other words, if one baboon's calls were played, only her sisters, her aunts and her cousins would reply. This type of 'altruism' has evolved in many animals since those who are related to one another share the same genes. The 'selfish gene' theory states that animals react to safeguard their own genes – whether those genes are in their own body, or if copies are in their relatives' bodies. Cheney and Seyfarth also discovered that female relatives only responded to the playbacks of the contact calls when they themselves were on the periphery of the group, right at the back of the troop or when there were no other females around. They concluded that the calls are used to keep in touch, but there is no mental understanding on the part of either the callers or the listeners. 'Monkeys [including baboons],' say Cheney and Seyfarth, 'see the world in terms of things that act, not things that think and feel.'

If monkeys do not have Theory of Mind, how do chimpanzees fare? Sarah, the original subject of Theory of Mind tasks, was taught to push a button that controlled the lock to a cabinet mounted on a wall just outside her cage. The cabinet was divided into two. One side contained pastries which her favourite trainer would share with her, the other side contained repulsive items such as rotting rubber and faeces. Every time the trainer came to see her, she pushed the button to release the lock to the good side of the cabinet. One day a villain wearing a mask entered her room and, while she watched, removed all the goodies and replaced them with the repulsive stuff from the other side of the cabinet. Sarah responded aggressively, hurling things at him from her cage. A few minutes later, the good trainer entered, yet Sarah showed no change to her normal behaviour. She made no obvious attempt to warn the trainer and neither did she hesitate before pushing the button. She acted as if she didn't recognise the discrepancy between her knowledge and the trainer's.

In contrast, Kanzi seems to have understood this distinction. Sue Savage-Rumbaugh told him he couldn't have any more M&Ms (sweets similar to Smarties). He then asked if he could go and play in the next room. He knew, although Savage-Rumbaugh did not, that there were M&Ms hidden in one of the cupboards. He ran into the other room, stole the sweets and returned.

At least one of three chimpanzees tested by Andrew Whiten appears to understand someone else's state of mind. The chimps' keeper would place food in one of two boxes, padlock them and hang the keys above the boxes. Whiten would then come in and unlock whichever box the chimps pointed to and, if they were correct, give them the food. Whiten was conducting this experiment with the symbol-using chimpanzees, Sherman, Austin and Panzee. He adopted an experimental procedure which went as follows: he asked Panzee what kind of food she would like to eat. He then put her choice of food in one of the boxes and locked both of them. He told her that he was just going out of the room and when he returned, he would then give her the treat. In the meantime, the keeper came in and hid the key. When Whiten came back, Panzee immediately pointed to where the key had been hidden and not to the box with food in as she had been trained to do. In other words, she seemed to understand that Whiten knew where the food was, but didn't know where the key was. In another version of this test, Whiten opened the boxes and hid the key. The keeper came in, placed food in one box and padlocked them. When Whiten came back, Panzee pointed to the box rather than the food – as if this time she knew that Whiten knew where the key was, but not the food. Austin and Sherman did less well on these tasks – they were able to point appropriately only after several trials. 'You could say that they had simply learnt whether it was correct to point to either the key or the box to get me to give them the food,' says Whiten. 'You could also say that Panzee is an exceptional chimpanzee.'

An experiment which I have conducted on four chimpanzees does seem to show that the brightest chimps can understand a false belief. I built a huge box which was so big that when a person crouched down behind it, a chimpanzee or a child facing the front of the box could not see the person. It had four drawers at the front, and a fan belt above the drawers. I used a large clothes peg, one of the old wooden ones, which I had painted bright red, as a signal to the chimps. The test involved a training phase prior to the experimental phase. In the training phase, each chimp had to learn that if I hooked the peg on to the fan belt above one of the drawers, there would be a sweet inside that drawer (after putting the peg above a drawer, I would go round the back of the box and place a sweet in the drawer; the box was pushed forward to the wire of the cage and the chimp reached through to pull the drawer handles and take out the reward). Once all the chimps had learnt this simple association, we progressed on to the experimental part. This time, I again put the peg above one of the drawers, but someone else moved the peg so that it was above another drawer. During half the trials the peg was moved while I was behind the box and could not see what was going on. The rest of the time I saw where the peg had been moved to. When I didn't see that the peg had been moved I put the sweet in the drawer above which *I* had placed the peg. The drawer beneath the peg which the other person had moved was empty. When I did see where the peg had been moved to I put the sweet in the drawer below it. I was alternately in a state of Knowledge and Ignorance. In Knowledge, I know where the peg is, but in Ignorance I do not know that the peg has been moved and thus I do not know where the peg is: I have a false belief about the peg's location and hence I bait the drawer where I wrongly think the peg is. To get this test right, the chimp has to understand my state of mind. Of course, the chimp could pick the drawer where the peg is and would be correct half the time – but this would obviously show that the chimp had learnt an association between the peg and the drawer. If the chimp was able to choose the correct drawer throughout the course of the experiment, she would have an understanding of my state of mind, knowing both when I knew and when I did not know.

One of the chimps was quite clearly not up to the task. He was much older than the others and had had little mental stimulation for years. He was given three times the number of trials in the training phase as the others. The other three chimps were young, between six and eight years old. Overall, they responded better than four-year-old children to this test, but not as well as five and six year olds. One female did exceptionally well and was able correctly to pick the drawer where the sweet was above chance levels in both the Ignorance and the Knowledge condition.

The children whom I tested with this non-verbal false belief task were able to pass it at the same age as they passed a verbal false belief task, the Smarties test. Autistic people could not do it at all. They consistently chose the drawer beneath the peg, no matter what the state of mind of the experimenter. One young man was able to do the task at first. We asked him how he knew which drawer to look in. The staff who cared for the autistic people had not wanted us to give them sweets, so we hid a bean instead. Mark said he could hear the slight click of the dried bean as we put it into the drawer and that gave him the clue!

A new Theory of Mind task has just been carried out on sign language-using bonobos and shows that bonobos with symbol use, at least, are capable of understanding a person's false belief. Panbanisha watched as a trainer hid some sweets in a box. When the trainer was out of the room, a second person substituted pine needles for the sweets. The trainer returned and attempted to open the box, Savage-Rumbaugh asked the bonobo what she was looking for. Panbanisha replied that the trainer was looking for sweets.

We've seen that normal children from four to five years onwards can understand false beliefs, as can Down's syndrome people. Most autistic people are unable to pass a false belief test, although a minority are able to give the correct answers. These false belief tasks that we've been using are all second order – the child *knows* that Sally does *not know* where her chocolate has been hidden. Josef Perner and Heinz Wimmer have gone a stage beyond this to discover at what age a third-order intentionality false belief task can be solved. They invented the following story, which is told with dolls to act out the events:

This is Mary and this is John. Today they are in the park. Along comes the ice-cream van. John wants to buy an ice-cream, but he has left his money at home. He'll have to go home first and get his money before he can buy an ice-cream. The ice-cream man tells John, 'It's all right John, I'll be here in the park all day, so you can go and get your money and come back and buy your ice-cream. I'll still be here.' John runs off home to get his money.

But when John has gone, the ice-cream man changes his mind. He decides he won't stay in the park all day, instead he'll go and sell ice-cream outside the church. He tells Mary, 'I won't stay in the park, like I said. I'm going to the church.'

So Mary goes home and the ice-cream man sets off for the church. But on his way he meets John. He tells John, 'I changed my mind, I won't be in the park, I'm going to sell ice-cream outside the church this afternoon.' The ice-cream man then drives to the church.

In the afternoon, Mary goes over to John's house and knocks on the door. John's mother answers the door and says, 'Oh, I'm sorry Mary, John's gone out. He's gone to buy an ice-cream.'

The false belief test is one question: 'Where does Mary think John has gone to buy an ice-cream?' The child has to think about one character's false belief about another character's belief. The child who passes the test *knows* that Mary *thinks* John doesn't *know* that the ice-cream van is at the church. Normal children are able to answer correctly at around five to seven years old.

About a fifth of the autistic children that Simon Baron-Cohen tested could give the correct answer to the Sally-Ann task. Although these children had a verbal age of between seven and seventeen, none of them could understand Perner's and Wimmer's more complex belief scenario. Some of the people he tested had Asperger's syndrome and they were able to understand what Mary thought about John; this is something we'll discuss in chapter eight.

People with autism and Asperger's syndrome are not the only ones to find Theory of Mind tasks difficult. Chris Frith, from the Wellcome Department of Cognitive Neurology, London, has shown that schizophrenics are also unable to understand false beliefs. In fact, the term autistic was initially invented in 1908 to describe people with schizophrenia. Although there are similarities between schizophrenics and autistics, the two disorders are quite different. Frith suggests that the inability of schizophrenics to represent the thoughts, beliefs and intentions of other people underlies their delusions of persecution. 'Some schizophrenic patients have a symptom in which they hear voices talking about them in the third person, for example, saying "He is stupid",' says Frith. 'I think that this might arise as follows: the patient believes that other people think that he, the patient, is stupid. This belief is represented (in his brain) and is normally labelled as a belief. The labelling goes wrong so the information is no longer experienced as a belief, but a perception. Rather than believing that other people think he is stupid, he hears other people saying that he is stupid.'

'Spider' is schizophrenic. He believes that his father has killed his mother and a whore has moved in to their house. Spider's doctor describes him as 'hallucinating floridly in the visual, auditory and olfactory spheres' and says that he has 'ideas of persecution and thought injection'. Discharged from a secure unit, he now believes his caretaker is his 'father's tart'. He writes in his diary, 'Despite further layers of brown paper taped to my torso, despite the layers of vests and shirts and jerseys on top, the smell of gas was with me until dawn [. . .] A new strategy from the creatures in the attic: I kept my light on all night, of course, and the bulb crackled at me as it usually did, and I paid it no attention – until, that is, the crackling grew suddenly louder and the *voices* were producing a sort of chant that came out of the bulb, and the chant went: KILL her kill her kill her kill her KILL her . . .' This is from Patrick McGrath's chilling but intriguing novel, *Spider*.

As Frith says, 'Paranoid patients make incorrect inferences about the mental states of others – believing that certain people are against you is an example of such an inference.' He has shown that people with schizophrenia have problems understanding the meaning behind words – just as autistic people do. For example, if you say, 'It's very cold in here' whilst looking pointedly at the window, they won't understand that you actually mean, 'Is it all right if we close the window?' Frith and Rhiannon Corcoran, from the Psychology Department at University College London, showed that both second- and third-order intentionality Theory of Mind tasks are especially difficult for schizophrenic patients with paranoia.

In this chapter we have seen that by the time a child is seven years old, her ability to understand the mental states of others is almost fully formed. She has a very sophisticated understanding of other people's desires and beliefs, a complex grasp of states of knowledge and how knowledge can be acquired, she can make fine distinctions between intentional and unintentional acts and can tell whether the consequences of a person's act could be foreseen or not. A child of seven, like an adult, is capable of passing a third-order false belief task; she, like many adults, will have trouble solving problems that require higher levels of intentionality. But her grasp of another person's mental states, her knowledge of what motivates a person and her ability to imagine what it is like to be them means that she is capable of showing an advanced degree of empathic understanding. In the next chapter we will explore the concept of empathy, compassion and the role of the imagination.

6

SOMEONE ELSE'S SHOES

In this struggle the old wisdom is cast out and man has to learn again that the foundation of justice is mercy, the beginning of knowledge is ignorance, and the wisdom of authority lies in benevolence.

Han Suyin, *A Many-Splendoured Thing*

Calvin bargains ferociously with his pet tiger, Hobbes. He agrees to pay him twenty-five cents if Hobbes has a bath instead of him. Hobbes is a stuffed toy and Calvin is a little kid with a fertile imagination, brainchild of cartoonist Bill Watterson. Hobbes splashes about in the bath while Calvin stands by yelling, 'I'm washing my ears now! Whoops! Dropped the soap!' When his mother comes to kiss him goodnight, he is tucked up in bed with his toy tiger. She immediately realises that he's filthy and packs him straight into the bath. We now see a Calvin eye-view: the stuffed tiger has metamorphosed into a large, live version of the toy lounging insouciantly against the bath. Calvin wants his quarter back and the tiger replies, 'Forget it. It's as good as spent.'

In his hilarious cartoons Watterson recreates the world of the imaginative child, full of tigers, space craft, giant flies and fearsome dinosaurs, and also what parents see – stuffed toys, a debris-strewn sitting-room and their grimacing son pretending to be a tyrannosaurus. This chapter is all about the power of the imagination and ultimately how this ability, combined with Theory of Mind, can lead to compassion and empathy for others. Empathy, at its most basic level, is the ability to put oneself in someone else's shoes, thus understanding how they feel and what the world looks like from their perspective. Imagination and self-awareness are crucial to developing empathy and, without empathy, human society as we know it could not function.

The imaginative faculty develops early in children and is first seen in their ability to use pretend play. Child's play is classified as pretence if the child plays in the following ways: first, by using one object as another object — Calvin uses his father's briefcase as a space ship (unfortunately, a trip to space necessitates taking along supplies and by the return journey to earth the briefcase stinks of tuna); second, the child attributes properties to the object which it does not have — Calvin treats his stuffed toy as if it's sentient; and third, the child refers to absent objects as if they are present — Calvin frequently imagines that things, such as aliens and elephants, are in the living-room.

At around eighteen months old, normal children start to treat dolls as if they're little people, but ones who cannot feel or think and have no independent life of their own. They are passive recipients to be washed, fed and put to bed. At about two to two and a half years old, children are able to make dolls talk and act out scenarios. The dolls now have their own desires and emotions. Between three and four years of age children endow their dolls with more explicit thought processes. They are characters with minds of their own who can voice plans and think aloud. As children get older, they rely less on props and can carry out long pretend scenarios: Calvin's pretend play generally lasts a whole lesson — or would were he not regularly hauled up to the front of the class for not paying attention. The imaginative capacity of children allows them to escape from current reality and, perhaps most importantly, to simulate or pretend to have emotions, to think what it would be like to be someone else and to imagine themselves in a situation that is different from their own.

The cardinal feature of pretend play is that in order to show pretence, one must understand how pretending is different from not pretending. Young children often get confused about this. One mother pretended to open out an umbrella and said to her son who was two and a half that he might like to feel the rain. But after he'd stretched out his palms, he held them to his face and inspected them closely to see if they were wet. Other reports tell of a child aged a year and a half carefully examining a cup to see where the pretend tea was, and a three year old who was pretending to be a monster bursting into tears after rather effectively frightening himself. So although two-year-old children can engage in symbolic play, they are not always able to maintain the distinction between the real world and the pretend world that they have created.

The onset of pretend play is an important step in a child's development. Paul Harris and Robert Kavanaugh, from Oxford University, devised an experiment to discover when children learn to use their imagination in this way. They demonstrated a pretend action to a child, such as pretending to squeeze toothpaste on to a toy hippo or shaking talcum powder on to a cat's head. They then showed the children three pictures of the scene, one which was irrelevant (red triangles stuck on the cat), one where the cat was exactly as the children saw it and one where the pretend action had been carried out for real (the cat was covered in talcum powder). Children younger than two chose any of these pictures at random, but once they were older than two to two and a half, they chose the picture showing the pretend-for-real scene. Harris says that this indicates that children at this age can begin to imagine scenes that are not real. This is one of the first basic steps along the road to pretence. (It's basic because imagining talcum powder on a cat's head does not require an ability to imagine what might be going on inside the cat's head.)

Pretence is all about pretending to believe what is false, so at first sight it seems strange that children so young can begin to pretend when it will be another three years before they are able to understand a false belief. When a child holds a banana to the side of her head and speaks into it, on the one hand she is acting as if the banana is a phone and on the other she seems to be aware that the banana is not a phone. Josef Perner thinks that the children are only acting 'as-if' and they are not aware of the falsity of the situation. Acting in this sense simply means pretending and is based on a compound of belief and pretence which he terms 'prelief'. The young child cannot as yet distinguish pretend actions from mistakes or pretence from false beliefs. A false belief is a *mistaken* acting 'as-if'; a pretend action is acting 'as-if'. Prelief is the mental state that underlies acting 'as-if'. A child under the age of four does not differentiate between play that is pretence, and actions based on a mistaken belief. Of course, adults also pretend and their play-acting is no more sophisticated than a young child's; the difference is that an adult is capable of understanding another person's mental states and hence is able to use this ability in everyday life, as well as on the stage. The proof that children prelieve is that below the age of four they cannot tell the difference between someone who is feeding a rabbit – but doesn't realise that the rabbit is no longer in its hutch; and a person who is pretending to feed a rabbit that they know is non-existent.

At the age of two and a half, when children are pretending, they are acting out an unreal situation, but they are not *mentally* representing what they are doing. Pretence certainly involves mental representation – you can't pretend a plastic crate is a horse unless you know what a horse is, what it looks like and you're thinking about a horse. And because of the power of the imagination, a plastic crate can be a horse without the child stirring a muscle and physically acting out her pretence. This does not mean that the child is able to imagine that it is she who is imagining. In fact, children are able to understand false beliefs earlier than they are able mentally to represent their pretend play, as Angeline Lillard, from San Francisco University, has elegantly demonstrated. She told children stories based on Moe and Luna who were trolls. Moe didn't know that there was such a thing as a bird, but he stretched out his arms and pretended to fly as if he were a bird. Luna didn't know that rabbits existed, but she hopped as if she were a rabbit. Children of four and under said that Moe and Luna were respectively pretending to be a bird and a rabbit. The children are imagining Moe pretending to be a rabbit, but don't understand that Moe is not imagining a rabbit. They also claimed that a child who was growling like a lion but was not thinking about a lion, or a child who was swinging like a

129

monkey but who had no thought of monkeys in his mind were pretending to be a lion and a monkey. Thus, children younger than four have an action-based understanding of pretence – they are prelieving; it is only when they are older than five that they are capable of mentally representing what they or others are doing when they engage in pretend play.

Young animals play frequently, but there are very few examples of animals engaging in pretend play. Vicki, a hand-reared chimp, pretended to drag a toy around on a bit of string. She even went so far as to pretend the string snagged on the bathroom door and she had to go back to retrieve it. Moja, one of Roger Fouts's chimps, played an imaginary game where she pretended a purse was a shoe. A captive dolphin was observed imitating the swimming mode and sleeping posture of a sea lion that shared its tank, and when a watching man blew a cloud of smoke out, a baby dolphin swam to her mother, sucked on her teat, returned to the man and blew out a cloud of milk, as if impersonating him.

Autistic children show such imaginative poverty that their lack of pretend play is one of three criteria (together with abnormality in their social development and an inability to communicate) used to diagnose autism. This lack of pretend play in autistic children was only noticed as recently as 1985 by Alan Leslie, Uta Frith and Simon Baron-Cohen. The way an autistic child typically plays is described by Baron-Cohen:

> He was very quick at jigsaws and could manage even difficult puzzles quite easily: at six years old, he did a 200-piece jigsaw puzzle on his own, and a 1,000-piece one upside down. Socially, however, he was unable to make any friends whatsoever. He would attempt to join in a game that he liked, but his approaches were so odd that other children tended to ignore him. Most of the time, John was to be found on his own, busying himself with one of his special interests, more absorbed in counting lampposts than playing with other school children.

Children with autism are interested in hobbies that are devoid of human contact, so, for example, they will study calendars and train timetables. They tend to bite or throw or spin a toy car rather than pretend to drive it, fill it up with petrol and crash it. Pretend play revolves around human drama and since autistic children have little emotional investment in people they have no interest in bathing a doll or pretending to give it a drink. However, their lack of pretend play is not due to their uninterested attitude towards people. As Paul Harris says, 'Just as they fail to understand the mental states of a real person in everyday life, or the mental states of the protagonist in a story that they hear, so, too, they fail to impute certain mental states to the dolls that they play with. To the extent that pretend play often calls for the attribution of psychological states to dolls, it will necessarily be impoverished.'

Even if autistic people are unable to mindread, they ought to be able to pretend that a doll can walk or eat, since this doesn't require endowing the doll with any special psychological state. If they are prompted, they can pretend that a blue serviette is a swimming pool and make a doll dive in. But such prompting is not always successful. One autistic child who was being encouraged to make-believe pointed to a piece of sponge that was green and cube-shaped and said, 'Are these potatoes? I don't know. They might be peas.'

Any pretend play that autistic people show is stereotypic and routinised. An autistic girl aged eight liked to pretend to be a waitress. At mealtimes she walked round the table asking each member of the family what they would like to eat or drink. She mimed writing it down or said that it wasn't available. But she said exactly the same thing every day and only rarely added new items to the menu. The customers never got anything they ordered.

Autistic people cannot understand a belief that is at odds with current reality, they can't distinguish between the appearance of an object and what it really is, they have problems telling the difference between a physical object and an imaginary one. Therefore, it is not surprising that they should not be capable of pretend play. Harris believes that there is a further skill which autistic people lack and which is vital when attempting to represent the mental states of oneself and others: an ability to monitor what one feels and thinks – self-awareness.

Being able to represent one's own mental states is critical when following a plan of action as it allows a hypothetical action to be held in mind and evaluated in the face of competing alternatives. For example, suppose you have to buy various items from several shops and you only have a limited amount of time. The best way of saving time and effort is to imagine the shops you need to visit and visualise the most economical route between them. This doesn't mean that everyone plans their shopping trip as if it's a military exercise; rather, most people have the ability if not the inclination to represent alternative courses of action.

Imagine an autistic child playing chess. She would not be able to reflect on whether she should move her bishop to check her opponent's queen or whether the pawn would be a better bet. If she's just about to move her pawn, but thinks about the bishop, his possible diagonal move will have no influence on her decision on whether to move the pawn or not. Neither would she be able to say, 'I've got an idea . . .' and mean it. Thus, although an autistic child may be capable of a limited amount of pretend play when prompted, because she is unable to identify and hold ideas in her mind or imagine alternative actions, her pretend play will be brief and impulsive and can only become routinised and stereotypic.

The ability to reflect on one's own actions changes play-acting to a more sophisticated type of pretence where a child is capable of reflecting on her own and other children's mental states. A child of five or six is able to imagine that she is imagining. A capacity for self-awareness is crucial both to the development of pretend play and, ultimately, empathy. It has been measured in a way that is both ingenious and crude at one and the same time: the moment one can recognise oneself in a mirror – or any reflective body, such as a pool of water – is thought to be the point at which self-awareness dawns. This dawning occurs only in a very select number of species: humans, chimpanzees, gorillas and orangutans are the only animals known to be capable of recognising themselves in mirrors.

In 1970 Gordon Gallup of the State University of New York, Albany, was the first person to realise that chimpanzees have this capacity. He supplied his chimps with mirrors and after three days they started to use the mirrors to groom the parts of their bodies they normally could not see and, like young children, they made faces at themselves. The crucial test was when he anaesthetised the chimps and daubed red paint on their wrists and foreheads. As soon as the animals came round they picked at the paint on their wrists. The marks on their heads were only visible to them if they looked in the mirror but, as each chimp caught sight of his reflection, he reached up and touched the mark.

When Gallup first conducted this test on chimps, he was attacked by Frederic Skinner, the leading behaviourist, who said that the mirror test revealed nothing about self-awareness. Skinner claimed his pigeons could also peck at marks on their feathers using the mirror to help them. A closer examination of Skinner's scientific methodology showed that he had trained the pigeons to peck at the marks. Gallup, whose chimpanzees spontaneously used the mirror, said that this was analogous to teaching someone how to do well in an IQ test – it wouldn't necessarily mean that they suddenly became more intelligent.

We spend a great deal of time looking in mirrors and take our reflection for granted, but apart from the great apes all other animals consistently treat their image in the mirror as if it is another animal. So far several species of macaques and baboons, spider monkeys, squirrel monkeys, capuchins, gorillas, dolphins, parrots and elephants have been tested. None of these animals has ever recognised itself, even after prolonged exposure to mirrors. Gallup left a mirror next to a pig-tailed macaque's cage for seven years, yet the monkey only ever threatened his reflection. A young rhesus monkey was shown a mirror from when he was born until he was four but, as he got older, he increasingly treated his image as if it were another monkey.

Children normally understand that they are staring at an image of themselves from the age of a year and a half. Chimpanzees, which develop more slowly than humans, recognise themselves when they are about three years old. Chantek, a sign language-using orangutan, began to pass the mark test and to point spontaneously to himself and label his image as 'Me Chantek' at the age of two. He would steal sunglasses and eyelash curlers and experiment with his appearance in front of the mirror. Koko, a sign language-using gorilla, could recognise herself from the age of three and a half, according to her caretaker, Francine Patterson, although she was never given the mark test using anaesthetic. She uses mirrors to clean her teeth and put lipstick on. As Gallup says, 'The mark test serves merely as a means of validating impressions that arise out of seeing animals use mirrors spontaneously for purposes of self-inspection.'

Recently, Irene Pepperberg gave Alo and Kyaaro, two of her speaking grey parrots, a mirror. They pecked at their image with open beaks as if attempting to 'beak wrestle' with their companion in the mirror. Kyaaro has said 'You come', 'You climb' and 'You tickle' to his image. However, the parrots are only two years old and as they live at least as long as chimpanzees and humans they may develop mirror self-recognition when they are older. Dolphins seem to be in the middle: sometimes they spend a long time in front of a live video-monitor when they can see that they have got white paint on their back, at other times they react to their image as if it's another dolphin.

Daniel Povinelli began his mirror tests with elephants, but although they could use the mirror to find hidden food, they showed no self-exploratory behaviour, failed the mark test and thought their mirror image was another elephant, at whom they trumpeted madly. To date, Povinelli has tested 105 chimps, aged between ten months and forty years and discovered that they start to recognise themselves at about four and a half years old. Chimps can also recognise themselves on video, but gorillas react as if the image is only of mild interest to them.

Povinelli invented another version of the mirror test for children. Whilst he was playing with a young child, he put a sticker on her head. Then he took a Polaroid of the child or showed her a video of herself taken whilst they had been playing. No two year olds, almost no three year olds but most four year olds were able to reach up and pull off the sticker when they saw themselves in the photo or on the television. Yet all the children could recognise themselves both in the mirror and even on television if the video was playing live.

Povinelli's explanation is that three year olds have difficulty understanding dual representations, just as they do in pretend play and false beliefs. They find it hard to understand that the Polaroid represents a past situation, so they defer to what they believe is true – they can't feel the sticker, so why should one be there? Three year olds spoke about themselves in the third person when they saw their video image – they understood that the person in the film bore a physical resemblance to them, but they didn't understand that the image was a representation of themselves. Until the age of three children are eternally rooted in the present; they cannot understand their past or their future, even though they may have rich memories: they can remember the green cake shaped like a dragon that they had for their birthday, but not that it was their past self that ate the cake. One child who did recognise a video of herself reached up and removed the sticker, but then could not understand why the girl in the video didn't peel her sticker off too. Povinelli, borrowing slightly from the psychologist William James, says that it takes a while for children to realise that, 'They are unique unduplicated selves trapped in the arrow of time.'

Being aware of oneself is indicative of an awareness of one's own mental states. A self-aware organism should be able to tell the difference between hunger, anger, fear, desire and so on, and should also be able to imagine those states when it's not actually experiencing them. An animal with a mind ought to be capable of imputing mental states to others. Mindless animals seem to show a very fast transition between mental states – macaques can vacillate between threatening behaviour and apparent uninterest with no apparent overlap of emotions whatsoever. A mindless animal should be incapable of showing empathy or deception.

However, whilst it certainly seems logical that self-awareness is necessary to be able to understand that others have an internal life, the ability to recognise oneself in a mirror doesn't necessarily indicate self-awareness. There does, however, seem to be a causal connection between understanding the psychological state of self-awareness and the behavioural ability to recognise that same self in the mirror. Young children under the age of one and a half to two and animals such as elephants and monkeys can learn that when they move, their mirror image moves with them. This allows them to modify their body posture and to manipulate objects. Elephants can find food using a mirror and a couple of Sue Savage-Rumbaugh's monkeys understand the displacement between self and mirror image so well that they easily transfer this same skill to video games, which they play with a joy-stick whilst looking at a monitor. Animals and children that use a mirror to find objects, and can react to their image in the mirror without believing that it is another animal, might, as Povinelli says, 'understand that the image in the mirror moving with them is about them and ultimately refers to or is equivalent to them'. However, this doesn't mean that they understand that the mirror image is a representation of themselves. Once children or an animal have a concept of self-awareness, they are able to understand that the image is them. At this stage they have a representation of who they are that withstands past events, so they can understand videos and photos taken in the past. This also explains why children in societies that seldom use mirrors can very quickly pass a mark test even if they have just been given a mirror for the first time in their life. So far only children and chimpanzees have shown this type of self-recognition and self-awareness. Without a concept of self-awareness, it is not possible to show empathy.

In the film *Blade Runner*, the only way to identify an escaped Replicant (an android) is to give it an empathy test. The film begins in a smoky film-noir atmosphere as one of the escapees, Leon, sits facing a Heath Robinson-type contraption focused on his eyes. He is told that as he walks across a desert he sees a tortoise. He flips it over on its back. The tortoise is baking in the hot sun, it's trying to turn itself over, but it can't. 'You're not helping, Leon,' says the experimenter. 'Why is that, Leon?' The android starts to twitch and sweat. The experimenter assures him that it's only a test. He continues, 'Describe in single words only the good things that come into your mind about your mother . . .' Leon replies, 'Let me tell you about my mother,' and shoots the experimenter dead.

Blade Runner is based rather loosely on the book *Do androids dream of electric sheep?* by Philip K. Dick, which is actually a detailed examination of empathy. In both stories the world is so polluted by radiation poisoning that most of the animals have died. Society has become obsessed with the need to show empathy. The acceptable way to do this is to own an animal but the ones that are still alive are hideously expensive so most people buy an electric animal which is serviced by engineers dressed in lab-coats driving vans marked *Vet*. Decker, the Blade Runner, is killing, or rather 'retiring' Replicants as a way of saving up to buy a real sheep.

> Empathy, he once had decided must be linked to herbivores, or anyhow, omnivores who could depart from a meat diet. Because ultimately, the empathic gift blurred the boundaries between hunter and victim, between the successful and the defeated [. . .] Oddly it resembled a sort of biological insurance, but double-edged. As long as some creatures experienced joy, then the condition for all other creatures included a fragment of joy. However, if any living being suffered, then for all the rest, the shadow could not be entirely cast off. A herd animal such as man would acquire a higher survival factor through this; an owl or a cobra would be destroyed.

Dick adds rather laconically that empathy 'would tend to abort a spider's ability to survive'.

There is some confusion between the terms empathy and sympathy. The word sympathy derives from the Greek *sympatheia* or the Latin *sympathia*, and means literally 'suffering with or pathos'. The Scottish philosopher David Hume used the term to explain how human beings could know about the feelings of others. Charles Darwin thought that sympathy was an 'all-important emotion' and was the key to the ability of animals and humans in particular to evolve a moral system. In *The Descent of Man* and *Selection in Relation to Sex* he wrote, 'Any animal whatever, endowed with well-marked social instincts, the parental and filial affections being here included, would inevitably acquire a moral sense or conscience as soon as its intellectual powers had become as well developed or nearly as well developed as in man.' Sympathy has its roots in the gregarious instinct, in the sharing of emotions. In psychology, we use the term 'Sympathy' to refer to how we feel when we are moved by another person. The pain of the other is experienced as one might experience it oneself and it can lead to an unselfish attempt to alleviate the other's suffering. Sympathy is more an emotional habit and is not necessarily to do with higher moral conduct.

In contrast, empathy is less of a distressed knee-jerk response. It refers to the attempt of one person to understand the subjective experience of another. Empathy is knowing what it would feel like to be in 'someone else's shoes'. To know what it would be like if I were the other person is empathy, to know what it would be like to be that other person is sympathy. In empathy I act 'as if'. In sympathy I *am* the other person. In sympathy we substitute others for ourselves, in empathy we substitute ourselves for others. Sympathy is a way of relating, empathy is a way of knowing. For instance, one might have precious little sympathy for a murderer, but one could empathise with him by trying to understand him while still disapproving of his actions.

Nazis used their capacity for empathy during World War II. They attached howling devices to dive bombs to create fear and panic amongst those about to be bombed. They showed an accurate understanding of how others would feel, if precious little sympathy for their victims.

The term 'empathy' was not coined until 1909. The word was invented by a psychologist, E. Titchener, in his book *Elementary Psychology of the Thought Processes*. Its root is in the Greek *empatheia*, but by way of the German word *Einfühlung*, which, at the turn of this century, meant the tendency for a person to project themselves into an object, blurring the boundaries between self and object. The subjective qualities of other objects would thus be experienced as if the perceiver were the object. Titchener thought one could not know about someone else's consciousness by reasoning analogically from one's own behaviour to theirs; he thought one had to go through a 'kinetic imaginative experience' using what he termed the 'mind's muscle'. Later he developed the concept to mean an imaginative awareness of the emotions of others which allowed a 'freemasonry among all men'. Empathy was thus both a way of knowing another's mental state and a kind of social bond.

'I think therefore I am is the statement of an intellectual who underrates toothaches,' wrote Milan Kundera in his novel *Immortality*. He adds, 'The basis of the self is not thought but suffering, which is the most fundamental of all feelings. While it suffers, not even a cat can doubt its own unique and uninterchangeable self [. . .] Suffering is the university of egocentrism.'

It is the power of the imagination that allows us to transcend this aloneness and decipher what it is like for others to suffer. That humans have powerful imaginations is beyond doubt. The central character Roberto in Umberto Eco's novel *The island of the day before* invents a brother, Ferrante, who he believes was banished from the family at an early age. Gradually he starts blaming Ferrante for his own misdemeanours. When he cuts down a young fruit tree that his father has just planted, Roberto manages to convince himself that it was Ferrante who committed the crime. His father summons all the boys who work on the estate and asks sternly who carried out such a wicked deed? Roberto steps forward and admits that it was he who axed the fruit tree. 'To us the story seems simple: the father, proud to have an offspring who does not lie, looks at the mother with ill-concealed contentment and administers a mild punishment to save face. But Roberto then embroidered this event at length, arriving at the conclusion that his father and mother had no doubt guessed that the culprit was Ferrante, had appreciated the fraternal heroism of their preferred son and had felt relieved not to have to bare the family secret.'

Jean Piaget thought that children were intensely egocentric until the age of seven. He and Hans Christian Andersen, incidentally, studied snails before embarking on the careers for which they have subsequently become famous. Few people have heard of Piaget's guide to the snails of Switzerland although it is still in use today. Quite possibly he should have stuck to conchology: children as young as two can show an awareness of others' distress. A toddler who holds out a toy to a crying child shows some understanding that the other child is unhappy.

At such an early age it is difficult to tell whether children are feeling empathy or sympathy. Kim Chisholm and Janet Strayer, from the Simon Fraser University in Vancouver, Canada, used a remote-control camera to film young girls aged nine to eleven years old as they were watching films. The technique allowed the two researchers to code the children's facial expressions every hundredth of a second. The film clips were designed to elicit some form of empathic response: for example, one showed a husband and wife having an argument while their daughter watched television. The man stormed out of the room and the woman angrily called her daughter to come to dinner. The girl accidentally knocked over a glass of milk and her mother slapped her.

The children's facial expressions corresponded with the emotions the characters were displaying in the films and with the emotion they reported feeling themselves. To positive emotions they responded positively, but when faced with a more unpleasant emotion, they often looked away – a reaction favoured by many viewing the more gory of Hollywood's current output. There was one exception to the rule: the girls looked angry six times more often than they reported feeling anger. This may be because girls are conditioned against showing anger or behaving in an angry fashion. Girls, in general, are better able to report their facial expressions and their own emotions than boys, presumably because they are more aware of what is a socially acceptable way for them to behave and so they monitor their expressions more closely. Boys, in contrast, rarely express negative emotions when faced with a person who is feeling sad or unhappy. This suppression of their emotions carries on into adulthood: men tend to express sympathy less often than women. However, although many empathy tests of adults have reported a large sex difference, this is in part due to the way in which empathy is tested. Women report their own emotions to a far greater extent than men, but when their empathic responses are recorded visually or by taking physiological measurements, there is actually little difference between the sexes.

Paul Harris and his colleagues found that children can deliberately engage in an empathic response to a character in a story or remain unattached. Those who were asked to identify with the character did so by pretending that the events that befell her also happened to them. They were also better able to remember and elaborate on sad episodes in the story. The children detached themselves by saying, 'It's only a story', which is the same approach some adults employ when attempting to distance themselves from Tarantino's *Reservoir Dogs* or Scorsese's savage *Casino*.

We are social animals. We are surrounded by others – even when we're alone, we have access to people via the phone, the radio, television, newspapers and novels. When we go for a solitary walk we take people with us, for the vast majority of us think about others most of the time. But is the human capacity for caring supremely egoistical? Do we treat others, as the philosopher Kant would say, as means and not ends? The parable of the Good Samaritan has been re-enacted in our time. The story is about a man half-dead by the side of the road who is ignored by a priest and a Levite, both supposedly religious and ethical men. He is helped by a passing Samaritan. Rather more recently, American theology students were told that their next lecture was to be about the Good Samaritan but that the talk would be held in a different building. In order to get to their lecture, the students had to walk past a person slumped on the ground groaning. Only forty per cent of the students stopped to ask what the matter was and even fewer did so when they had been told to make haste to get to their lecture on time.

Many would cynically argue that we care for others because if we did not we would feel guilty. We want to help because in doing so we reduce our own personal distress and, like the dystopic society in *Do androids dream of electric sheep?*, we need to show empathy in order to be socially acceptable.

Abraham Lincoln argued that all altruistic behaviour was prompted by selfishness. Lincoln was explaining his theory to a fellow passenger on an old-fashioned coach; at that moment they drove over a bridge above a muddy ditch. A sow was standing on the bank making a terrible noise because her piglets had fallen into the mud and were drowning. Lincoln asked the driver to stop, got out and rescued the piglets. His companion pointed out that he had refuted his argument himself. Lincoln replied that it was quite the contrary, he had rescued the piglets for purely selfish motivations – if he hadn't, he would have had no peace of mind all day.

Yet throughout history there are extraordinary examples of personal courage and selfless acts of charity. Anne Frank and her family would not have survived in their Dutch hiding place for two years without the aid of Miep Gies, who brought them food every day and who risked her life to save them when the Germans finally uncovered their secret annexe. Two of Otto Frank's business partners, Mr Kraler and Mr Koophuis, continued to run the business, using the profits to feed and clothe the family. Kraler supplied Anne, her sister and Peter van Daan with school books. Unfortunately, their unfailing support was not enough to protect Anne and the other occupants of the annexe from the horror of Bergen-Belsen.

When we become personally distressed, our heart rate increases, but when we are showing empathy towards others, our heart rate actually drops and our expression registers sadness and concern. The reason for the decrease in heart rate is because we are focusing on another person and not merely reacting towards them on the basis of our own personal distress. Thus people *are* capable of unselfishly helping others and are not simply motivated by the desire to relieve their own anxiety. This is in some measure taught: how we express our emotions is partially conditioned by our upbringing. Those people whose parents punished them for displaying any emotions, suppress how they feel, but feel bad inside themselves when faced with another's distress. Those who do express negative emotion were encouraged as children to show how they felt about others.

In general, we only help people for whom we are capable of feeling empathy. If we have no understanding of them, but help them anyway, it is more for our own sake than theirs. Not everyone is equally caring, but if we are not a society of Mother Teresas, at least the number of Genghis Khans is also small. There is a continuum of people ranging from those with very low empathy who will help others only to avoid punishment, through to those who feel a lot of empathy and are undeterred by the difficulty of helping others. Daniel Batson, from the University of Kansas, designed an empathy test which involved telling each volunteer that another student was to be given uncomfortable electric shocks. They could relieve this person's suffering by taking some shocks themselves – but, if they didn't want to, they had to watch the person being given the shocks. However, only those people who passed a test could help the student out. Batson hypothesised that if an individual was not particularly empathic, he or she would use the test as an excuse to duck out of the whole scenario. Batson gave exactly the same test to all his volunteers, but he told half of them that the test was very easy, and half of them that it was difficult and that they shouldn't feel bad if they failed. As he predicted, those individuals who did not feel that much empathy did badly when they thought the test questions were hard – indicating that they were using the test as an excuse – but caring individuals actually did better on the test when they thought it was harder. In a similar experiment, the subjects were more willing to take the shocks if they anticipated being reminded of their failure to be altruistic.

On a daily basis we are surrounded by the distress of others: carnage in Bosnia, famine in Rwanda, genocide in Angola, torture in Libya, environmental devastation in Nigeria, and by hundreds of hungry and homeless people on our own doorstep. Although we are capable of showing empathy and altruism to achieve our own goals, we do not always show empathy for its own sake. Indeed, there is so much suffering around us that many of us deliberately ignore it. Concern for others is indeed 'a fragile flower, easily crushed by self-concern', as Daniel Batson says.

'We have chosen to put profits before people, money before morality, dividends before decency, fanaticism before fairness and our own trivial comforts before the unspeakable agonies of others,' says killer Andy Gould in *Complicity* by Iain Banks. Andy is quoting one of his journalist friends, Cameron Colley's, own articles back at him and using it to exonerate himself for the horrific murders he, Andy, has committed in the name of justice. Interestingly, Iain Banks's novel is a brilliant case-study in empathy. Whilst appalled at Andy's behaviour, we can understand it to some extent. He only kills people who are evil and who have, however indirectly, sanctioned the deaths of others. His empathy for their victims outweighs any empathy he feels for his own victims. Cameron, on the other hand, is a man one can sympathise with. He had lots of high-minded moral ideas when he was a student. Now, he's a hack on a Scottish newspaper who drinks and smokes too much, does illegal drugs, plays computer games and lusts after a friend's wife. By no longer following his ideals, Cameron also becomes part of the system of avarice and corruption that Andy rails against: he is complicit in Andy's crimes. He symbolises the everyday man or woman who, however much he or she might care about others, can do little in practice to relieve their pain. The overall structure of the novel shows how one needs to have empathy for the characters in a novel to be concerned for their welfare: Cameron needs to be plausibly nasty enough at the beginning for us to have a twinge of doubt about his innocence (it's unclear at first who has committed the murders), yet a sensitive and caring person must emerge for us to want him to be acquitted. The murders themselves are described in the second person: 'You took the gun out once, reaching round under your thin canvas jacket to the small of your back and easing it from between shirt and jeans. The Browning felt warm through your thin leather gloves . . .' This has the effect of drawing the reader in as an accomplice to the crimes described.

Many autistic people are largely indifferent to the distress of others and are unable to offer comfort or to receive it themselves. Leo Kanner said that to the autistic child people 'figured in about the same manner as did the desk, the bookshelf, the filing cabinet'. They are unable to show empathy; even high-functioning autistic people have difficulties imagining being in someone else's situation. They can, however, show limited sympathy. If a newsreader discusses famine, some autistic people are capable of showing compassion because they too have been hungry and can thus feel sympathy for people who suffer in situations which have caused them distress. They also sometimes reflexively laugh or cry as if mimicking another's emotion. This is known as emotional contagion and is also seen in very young children.

There is yet another category of people who lack empathy, but for a quite different reason: psychopaths. One scientist who studies psychopaths says that it is as if they know the words of emotion, but not the music. Remorse, guilt and empathy are not merely large lacunas in their social vocabulary, psychopaths also lack the physiological capacity to react to the distress of others. James Blair, a young psychologist from University College London, gave empathy tests to psychopaths and 'normal' murderers at Wormwood Scrubs Prison and Broadmoor Special Hospital. All had killed and all were male. He measured their skin conductance − the electrical activity on the fingertips − while they were watching a series of slides designed to elicit either fear (such as a tarantula) or empathy (a child crying). Unlike the murderers, the psychopaths showed no arousal when faced with the distressing pictures. Although the fear-enducing pictures sometimes elicited a response from the psychopaths, other people's trauma held no interest for them. Included in the slide set were supposedly neutral pictures. Prior to testing in prison, Blair gave his test to his students, all of whom responded normally, apart from one girl who showed no arousal level for any of the pictures, except for one of the 'neutral' ones, which was of a horse!

Blair also told the psychopaths short stories to which normal people would react by feeling happy, sad, embarrassed or guilty on behalf of the central character. For example, when one boy punches another, we would normally attribute the feeling of guilt to the bully. The psychopaths were perfectly capable of attributing most emotions to the characters in the stories, but they had severe problems with two: guilt and remorse. They could answer Theory of Mind tasks. Their inability to show empathy, guilt and remorse does not occur because they are unable to understand other people's mental states. Blair reasons that it is because they have a deficit in

VIM, the Violence Inhibiting Mechanism, in the brain. Subordinate animals will often make gestures of submission to dominant ones – dogs wag their tails, cower and roll over on their backs, exposing their stomachs – and these gestures usually serve to appease the dominant animal. Blair believes that this facility in humans is a prerequisite for being able to feel sympathy, guilt, remorse and empathy. It also allows us to make a distinction between conventional and moral rules.

Oscar Wilde may have cynically believed that 'Morality is simply the attitude we adopt towards people we personally dislike' but most people regard moral rules as unbreakable, unlike conventional rules. Moral rules are those that safeguard people from being victimised and minimise their distress, whereas conventional rules uphold the strictures of society. For example, a moral rule is 'Do not Kill', a conventional rule 'Do not speak when your mouth's full of food'. Psychopaths treat conventional and moral rules in the same manner and, in general, pay them little heed. They make little reference to the welfare and the pain of others when deciding whether or not to break a rule. Some of the psychopaths Blair tested did see moral rules as more serious, but, as Blair says, 'Given that all the subjects were incarcerated because of actions similar to the moral trans-gressions described – violence, theft – and not for committing conventional transgressions – talking in class – this is perhaps less surprising.'

Normal children can distinguish between moral and conventional rules by the age of three and a half. Although one might think that, as autistic people do not have Theory of Mind and so cannot empathise, they would not be able to tell the difference between moral and conventional rules. Blair argues that they can and that this ability bears no relation to whether or not they are able to pass the Sally-Ann task. Autistic people are good at learning rules – what is or is not acceptable in society – and they are capable of reacting sympathetically to the distress of others.

Are animals able to show empathy? A reprehensible study con-ducted in the sixties involved fifteen rhesus macaques who had two chains in their cage. Pulling on either of these chains provided them with food. The experiment was then altered: pulling one of the chains would result in a monkey in the next cage receiving an electric shock. Two-thirds of the monkeys preferred to pull the chain for food and two refused to touch either chain. The monkeys were more likely not to inflict a shock on another monkey if they had interacted with it or had been given a shock themselves.

I conducted a study to discover whether chimpanzees can show empathy. They seemed the most likely candidates to be able to do this since they may have Theory of Mind. I collated examples of empathy from other scientists who study chimps and from work that had already been published in order to create a classification of empathic acts. Understanding another's perspective involves four different types of empathy: first, an understanding of the visual perspective of another individual; second, an understanding of their emotions; third, the ability to understand their non-emotional mental state – such as ignorance, or thirst; and, finally (a combination of the first, second and third types), an understanding of their mental state and the physical situation in which they find themselves – to be in another's shoes, at it were, both mentally and physically.

The ability of chimps to understand the visual perspective of others is demonstrated in one of Daniel Povinelli's experiments on role reversal. The chimpanzees were shown a strange contraption which was a little like a pinball table. There were eight covered cups in the middle, arranged in pairs, and four handles at either end of the table. A chimp stood at one end of the table, a person at the other. When one person or chimp pulled a handle, one pair of cups travelled to either end of the table. The other six cups remained in the middle. The idea was that a person and a chimp would take on separate roles to operate this contraption. One became the Informant. He knew in which pair of cups food had been hidden and he had to point this out to the Operator, who pulled the appropriate handle. The two cups would slide to opposite ends of the table so that both Operator and Informant could share the food. Two chimps acted as Informants and two as Operators and then they swapped round. Three out of the four chimps immediately understood their new role, thus showing that they understood the

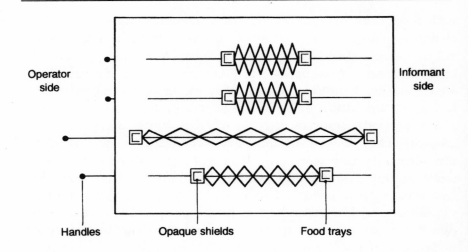

Operator side

Informant side

Handles   Opaque shields   Food trays

A diagram of the apparatus used in the role reversal experiment. Opaque shields covered the food trays so that the Operator could not see where the food had been hidden but has to rely on the Informant. By pulling the handles, the food trays would slide to opposite ends of the table so that both Operator and Informant could share the food. The chimp and the person taking part in this experiment would then swap roles. By Daniel Povinelli.

visual perspective of their partner. No rhesus macaques were able to swap roles in this way.

An example of emotional understanding is shown by Austin, one of Sue Savage-Rumbaugh's chimps, who is able to understand his companion Sherman's emotions and how to manipulate them. Sherman continually bullies Austin, the smaller chimp, but Sherman is afraid of the dark and Austin has learnt to exploit his fear. At night, Austin goes outside their indoor cage and makes noises, banging and scraping on the metal walls. He then rushes back inside, looking fearfully behind him. Sherman becomes frightened and runs over to Austin and hugs him, demanding reassurance. For a short while the bullying stops and Austin is in a position of power.

Another example of a chimp understanding the emotional state of a second chimp is given by David Premack. In an experiment, one chimpanzee, Sadie, was being taught by another, Jessie. Jessie took into account Sadie's fear of her by never running after her when Sadie fled. Sometimes she reassured Sadie by patting her.

Teaching another animal may indicate an awareness of their non-emotional state, in other words knowing that they are ignorant about whatever it is the other animal knows. In 1925, primatologist Wolfgang Köhler reported an example of how one of the chimps in his care seemed to understand what he was trying to teach another chimp. He was showing Chica how to fit two sticks together to obtain fruit that was out of her reach. He gave up and passed the sticks to a second chimp, Sultan, who was watching. Sultan fitted the sticks together and raked the fruit in, but towards Chica. It is possible that Sultan understood Köhler's desire to teach Chica and Chica's lack of knowledge; he also assumed that Köhler desired that he, Sultan, show Chica how to obtain the fruit. A simpler explanation, but one which still shows Sultan using Theory of Mind, is that Sultan knew that Köhler wanted Chica to have the fruit.

Chimpanzees rarely actively teach their youngsters in the way that we do; chimps learn from their elders by watching. However, Christophe Boesch, from the University of Zürich in Switzerland, has noted several examples of both active and passive teaching in wild chimps in the Taï National Park on the Ivory Coast. This particular group of chimps crack palm nuts using a stone hammer and anvil. It's a difficult and specialised task, one that is tricky for a human to learn, but the technique is alike whether it is the chimps or the local tribespeople who crack the nuts. Hammers and anvils are prized possessions. Chimps will often walk a great distance to get to their favourite anvil, carrying their hammer with them. Mothers 'teach' their infants how to crack nuts by placing nuts for them on the anvil and giving them hammers. On a couple of occasions Boesch noticed a mother altering her infant's grip on the hammer, demonstrating to him how to crack the nut and then replacing the hammer, correctly, in his hand.

Another example of this type of empathy involved David Premack's chimp, Jessie. This time Jessie understood another chimp's non-emotional state. 'Jessie filled her mouth at the drinking fountain on the edge of the half-acre compound, crossed the compound, climbed a high structure and delivered a drink into the mouth of her reclining friend. She did this recurrently, always with respect to the same "friend". Did her friend "request" a drink or indicate thirst? Not in any way we could detect.'

The final kind of empathy – understanding someone else's mental and physical situation – is more complex. Kathleen Gibson, a primatologist from the University of Texas, gives this example: a chimp called Tania had been taught sign language and as Gibson was walking past her cage, she signed, 'Hurry, hurry, come here, hurt, hurry, hurt, come here' and tried to reach Gibson's leg. A young woman then pointed out that there was a mosquito on Gibson's calf, which subsequently bit her. Gibson said, 'I am certain that Tania's response was spontaneous and not conditioned.' In addition, Kathleen Gibson added that she had had very few interactions with Tania prior to this incident.

Ironically, revenge is a good indicator of empathy. The chimp code of conduct is such that if a friend or ally loses in a conflict, the other chimp will support the victim by attacking the aggressor at a later date. Frans de Waal noticed this example at Arnhem Zoo in Holland. Tarzan, a one-year-old chimp, was 'kidnapped' by his 'aunt' Puist, who climbed up a tree with him. Both Tarzan and his mother, Tepel, who was on the ground, became extremely anxious. When Puist finally descended, Tepel attacked the larger and more dominant female. An adult male, Yeroen, intervened and flung Puist a few metres away. In de Waal's words, this intervention was remarkable because, on other occasions, Yeroen had always intervened in Puist's favour. It can be argued that Tepel was supporting her infant Tarzan and revenging herself on Puist, but that is more likely to be a straightforward instance of maternal instinct. Yeroen was a more objective observer and was unrelated to Tarzan.

De Waal also witnessed a full-scale conflict being staved off by the social understanding of a chimp called Mama. 'Jimmie and Tepel are sitting in the shadow of an oak tree while their respective two children play in the sand at their feet. Between the two others, the oldest female, Mama, lies asleep. Suddenly the children start screaming and hitting [. . .] each other. Jimmie admonishes them with a soft, threatening grunt and Tepel anxiously shifts her position. The children go on quarrelling and eventually Tepel wakes Mama by poking her in the ribs several times. As Mama gets up, Tepel points to the two quarrelling children. As soon as Mama takes a step forward, waves her arm in the air and barks loudly, the children stop quarrelling. Mama then lies down again and continues her siesta.'

Neither of the two mothers could have intervened because it might have sparked off a fight between them. They understood the possible consequences of their actions and exploited another chimp to resolve the problem. Mama understood the situation and responded accordingly, without being tricked or deceived into doing so. The very fact that she could perceive the situation from another's point of view, predict the consequences of their action, as well as her own, constitutes empathic understanding.

There is a branch of biology known as altruism, although it does not refer to altruism as we know it. This biological altruism is carefully calculated and mindless. One animal will help another only if they are related and thus share the same genes. In his book, *The Selfish Gene*, Oxford biologist Richard Dawkins wrote that we are 'survival machines – robot vehicles blindly programmed to preserve these selfish molecules known as genes'. I share fifty per cent of my mother's genes and fifty per cent of my father's, half of my genes are the same as my sister's, and although half of my genes will be in my child, I will only share a quarter of my genes with my grandchild. The biologist John Haldane once remarked in the pub that he would only risk drowning for two of his brothers or ten of his cousins. (Actually, he ought to have said eight of his cousins, since each cousin shares an eighth of his genes, but, as he pointed out at the time, he wanted to be on the safe side.) The desire to maximise our genetic output fuels reproduction but also altruism. Robin Dunbar, from the University of Liverpool, and colleagues carried out an experiment to test this theory. He asked people to take up a sitting position leaning against a wall with legs bent as if they were exercising for skiing. Because the leg muscles are under considerable stress, most people find this painful after about half a minute. Dunbar offered the subjects seventy-five pence for every twenty seconds they could remain in this position, but the money was either to be given to a relative, a charity or to themselves. The subject nominated the recipient of their choice and had six attempts. The results were clear cut: all the subjects endured more pain for themselves or close relatives (such as a sister or a parent) than a distant relative or a charity.

Florida scrub jays are a classic example of biological altruism. The elder brothers remain behind to help rear their mother's new fledglings, often forgoing mating and establishing a territory of their own. This seemingly selfless behaviour is not as altruistic as it sounds. The land is poor in the scrub and the jays would not survive were rearing chicks not a family affair. Genetically speaking, feeding siblings is nearly as good as mating, since the youngsters are so closely related to their elder brothers. A male who tried to go it alone would probably raise fewer of his own chicks than the siblings he can help rear if he stays because he would lack a large territory and fraternal help. Hanging around usually pays off in the end as the oldest brother inherits his father's territory when he dies.

There are very few cases of altruistic behaviour in the animal kingdom where help is not directed towards relatives. One species exhibiting such altruistic behaviour is the Vampire bat. The bats live up to their name, flying into the New Mexico dusk to drink blood from cows and chickens. It's a hard life: there are fewer calories in a pint of blood than in a small pot of fruit yoghurt. If a bat fails to feed, it will survive less than three days. But any hungry bats are saved by their companions who will regurgitate enough blood to prevent them from starving. However, bat altruism works according to carefully regulated rules. Two females take it in turns to regurgitate blood to each other. As groups of females share a roost, these 'friends' can be together for up to fourteen years – a long time to build up a relationship of trust, a you-scratched-my-back-I'll-scratch-yours routine.

Are chimpanzees capable of showing empathy to other chimps to whom they are not related and with whom they have not lived over a long period or shared an exclusive friendship? In fact, as I discovered, proportionately more of the life-threatening risks taken by chimpanzees were for strangers, or another species, or apes that were unrelated to them. Indeed, chimps do often die in the process of saving others: a male at Lion Country Safaris in Florida drowned attempting to rescue an infant chimp who had fallen into the moat surrounding their enclosure. Jane Goodall gives another example: 'Washoe spent some time (at Norman, Oklahoma) on an island ringed with an electric fence. One day a three-year-old female, Cindy, somehow jumped this fence. She fell into the moat, splashed wildly and sank. As she reappeared, Washoe leapt over the fence, landed on a strip of ground at the water's edge and managed to seize one of Cindy's arms as the infant resurfaced again. Washoe was about nine years old at the time; she was not related to Cindy and had not known her for very long.' (Chimpanzees are terrified of water and have been known to panic and drown in very shallow depths.)

Chimpanzees are not the only animals to show empathy for non-related animals or even those from another species. An incident recounted by Jeffrey Masson and Susan McCarthy in *When animals weep: the emotional lives of animals* concerned a baby black rhino calf which got trapped in a salt lick during the rainy season in Kenya. As its mother was returning to the forest, the baby called out to her. She came back for it, sniffed at the baby and trotted towards the forest. The baby called again and the mother returned. This went on for some time, as if the mother could not see what the problem was. A group of elephants arrived at the lick and the mother rhino charged their leader. The group moved to a lick further away. The rhino started to forage on the edge of the forest. One of the adult male elephants then came over to the baby rhino, put its tusks underneath and began to lift it. The mother came charging back and the elephant quickly got out of the way. Over several hours the elephant continued to try to help the baby and the mother attempted to attack it. Finally, the elephants left for the night; fortunately, by the morning, the young rhino had managed to struggle free by itself.

A second example Masson gives is of a woman who'd given birth earlier in the day and who was woken at night by her border collie. The collie ran between her bedroom and the child's cot: the baby was still and blue and had choked in the night. Fortunately, the family had been alerted early enough by the dog and the infant survived.

Grieving for a loved one is one of the hallmarks of being human, but, arguably, some other animals show grief in a way that is not merely a cursory look for a lost partner or a dead infant before continuing with normal life. Grief can also indicate empathy since it shows some understanding of loss or death. Roger Fouts recorded in his diary the moving story of Washoe, a sign language-using chimp, and her son, Sequoyah, who died despite Washoe's attempts to care for him and diligent veterinary attention. Fouts was particularly worried about Washoe, 'I began to fear for her life, since it is well known that chimps can mourn themselves to death. Jane Goodall observed this in the wild when nine-year-old Flint starved himself to death after losing his mother. And we had personally seen several such outcomes in captivity when the mother-child bond was broken.' After the death of Washoe's baby, Fouts called everyone he could think of and eventually found a young chimp called Loulis who was ten months old. He 'borrowed' Loulis from Yerkes Primate Centre for Washoe to foster. At first she wanted nothing to do with Loulis; he was not her baby. But after some persuasion she adopted him whole-heartedly and even, in another rare example of teaching, began to show him how to use sign language.

As I write this, the people of Dunblane are quietly and sorrowfully trying to repair the fabric of their lives. Thomas Hamilton opened fire in the small Scottish village killing sixteen children and their teacher. The blood-stained gym in which this occurred has just been pulled down and a garden planted in its place. I can't help feeling that despite all our intelligence and extensive capacity for Theory of Mind, Philip K. Dick was right when he said, 'Mankind needs more empathy.'

7

THE TANGLED WEB

My mother . . . predicted that
Future rulers would conquer and control
Not by strength, nor by violence,
But by cunning.
    Aeschylus, *Prometheus Bound*

'The probability that a monkey with a typewriter would produce the complete works of Shakespeare is one in many billions. Even if given thousands of years, the right combinations of letters and spaces would simply never arise by chance. Monkeys would have to rely on chance because they lack a Theory of Mind. Even if a monkey could type and describe his characters' behaviour, he could not reveal their minds. And without such attribution there could be no tragedy or comedy, no irony and no paradox,' wrote primatologists Dorothy Cheney and Roger Seyfarth.

We are primates who are experts in deceit, double-dealing, lying, cheating, conniving and concealing. Some psychologists think that our whole life is one big act where we try to dramatise our lives and enact an image of ourselves for others. Others view human society as a network of deceit and treachery bound by social rules which sanctify and conventionalise the telling of lies.

This may seem overly cynical, but we are initiated into the hallowed halls of deception at an early age, progressing from complete innocence to the fine art of lying, telling two lies a day to our nearest and dearest by the time we are eighteen. We owe our allegiance to deceit in great measure to our primate inheritance. Skilled social manipulators, great apes and monkeys have a certain Machiavellian streak and have learnt how to cheat on each other to obtain food, sex and to avoid fights. Our ability to lie depends crucially on Theory of Mind. When we attempt to deceive another, we are altering another person's beliefs and thus, for full-scale deception, we need to be able to mindread. To understand comedy and irony, we also have to understand the speaker's intention. If Nathalie tells a lie, she is trying to get Nathan to believe something which she herself does not believe. But if Nathalie is merely being ironic, although her statement will still be false, she now intends Nathan not to believe her. In *The Crocodile Bird*, Ruth Rendell writes, 'Liza listened outside the door. She heard Eve tell Jonathan it was half-term. Perhaps it was. In that case what she said wasn't really untrue. Of course, that depended on what you meant by a lie. It was a lie if by lying you meant to deceive. Eve certainly intended to deceive Jonathan into thinking Liza went to school.'

Without an understanding of intention, we would not know for what purpose or in what way the speaker was altering the listener's mental state and thus we would not be able to tell the difference between a lie and an ironical statement. Of course, some people never manage to tell the difference between the two. Americans in particular are not hot on irony and have recently been offended by in-office satire appearing on their notice boards. One American humour consultant told the *Wall Street Journal*, 'Once in a while, you come up against someone above you who doesn't get it. Don't put your career in jeopardy!'

Children usually begin to tell lies just before their third birthday, but at first they are not very good at it, witness the child who, covered from ear to ear in chocolate, denies having eaten any chocolate biscuits and the one who says, 'I didn't break the vase and I won't do it again!' Michael, aged two years and ten months, wanted to take a pair of crocodile scissors to bed with him. His mother, quite obviously, didn't want him to. He wrapped them up in a blanket and said to his father that he was hiding them from mummy. When she asked him, 'What's in your blanket?', he charmingly replied, 'Scissors hiding.' But at a much younger age, even before babies are a year old, they prepare for their entrance into the world of deceit by mildly teasing their parents.

Stephanie, at the age of seven months old, was bundled into a shopping trolley and wheeled round the supermarket. Her mother had left her briefly to look in the next aisle when she heard a terrible screaming. She rushed back only to find Stephanie sitting grinning at her. Carla, at eight months of age, would cry bitterly – but without tears – when she was put to bed. Her mother hid behind a door and watched and sure enough, every thirty seconds or so, Carla stopped crying and listened to see if anyone was coming to rescue her. Babies will steal things and then hand them back over and over again, or drop them several times before grabbing them firmly. They will also do exactly the kind of things they know they're not supposed to, such as crawl in front of the television or towards the fire, smiling and waiting for the predictable adult response. Teasing is a mild form of deception because, unlike a deceptive action, teasing need not affect a person's behaviour or their mental state. Teasing elicits an emotional reaction and in tolerant and loving parents this is usually laughter, surprise, amusement and smiles. Laughter, in particular, will stimulate the infant to build her teasing gestures into a little game. So although teasing requires no understanding of a mental state, it does teach the young infant some understanding of other people's expectations about certain actions.

Most children do not learn to deceive others until they are at least five years old. When researchers asked children to hide a toy bear in either a Wendy house, a play tower or a plastic truck and then try to fool an adult who wanted to find the bear, two year olds were happy to tell the adult straight away where they had hidden the bear! Three to four year olds, although not quite so enthusiastic about disclosing the bear's location, could not conceal from the experimenter where they had hidden it.

Just as vervet monkeys appear unable to infer the presence of a leopard from an antelope carcass, young children cannot cover their traces of guilt. Beate Sodian, from Munich University in Germany, and Uta Frith made a puppet hide treasure. The children were asked to make it difficult for another person to find the treasure. The puppet, on its way to the treasure chest, had left visible footprints, but until the age of four, children would not wipe away the tracks unless they were asked, 'What about the tracks?' – a giveaway question if ever there was one. Neither did the children lay a false set of tracks to muddle their opponent.

In a version of this test where the person looking for the treasure would either share it with the children or keep it all to herself, the three year olds only laid a false set of tracks if they were shown how to do so by the experimenter. The children then happily dotted footprints all over the place for both the competitor and the co-operating adults alike. Sodian says this shows that three year olds are capable of using deceptive ploys, but they have no understanding of their effect.

The same children were given boxes with windows cut out of them so that they, but not the experimenter, could see that there was chocolate inside one of the boxes. A competitive experimenter kept all the chocolate if the child pointed to the box containing the sweets, a co-operative one shared the reward. Yet despite having more than twenty attempts at this task, and with mounting frustration, three year olds could not point to the empty box when faced with the competitive adult.

The inability of young children to deceive adults is a specific deficit: all three year olds are perfectly capable of physically excluding others from a game or preventing them from eating a sweet. When presented with two boxes, one empty, one full of sweets, and a co-operative and a competitive experimenter, the children were able to lock the empty box for their co-operative partner, or lock the full one to thwart their opponent. But no three year olds and few four year olds could lie about which box was locked, or deceptively point to the empty box. Sodian says the children understood the need to hinder their opponent and were certainly motivated by the chocolate to do so. In fact, when they had no lock and they saw the competitive experimenter, they would grab the box, or try and hold the lid down with their hands – thereby showing their opponent exactly which box contained the sweets.

The only children capable of understanding a lie are those who can understand a false belief, as Heinz Wimmer and Josef Perner, from Salzburg University, Austria, elegantly demonstrated. They told children between the ages of four and six the following stories: Maxi has put his chocolate bar in a cupboard, but his mother has moved it to a different cupboard. Maxi's brother asks him where the chocolate is, but Maxi doesn't want to share his chocolate. He lies to his brother – in doing so he tells him where the chocolate actually is. Alternatively, Maxi decides he wants to eat his chocolate and he asks his grandpa to reach up to fetch it for him. He shows him where he thinks his chocolate is, but actually tells his grandfather the wrong location of the chocolate.

No matter what the age of the children who were given this test, only those who could understand a false belief could understand whether Maxi was being truthful or dishonest. The children who could not give a correct answer to a primary false belief question were prevented from answering straight away to give them time to think. They were then able to answer the false belief questions in Maxi's story, but they were still unable to tell the experimenters what Maxi would say when he wanted to lie or be truthful about the whereabouts of his chocolate bar. Making Maxi's belief correct also made no difference: in this scenario, Maxi's mother put the chocolate back in the same cupboard where Maxi had hidden it. Therefore, even when children do not need to make any complicated assumptions about the wrongness of Maxi's belief, four to six year olds still find it difficult to construct a deceitful statement.

Children between the ages of four and eight are often characterised as being at the 'Fairy Tale Age'. Many of the plots of stories such as *Hansel and Gretel* involve complicated deceptive ploys. As the story unfolds, children are often told the hero's goal, the villain's goal and what the hero says, and from this information children have to infer a deceptive plot:

'Creep in,' said the witch, 'and see if it's properly heated, so that we can shove in the bread.' For when she got Gretel in she meant to close the oven and let the girl bake, that she might eat her up too. But Gretel perceived her intention, and spoke: 'I don't know how I'm to do it; how do I get in?' 'You silly goose!' said the hag. 'The opening is big enough; see, I could get in myself'; and she crawled towards it, and poked her head into the oven. Then Gretel gave her a shove that sent her right in, shut the iron door and drew the bolt. Gracious! how she yelled! it was quite horrible; but Gretel fled, and the wretched old woman was left to perish miserably.

Wimmer and Perner thought that actually voicing a lie, as the children had to do for the Maxi story test, might be difficult for them, and instead told them a playground story based on a typical fairy tale construction with naughty children but no magic: Nancy meets Thomas's mother on her way to the playground. She says to Nancy to tell Thomas he must wait for her in the playground. But when Nancy sees Thomas, he is using the swing and she wants a go, so she says, 'Thomas, your mum needs you right away.' Children were asked why Nancy said what she did and if she was speaking the truth. Four to five year olds were unable to recognise that Nancy was being deceitful, although older five year olds and children from six upwards could. It seems that even though children can understand false beliefs from the age of four, they only begin to lie and understand lies towards the end of their fifth year.

Like very young children, autistic people show a striking absence of deceptive behaviour. One mother of a sixteen year old was concerned because he used to attack her physically and throw food and furniture, but she was even more worried by his social naïvety. She said he was, 'too good, totally honest and unable to lie'. He would religiously stick to an instruction such as 'Go to bed at ten p.m.' whether she was there to enforce it or not.

Although children with Down's syndrome could deceptively point to the empty box when they could see which one had chocolate in, autistic children could not. They could happily lock a competitor out of a box of sweets and leave it open for a co-operative partner, but they couldn't lie about which box contained chocolate. Even sophisticated behavioural manipulations were beyond many of them: if the experimenter was co-operative and they still had to lock one box, they couldn't lock the empty one.

Most autistic adolescents with a high mean verbal age (from seven years old onwards) can learn how to point deceptively, but simply because they can point to deceive an opponent does not mean the child intends to trick him or her. This may seem a strange thing to say, and we will return to the idea that children may not understand deception even when they are being deceitful. Similarly, autistic children can hide objects because they know the facts of vision, but they can't do it deceptively. For example, if asked to hide a penny, they may do so in full view of the person who is supposed to try to find it. They will not pretend to transfer the penny to another hand behind their back, or, if they do hide the penny in their closed fist, they keep the other hand open.

Below the age of four or five, children understand lies only as false statements, no matter whether they are errors, jokes, sarcasm and so on. Saying that nextdoor's dog is very thin when the neighbours have an obese labrador is a blatant lie to a child, whereas an adult interprets the comment as sarcasm. At about the age of five children first begin to deceive one another and start to understand the difference between a joke and a lie. Their burgeoning understanding of falsehood is related to their developing comprehension of other people's intentions and beliefs. Only when a child is capable of understanding a false belief can she start to tell the difference between a lie and a mistake and begin to comprehend jokes. A complex set of mental states is related to the idea of jokes and lies: at the simplest level, jokes and lies are both seen as intended falsehoods and are distinct from falsehoods which are genuine mistakes. The distinction between these two levels depends on the speaker's intention to deceive the listener. The deceitful speaker's sole aim is to dupe the listener, but the joking speaker wants to be disbelieved. A higher level of mental understanding is required to understand white lies and ironical statements. Being able to tell a white lie from irony depends on whether the child can understand third-order deception and this skill is not usually acquired until the child is older than six.

Sue Leekam, from Sussex University, designed a test depicting a familiar scenario: a boy is picked up from school by his mother. He points to a picture pinned on the wall and says, 'I did that.' But then the children are either told that the boy points to the name at the bottom of the picture, which is that of a classmate, or else the children learn that the two go home and the following day his mother, on closer examination of the painting, discovers by herself that it was not painted by her son. Children were asked which boy thinks his mother still believes him and which boy was joking. Although children from the age of six onwards could answer the belief question, only eight year olds were consistently correct at deciphering the lie from the joke. The problem children have with this, according to Leekam, is that they don't know what the boy *wants* his mother to know. Leekam then made the boy who points to the other child's name say that he had not painted the picture. It is now clear what this boy's intention is. However, comprehending this task is still difficult. The child listening to this story has to be able to understand a third-order intention: he has to *know* that the boy *wants* his mother to *know* who has painted the picture; and third-order belief: the child *knows* that the boy *knows* his mother *knows* who is the artist. When the boy's intention was made clear and the child was asked which boy wants his mother to know who did the picture, which boy is lying and which one is joking, even some of the four year olds were able to answer the questions. The critical distinction here is between intentions and beliefs. When both boys knew that their mother knew they had not painted the picture (the boy who lied saw his mother examining the name on the painting the next morning), most of the four year olds were able to discern who was being deceitful.

In normal everyday life we infer people's intentions, but it is difficult to know whether a person, and especially an animal, is intending to manipulate another's behaviour and it is even harder to determine whether they intend to alter another's beliefs. It is perfectly plausible to deceive someone because you don't want them to discover the truth, without knowing or understanding how they will view your false statement. Children often seem to deceive people at an early age, but their acts of deception are very rigidly tuned to specific situations – they are manipulating behaviour without knowing that they are being deceptive. And what follows from this is that in order to influence someone else's thoughts, it is not necessary to represent their state of mind.

As Leekam says, 'In everyday life we *need* not make the complex kinds of distinctions required here. We rarely, for example, need to make complex attributions of higher-order mental states or consider someone's representation of a situation even in the case of deception. This does not mean that we do not do so, especially when things go wrong. In the case of mistakes, misunderstandings and failed jokes, we are often forced to replay the situation in order to understand it. We say things like: "I thought you knew"; "Do you expect me to believe that?" My point is that we don't always have to use complex mental state attributions in order to be effective communicators and effective deceivers. We can get by with far less. After all, why should we bother to represent the mind if we don't need to? However, being able to understand mental states enables us to incorporate such understanding into our social interactions and allows for greater flexibility and efficiency in our dealings with others.'

Once children can understand false beliefs, they are able to manipulate the mind as well as someone's behaviour. Children older than five understand the difference between jokes and lies and can grasp complex embedded mental states related to this distinction.

Crucial to an understanding of a joke is the ability to appreciate the mind of the comic or the cartoonist when he or she conceived of the joke. First, we need to understand a very basic fact: jokes are funny, or, more accurately, that a joke is *meant* to be funny. Knowing that a statement is supposed to be a joke makes us persevere when initially we don't 'get it'. Second, we need to appreciate what is supposed to be funny and why. Rhiannon Corcoran, from University College London, Connie Cahill, who is based at Hammersmith Hospital, and Chris Frith, from the Wellcome Department of Cognitive Neurology, in London, gave a whole series of jokes to patients with schizophrenia as well as to non-psychotic patients with depression. Initially they were concerned that their depressed patients would simply not realise that the cartoons were actually meant to be funny, but they need not have worried. All the patients recognised that the jokes were supposed to be humorous. Corcoran and her colleagues thought that schizophrenics who hear voices and who have trouble with Theory of Mind would be able to understand slapstick cartoons, but if a reading of a character's mind was involved, they would fail to understand what was funny. The researchers were proved correct: all the patients generally thought the slapstick cartoons were humorous even if the patients with schizophrenia did not understand why. For example, one cartoon involved a fisherman who had caught a crab and turns to show his friend, blissfully unaware that a huge shark is coming up behind him. His friend turns tail and runs, but the fisherman thinks he is afraid of the crab. The caption reads, 'Ho ho ho! Fancy being afraid of a little crab!' One of the patients explained the joke by saying, 'The crab is the bait and the shark has come up to get it' and another said, 'He sees a whale and calls a whale a crab.' The schizophrenics had enough general comprehension of intentionality to realise that the jokes were supposed to be funny but not enough to decipher them when an understanding of someone's mental state was required.

Everybody lies regularly. Undergraduates lie to their mothers in half of their conversations and to complete strangers eighty per cent of the time. They tell twice as many lies as other people – two a day – usually for financial gain (there is one price for books in the bookshop and another when parents ask), to make their friends feel better about themselves and to con their family into thinking they were studying and not in the pub the night before. People tell fewer lies to those who are close to them, but partners are likely to be lied to a third of the time, which is more than people lie to their best friends. Although children rarely lie to their fathers, this is because they interact with them so seldom. When people are deliberately lying, they tend to try to control their facial expression and look the person to whom they are lying directly in the eye. However, there are a number of so-called reliable muscles which, to a well-trained observer, give the game away. Gladness, sadness, disgust and anger all have their reliable muscles – the disgust one causes a slight puckering of the nose; a genuine smile can be detected from a fake one by the *orbicularis oculi*, a muscle that wraps round the eyes and which raises the cheeks and makes the skin near the eyes furrow into crow's-feet. This muscle only contracts when people are genuinely happy when they smile. Body language can also let a liar down: people who are lying gesticulate less with their hands, blink more, their pupils dilate, their voice rises and they tend to fiddle with their clothes or their hair. Despite all these signals, most people are easily duped by liars telling ordinary and white lies.

Even that pillar of English values, Winston Churchill, believed in the value of deception. He said, 'In time of war, the truth is so precious it must be attended by a bodyguard of lies.' Josef Goebbels was one of the world's most famous liars; he turned deception into an art form through his propaganda machine. In his personal life he was notoriously deceitful, conducting affairs obsessively and consistently lying to his wife and to Hitler about his faithfulness. During the war he lied continuously to the German people about so-called Wonder Weapons that were always just about to be released. He knew perfectly well that no new weapons would be launched during the war because Germany lacked sufficient raw materials.

Francesca Happé told a series of what she called 'Strange Stories' to people with autism who could understand simple false beliefs. The stories dealt with a cast of characters who lied, joked, double-bluffed and were ironic. The results reveal much about the mind of an autistic person. For example, one story is a typical tale of deceit: Anna has just knocked over her mother's favourite crystal vase which smashes into smithereens. She knows her mother will be cross so she tells her that the dog knocked it over. What Happé wanted to know was whether Anna was telling the truth and why she said what she did. An example of double-bluff featured the Blue Army and the Red Army. During the war the Red Army captures a member of the Blue Army. They want him to tell them where his army's tanks are; they know they are either by the sea or in the mountains. They know that the prisoner will want to save his army and so he will certainly lie to them. The prisoner is very brave and very clever, he will not let them find his tanks. The tanks are really in the mountains. Now, when the other side asks him where his tanks are, he says, 'They are in the mountains.' Again, Happé asked whether the prisoner was telling the truth and why he said what he did.

The autistic people were unable to answer these questions correctly. Even though they often used terms that described mental states, their responses showed that they had little understanding of what the terms actually meant. For instance, when one character was described as having a 'frog in her throat', some people thought she had really swallowed a frog and in another story where a child pretended a banana was a phone, an intelligent twenty-four-year-old man said the reason was because some cordless phones are made to look like fruit. Some of the autistics could pass a Sally-Ann test, and these people were better at the Strange Stories which suggests that understanding false beliefs is closely linked to the ability to understand jokes and lies. However, all the autistic people made what Happé refers to as 'glaring errors'. In order to understand her stories, the autistic people needed to know what the main characters' speech meant in the context of the story – taken in isolation, many of the characters' responses would be ambiguous. For example, if your friend says, 'How nice', without any background information, it is impossible to tell if she is being truthful, sarcastic, telling a white lie, pretending or double-bluffing. By integrating your friend's motivation with the other relevant information, it is possible to work out what she actually means, and it is this integration that proves so hard for autistic people. Because of this inability, even those autistic people who can understand some mental states are still handicapped in everyday life.

Animals are capable of deceiving us and each other. Crab spiders blend to the exact colour of the flower they hide in and Sri Lankan jumping spiders mimic ants all the better to sink their poison fangs into unsuspecting prey. A type of moth caterpillar from Costa Rica bears more than a passing resemblance to a viper about to strike and consequently is left alone by potential predators. But these disguises are not conscious deceptions. Animals with mutations that make them better at mimicking vipers or changing the colour of their coats will survive longer, produce more offspring and pass on those precious genes to the next generation. When studying Theory of Mind, it is only worth looking at an animal's behaviour if it either influences another animal's behaviour or their beliefs and if the deceptive animal *intends* to be deceptive.

Plovers nest on the ground and are at risk from animals that could crush their eggs or those which actively seek out the eggs as a delicacy. The adult birds and their eggs are superbly camouflaged, but should a predator get too close, the nesting bird will launch into a pitiful display, its wing twisted at a tortuous angle, as it attempts to fly but falls painfully from the sky. As a predator such as a fox follows the bird, drooling with anticipation at the ease with which it will catch the disabled plover, the bird is actually leading the fox away from its nest. Once the plover has put a sufficient distance between the fox and its eggs, it flies from the fox's jaws, circles and returns to the nest. Plovers can correctly gauge that it is the eyes that are crucial and will stay away from their nests longer when an intruder is looking at them. If the intruder being distracted from the eggs stops gazing at the plover, the bird will move closer and resume its display with renewed intensity. As if they have learnt that cows do not eat birds, they do not bother with the broken wing display but lunge at cattle to stop them trampling on the nest.

It is difficult to know whether the plovers intend to deceive predators. Plovers clearly change a predator's *behaviour*, but we do not know whether their behaviour is innate or learnt, nor whether the plover intends to change a predator's *belief* about its flying capacity. However, even though the plover's behaviour is flexible to some degree, it is a behaviour shown by every member of the species and throughout an individual plover's life will be repeated countless times, allowing the plover to learn a simple rule: unless I make sure the fox's eyes are on me, the fox will abandon the chase and head for my nest. True deceptive capacity is most likely to be found in animals with a high degree of intelligence and whose deceit lies not in a pattern that is witnessed throughout the species, nor in a pattern that is seen repeated many times in one individual's life.

Like human infants, young chimpanzees tease their elders and betters. A chimp resting peacefully is fair game for an infant who will pull his or her hair, kick, bite and dangle from branches directly above the adult. After 'teasing' for a short while, infants often make a 'play face', a kind of open-mouthed grin which usually serves as an invitation to play. Adults and sub-adult chimpanzees react by screaming or hitting the teasing infant as if the play face in this context is derisory. Adult chimps rarely play with infants – those that do tend to be relatives – but teasing by young chimps is cordially extended to any members of the group. It is likely that it serves as a means of social exploration for youngsters, allowing them to probe the limits of their troop-mates' social tolerance. If chimpanzees are capable of deception, teasing may serve as the first step in their development of this ability, just as it does in human infants.

Guy Woodruff and David Premack carried out an experiment on young chimpanzees to see if they could conceal the truth and if they could actively lie. Four young chimpanzees saw food being hidden but they could not reach it themselves. Their task was to inform a friendly trainer where the food was so that it could be shared among the chimps. A hostile human – dressed in dark glasses, boots and with a bandit-style scarf wrapped round his mouth – kept the food to himself if he found it. Initially, the chimps made no attempt to match their behaviour to each trainer. However, they soon learnt to stifle their pointing gestures and stopped looking at the location of the food when the hostile human was present and two of the chimps, Bert and Sadie, learnt to misinform him by pointing with one leg at the empty container. Sadie, the oldest, was the first to withhold information and Jessie, the youngest, took the longest to learn to do so.

Woodruff and Premack then reversed the roles so that the people knew where the food was but the chimps did not. They modelled their gestures on those of the chimps. Sadie and Luvie were capable of finding food in the baited container both when the hostile trainer lied to them and when the friendly informant was truthful, but the other two chimps, Bert and Jessie, were only able to complete one half of the task: Bert could follow the truthful person and Jessie could avoid the container that the competitive trainer pointed to.

In the wild, primates have become renowned for their capacity to cheat on one another. As Machiavelli says, 'It is good to appear clement, trustworthy, humane, religious and honest and also to be so, but always with the mind so disposed that, when the occasion arises not to be so, you can become the opposite.' In general, there are four types of deception that have been witnessed by primatologists in the field: concealment, distraction, creation of an image and manipulation of another individual who acts as a 'stooge'.

Primates have perfected the art of concealment. Subordinate males who are not supposed to mate with females suppress their copulation calls. 'Undoubtedly, the penis is one of the most "independently" behaving body parts,' says primatologist Frans de Waal. 'In chimpanzees, it has an important signal function: it is of a bright pink colour, which strongly contrasts with the dark fur. This, together with the difficulty of rapidly losing an erection once it is there, makes the penis an important piece of evidence for dominant males who watch over the sexual contacts of other males.' Male chimpanzees are aware of this: a typical stance of a male chimpanzee is to sit legs apart displaying to a female, but with his hands carefully positioned at the sides so that other males cannot see what he is revealing.

Two of Sue Savage-Rumbaugh's chimps, Austin and Sherman, have developed a neat way of escaping from their cage. They bang a heavy-duty plastic cube against a wall made of lexan (a strong clear plastic building material) until it stresses and splits apart. The chimps make a terrific noise, but whenever anyone goes to see what they're up to, Austin and Sherman are always sitting quietly, minding their own business. Panzee, Kanzi's sister, also concealed her behaviour. She had a strange habit of drinking from other people's glasses and plates. When she was told not to do this and given her own set of tableware, she started to monitor other people and as soon as she thought they weren't looking, she would take a quick swig from someone else's glass and then replace it.

Distracting another individual's attention is a deception classically employed in slapstick comedy. In *Easy Street*, made in 1917, Charlie Chaplin is given a job as a policeman. He runs into a bully who towers over him (Eric Campbell). Chaplin, ironically, wants to telephone the police, but the thug won't let him near the phone. The quaking policeman makes a big show of looking away as if he has just seen something incredibly fascinating. The bully follows his gaze and Chaplin grabs the phone. Needless to say, he does not succeed in calling the cops.

One young chacma baboon tried this trick with rather more success. He had been tormenting some juveniles and their screams attracted the attention of the group's males who came racing over the brow of the hill. Immediately, the young baboon stood on his hindlegs and looked around. The older males began to scan the horizon for imminent danger and forgot to punish the youngster. Roger Fousts's sign language-using chimp, Bruno, used the same trick to get one over on his playmate Booee. The two were squabbling over a hose. Bruno suddenly dropped everything, raced to his cage door and gave a chimp alarm call. Booee rushed to the door and peered anxiously out. Meanwhile Bruno crept back and stole the hose.

Frans de Waal says that chimps often turn their attention to something unimportant as a way of hiding apparent embarrassment or disappointment, though whether this is to distract themselves or their opponent is not clear. Of this second type of deception, he says, 'After a negative experience, they may carefully inspect details of their own body, similar to the way a tennis player concentrates on the strings of his or her racket after a bad return.' Social harmony cannot be restored after a fight until both parties are reconciled, but no one wants to be the first to lose honour by making up. De Waal has witnessed several occasions when chimpanzees feign interest in small objects to break the tension. In one instance, a male discovered something in the grass and hooted loudly. A number of chimps, including his adversary, rushed over. The others rapidly lost interest but the two rival males stayed. They avoided eye-contact, but made all kinds of excited sounds while touching and sniffing the discovery (which de Waal was never able to identify). After a few minutes they calmed down and started grooming each other. 'These reconciliations gave the impression of being intentionally facilitated by the use of an "excuse". The fact that, besides the discoverer, his adversary was equally fascinated by an object that induced so little interest in others suggests that the adversary also understood the purpose. It is tempting to regard this face-saving tactic as a *collective lie*, in other words, one party deceiving, and the other acting deceived.'

Distracting top secret service agents such as 007 with beautiful women in order to extract secrets or weapons is the stuff of James Bond films. Rather more down to earth, one primatologist witnessed a female grooming a male olive baboon who had just caught an antelope. He relaxed into her tender administrations and lolled back. She immediately grabbed the carcass and ran off.

The third main type of deceptive behaviour is to create an image of oneself which is untruthful. Often this is simply a neutral image: a young female gorilla was fascinated by another female's infant. In order to get close to the infant she built a nest a little way away, then another one slightly closer, and a third, until finally she was right by the infant without the mother thinking that the female intended to try to play with her baby. At Arnhem Zoo, one of the keepers buried some grapefruits in the sand. A young adult male, Dandy, walked over the spot, but without hesitating or altering his usual behaviour. A good three hours later, once all the other males were asleep, he headed straight for the fruit and dug them up. Zwart, a female adolescent in the same group, also managed to perfect a neutral image for the sake of food. She was the only chimp who saw a visitor throw an apple into the outdoor enclosure. She walked over to the apple without looking at it and sat down. Then very casually she stretched out her hand, blindly closed it round the apple and walked away using all four limbs (chimps normally carry food in one hand and hobble on three limbs). Still without making a sound – impressive in a species renowned for its excited calls when food has been spotted – she sat down behind a pile of car tyres where no one could see her and consumed the apple in peace.

There are counter-strategies to such devious behaviour. Figan, a male chimp at Gombe, had seen a box full of bananas. He was about to eat them when he heard another chimp approaching. He shut the box, sat down and looked around as if nothing had happened. The second chimp left the clearing and Figan turned to retrieve the fruit. Just as he was about to help himself, the second male, who had been hiding behind a tree, leapt out and took the bananas from him. Back at Arnhem, Frans de Waal saw a male who was about to get into a fight give a fear grin. Three times he pushed his lips back to a normal expression, each time failing to stifle his innate fearful response. The third time he succeeded in wiping the grin off his face and only then turned to present his rival with a face devoid of fear.

A rather less benign form of deception was seen in Lucy, one of the first sign language-using chimps. When Sue Savage-Rumbaugh met her, Lucy offered her a plastic flower. Savage-Rumbaugh thought she was being friendly and reached out to take the flower, whereupon Lucy promptly bit her hand.

The final major category of deception is the manipulation of a victim who is to be deceived using another animal as a fall guy. Often this kind of deception takes the form of teasing. Sub-adult patas monkeys will often carry infants around and pester a male until he reacts. The infant then screams and all the females in the group descend on the hapless male.

Weaning is a trying time for all. One gelada baboon was desperately trying to suckle only to be rebuffed by his mother. He went to a male baboon and started to hit him and pull his hair. The male ignored him, but eventually he lashed out at the annoying infant who shrieked loudly. His mother ran over, put the infant to her nipple and took him out of the male's way. Chimpanzees have also been observed engaging in behaviour which it is tempting to see as telling tales: Dandy was close friends with a female called Spin but he once found her mating with another male. Both 'knew' they shouldn't be mating with each other since only the alpha male is supposed to mate with the females. Dandy ran barking to the dominant male and led him over to where the pair were having their clandestine liaison.

Chimps can make humans their stooges, too. Sue Savage-Rumbaugh introduced a young woman to Matata, Kanzi's mother. Matata initially wouldn't let the visitor touch any of her possessions. She handed her bowl to Savage-Rumbaugh and asked for food. As soon as Sue had gone, she heard Matata shrieking. She ran back in and saw the woman holding Matata's bowl; the chimp was screaming at her and threatening to bite. She looked from the visitor to the bowl and back to Savage-Rumbaugh as if trying to get her to attack this mean individual who had stolen her bowl. Since neither Savage-Rumbaugh nor the young woman follow chimp etiquette, the woman was able to explain that Matata had placed the bowl in her hands and then started to yell.

Deceptive acts have been witnessed in all the great apes and some monkeys, but never in prosimians such as lemurs. This is not surprising since lemurs and their ilk evolved over forty-five million years ago, whereas the great apes split from what was to become the human line much later. Chimpanzees only branched off between four and five million years ago and are, apart from humans, the biggest cheaters. Their deceptive strategies work because they have the ability to compute visually another animal's perspective. Deceptive acts do occur at low frequencies, but that is to be expected. If you spend all your life surrounded by the same individuals, it is hard to dupe them and it is likely that they will be able to employ counter-measures. It is also perfectly possible that some of these acts of deception were conditioned. For example, Zwart could have previously picked up pieces of fruit thrown to her by visitors. Each time every member of her group promptly descended on her, so she quickly learnt that the only way to safeguard her fruit would be by keeping very quiet and displaying no outward sign of her discovery. This is rather different from thinking, 'If I keep quiet, everyone will believe that I have not found some food.' At the moment it is difficult to say for sure whether deceptive acts by great apes, and especially chimpanzees, show a full comprehension of another's state of mind and an intent to alter how the victim of the deceptive act thinks, rather than how they act.

Teaching apes language may affect their ability to lie. Koko, a gorilla who uses American sign language for the deaf, has a sense of humour and will tease her caregivers. This is a transcript of a conversation between her and one of her caregivers, Barbera, who has just shown her a picture of a bird feeding its young.

K: That me. (Pointing to the adult bird.)

B: Is that really you?

K: Koko good bird.

B: I thought you were a gorilla.

K: Koko bird.

B: Can you fly?

K: Good. ('Good' can mean 'yes'.)

B: Show me.

K: Fake bird, clown. (Koko laughs.)

B: You're teasing me. (Koko laughs.) What are you really? (Koko laughs again and after a minute signs:)

K: Gorilla Koko.

A favourite tease of Koko's is to chase people with a toy alligator. They are supposed to act as if they're frightened by screaming and running. As Francine Patterson, who is in charge of Koko, says, it's wonderful that a fully grown adult gorilla thinks she can scare people with a toy alligator. Koko likes to rough and tumble with wrestler, Eugene Linden. In the course of one game, she bit him. Patterson instantly demanded to know what she had done. *Not teeth*, was her innocent reply. 'Koko, you lied!' said Patterson and Koko responded by signing, *Bad again Koko bad again.*

Patterson also reports the following lie. 'When Koko was five she sat on the sink in the kitchen, causing it to cave slightly away from the counter. I then had an assistant named Kate Mann, a deaf woman Koko loved to blame things on. Kate was not, so far as I had noticed, prone to fits of violence. Thus, when I saw the broken sink and asked, "What happened here?" I was not disposed to believe Koko when she signed, *Kate there bad.* In fact, the image of a gorilla accusing a good-natured young woman of breaking the sink made it hard for me to maintain my pretence of irritation.'

Once, when Patterson caught Koko eating a crayon, she signed *lip*, and began moving the crayon across her lips as if applying lipstick. Another time she tried to break a window using a chopstick (in itself a somewhat ridiculous image) which she'd stolen from the cutlery drawer. When she was asked what she was doing she said,

Smoke mouth and put the stick in her mouth as if she were smoking a cigarette.

Chantek, a sign language-using orangutan who was taught by Lynn Miles, from the University of Chattanooga, Tennessee, also lies using signs. He frequently signs *dirty*, meaning that he wants to go to the toilet. Chantek has to ask permission because he is only allowed in the bathroom with a caregiver. As Miles says, 'Bathrooms are as much fun for apes as they are for young children: when in the bathroom, Chantek would turn on the faucets, flush the toilet, play with the soap, turn knobs and buzzers on the washer/dryer and pull towels from the shelves.' He often asked to go to the bathroom when he was bored of what he was doing and not when he actually needed to go. 'Once when his caregiver became angry, Chantek quickly sat on the toilet and pressed his penis to try to extract a few drops, but failed.' A statistical analysis of Chantek's deviousness revealed that the two most common goals of his 'lies' were to go to the bathroom when he didn't need to and to distract his caregiver's attention to Chantek's advantage.

Kanzi, by contrast, is adept at all kinds of deceitful behaviour. He can hide himself and remain motionless for nearly half an hour – once under a pile of blankets in the room Sue Savage-Rumbaugh was searching. He also hides objects exceptionally well, such as the keys to his cage, but will diligently pretend to search for them with Savage-Rumbaugh when she complains of their loss.

He and Savage-Rumbaugh frequently walk in the woods together and Kanzi is expressly forbidden to eat any toadstools or mushrooms he finds. However, since he is quicker and has keener eyesight than his companion, he often spots toadstools before she does and may hide them until he thinks he can eat them without anyone noticing. As a counter-strategy, Savage-Rumbaugh has taken to carrying a rock with her. As soon as Kanzi scampers off, she chucks the rock at the toadstool he is heading for, hoping to destroy it before he reaches it. Kanzi now asks for the rock when they're walking on the pretext of playing with it or incorporating it into a nest he is building. Once in possession of the rock, he races off to pick the forbidden fungi. One day Savage-Rumbaugh climbed into their tree house, expecting Kanzi to follow her. She waited for ten minutes, calling him all the time. Eventually, she climbed down only to find Kanzi sitting quietly at the base of the tree as if waiting patiently for her. Just as she was about to reach him, he whipped out a giant toadstool, a good six inches in diameter, and bit into it.

Children and apes are both capable of lying and deceiving. When children begin to deceive, however, they do not mentally represent another person's state of mind. To us, their lies and deceptions seem as sophisticated as our own but this is because we interpret everything in a mentalistic way. Young children are not reading minds, but they have a disposition to behave in a certain way which derives from biological evolution. We call their behaviour deceptive. Adults and children over five or six years of age do truly deceive and manipulate others and have access to their Theory of Mind. Sometimes we consciously plan how to deceive others, but we often deceive unintentionally or unconsciously. We're also amazingly good at reinterpreting behaviour. Our ability to be empathic or deceptive has evolved over millions of years. Within our own species we begin simple acts of empathy and deception without aforethought, but our mentalistic framework is implicit. We build upon behaviour and overlay that with psychology.

As William James might have said, we never step into the same stream of consciousness twice. Our mental states are constantly changing. Our beliefs change as we learn more, our desires change as they become satiated, our intentions change as we invent new ideas about what we want to do, our perceptions change as we alter our point of view. As adults we know about the changes in our mental states and we can remember and describe our past mental states. Young children have as little access to their own mental states as they have to anyone else's. First, they begin to understand joint attention, they start to recognise themselves in the mirror and use pretend play. By the age of three they can understand their own and other people's desires and they have an implicit concept of belief. They understand that seeing leads to knowledge. By four they can understand others' beliefs and begin selectively to comprehend attention. By five they can understand a false belief. At six they are capable of telling a lie from a mistake and a joke from a lie. They also have a representational attitude towards pretend play. By the time they are seven or eight years old they are capable of understanding irony and they can understand third-order false beliefs.

Apes are by far the cleverest animals that we have come across. Their ability to manipulate others and their flexibility are unmatched in the animal kingdom. Chimpanzees, at least, show full self-awareness and they and other great apes can recognise themselves in mirrors. They can use joint attention, the brightest of them appear to understand that seeing leads to knowing, they are capable of responding better than a four-year-old child to a false belief task, they are able to show empathy and deception. Many apes have learnt our own language through signs and symbols and can, to a limited extent, communicate with us.

During fifty-six hours of recording five signing chimps, Dar, Loulis, Washoe, Tatu and Moja, there were 368 instances of private signing where the chimps talked to themselves in the same way that young children do. Between twelve and fourteen per cent of the time they signed about objects, people or chimps that were not present and five per cent of the time their signs concerned imaginary things. When Loulis stole her magazine, Washoe signed to herself, *Dirty, Dirty*, a chimp insult. The chimps also have a concept of themselves related to time. Roger Fouts makes a point about celebrating birthdays and Christmas because he says that captivity is so boring. For Christmas, he and his wife Debbi hang strings of dried fruit around the chimps' enclosure and decorate a tree with them. The chimps spontaneously came up with the name *candy tree*.

On the Friday after Thanksgiving in 1989, it began to snow and Tatu asked for the *candy tree*. She had not only remembered the Christmas tree, but knew that this was the season for it. Debbi Fouts's birthday is on the first of August and Dar's is on the second. The Foutses and the chimps were celebrating Debbi's birthday when Tatu asked, *Dar ice-cream*? Ice-cream is usually eaten on Dar's birthday and Tatu may have been aware that the following day would be Dar's celebration.

However, there are many things which chimpanzees cannot do.

They have to learn how to deceive others in a laboratory situation (such as Premack's attempt to get them to dupe an uncooperative trainer), just as they appear to have to learn who is paying attention to them in Povinelli's experiment where one trainer could see the chimp and one could not. They very rarely point or gesture protodeclaratively, they don't share or show, and they seldom teach infants or those who lack knowledge. Although they can be empathic and deceptive, how much of this behaviour is truly mentalistic? Like young children, they may attempt to manipulate another's behaviour rather than their mind, and they, like us, have had millions of years of social living to be primed to be deceptive in group situations in order to obtain those things they hold dear, such as food and sex. They are exceptionally rapid at learning cues that they are already primed by evolution to respond to.

My guess is that chimpanzees, and other great apes, have an implicit mental understanding. They are on the cusp of the human mind. They share many similarities with us and with other animals, yet they are very different to us. There is both gradation and discontinuity between us, them, and other animals. Similarly, we are animals ruled by our culture, environment and biology. None of these factors can be separated out and treated in isolation. We share a biological nature with chimps, but we can transcend that, just as chimps share a biological nature with monkeys, but they can transcend a monkey code of conduct by showing empathy, through their protoculture, mirror self-recognition, symbol acquisition and a 'weak' Theory of Mind. Chimpanzees live in a less mentally complex world, where the workings of other minds, though present, are only dimly understood.

As I was puzzling over the triumphs chimps and other animals have achieved in some areas of Theory of Mind and their deficits in related areas of mindreading, I started to reread Daniel Dennett's work and found that, as usual, the philosopher had got there first. The quote from his essay, 'The intentional stance in theory and practice', is long, but I think it worth reproducing at length.

It will turn out on further exploration that vervet monkeys (and

178

chimps and dolphins and all other higher non-human animals) exhibit mixed and confusing symptoms of higher-order intentionality. They will pass some higher-order tests and fail others; they will in some regards reveal themselves to be alert to third-order sophistications, while disappointing us with their failure to grasp some simpler second-order points. No crisp, rigorous set of intentional hypotheses of any order will be clearly confirmed. The reason I am willing to make this prediction is not that I think I have special insight [. . .] just that I have noted, as anyone can, that much the same is true of us human beings. We are not ourselves unproblematic exemplars of third-, fourth-, or fifth-order intentional systems [. . .] I expect the results of the effort at intentional interpretation of monkeys, [as with] small children, to be riddled with the sorts of gaps and foggy places that are inevitable in the interpretation of systems that are, after all, only imperfectly rational.

In the next chapter we are going to delve into how the brain computes Theory of Mind. When the human mind cannot understand other minds, autism is the result, and we will examine the strange, bizarre and often tragic world of people with high-functioning autism: those who have Asperger's syndrome.

8

THE WATER LILIES HAVE
OPENED THEIR EYES

I shall be telling with a sigh
Somewhere ages and ages hence:
Two roads diverged into a wood, and I –
I took the one less travelled by,
And that has made all the difference.
      Robert Frost, 'The Road Not Taken'

Brother Juniper featured on more than one occasion in *The Little Flowers of St Francis*, a collection of legends written in the thirteenth century. One of the legends tells of the time that Brother Juniper went to visit a sick man at the convent of St Mary of the Angels. He asked, 'Can I do thee any service?' The sick man replied that he'd like a pig's foot to eat. Without further ado, Brother Juniper took a knife from the kitchen, found a herd of pigs, caught one of them and cut its foot off. He took the foot back, cooked it and gave it to the sick man. Meanwhile, the swineherd, who had seen Brother Juniper, went to the convent and called the friars hypocrites, deceivers, robbers and evil men. St Francis apologised to him on behalf of all the friars and upbraided Brother Juniper.

'Brother Juniper was much amazed, wondering that anyone should have been angered at so charitable an action. And so he went on his way, and coming to the man, who was still chafing and past all patience, he told him for what reason he had cut off the pig's foot, and all with such fervour, exultation and joy, as if he were telling him of some great benefit he had done him which deserved to be highly rewarded.' The man then realised the 'charity and simplicity of his story' and, after weeping copiously, killed the pig and presented it to the convent.

Another legend tells of the time Brother Juniper cooked food for the entire fortnight not realising that it would spoil. The Brother Superior shouted at him, but the only thing that Brother Juniper noticed was that his Superior's voice had grown hoarse with shouting and he cooked him some porridge. His Superior refused to eat it. Brother Juniper eventually gave up trying to persuade him to take the porridge, but he asked him to come down and hold a candle for him so that he had light enough to eat it himself. The Brother interpreted this as Brother Juniper's simplicity and piety and shared the meal with him.

Brother Juniper was well known for his literal interpretation of the Franciscan virtues of poverty and charity and would give away all his clothes and once even cut the bells off the altar-cloth in order to give them to a poor woman. Uta Frith believes that Brother Juniper probably had Asperger's syndrome. She says, 'What the case of Brother Juniper highlights is one of the many astonishing aspects of autism, namely utter guilelessness.' Another more recent literal interpretation of the bible was given by an eight-year-old child with Asperger's syndrome. He was looking at a film about Abraham, who was told to sacrifice his son to God. He watched passively enough and at the end uttered one word: 'Cannibals.'

In Asperger's own words, these children seem to have 'fallen from the sky'. Autism can now be diagnosed when a child is as young as eighteen months and some people who have Asperger's are initially diagnosed as autistic before the prognosis is corrected. Others may go for many years without being diagnosed at all or are treated for schizophrenia. The criteria for diagnosing Asperger's syndrome are the same as those for diagnosing autism: impaired social communication, lack of pretend play and poor communication skills. However, language and cognitive development of Asperger's sufferers are usually not significantly delayed. Their speech is often pedantic and stereotyped, their movements clumsy, they interact in a peculiar way socially, cannot show empathy and have a very narrow range of odd all-absorbing interests. Many are very intelligent and for this reason they are often referred to as 'high-functioning autistics'. The two terms, autism and Asperger's syndrome, are even used inter-changeably.

Ben was one of the lucky ones. He was diagnosed early, before his fourth birthday. His mother says, 'He was a spectacular baby. He stood alone at seven months, walked unaided at nine. By eighteen months he knew dozens of rhymes and stories by heart, could identify every colour and knew most of the letters of the alphabet. We were delighted and complacent. When you have a child who can sing, tunefully, every verse of "Good King Wenceslas" before the age of two, you don't tend to look for problems.'

Ben's parents initially ignored the strange side of their child, the fact that he didn't share toys or copy people's actions. 'He didn't babble and he had no baby words. He applied his quotations to appropriate situations: "And there in the doorway stood a huge green alligator," he said, looking at our stout cleaning lady wearing a green dress.'

When the family finally realised that Ben had a problem, his mother tried to look at the positive aspects of his condition. As she says, 'There are some advantages for a parent in having a child who would rather watch dust motes in sunlight than Power Rangers and who lets us know that he wants to visit the pond by saying, "The water lilies have opened their eyes now." ' When asked what he wanted for Christmas, he replied, 'Aphids.' Even so, Ben, like all other people with Asperger's syndrome, has an incurable disorder. His mother says, 'The fear that one's child may never sustain normal relationships or even be tolerated by other people is harrowing.'

Despite their inability to show pretend play, people with Asperger's often have vivid imaginations and can use striking imagery. James always asks strangers, 'What would you do if a tall man with yellow hair came and swung you up on his shoulders?' When he was younger, he wrote a short story to explain his question, part of which is reproduced here.

This wicked witch thought it would be great fun to make someone suffer for all absolute endless eternity. So one night, after I started school, the wicked witch came to my house and crept upstairs to my bedroom. Then the wicked witch put a spell into my mouth and gave me a drink of water to swallow the spell so that it would work. The magic spell was to make me fall in love with that man who was nine feet tall with long, straight, light yellow hair down to his elbows, who was wearing a dark brown three-piece suit . . .'

And then one day, when I had been at that school for six or seven years, this man at my school who looked so fine to me and made me feel so great decided to leave school and go to live somewhere else millions and millions of miles away. When I came back to school on the first day of the following term, I looked all round and about the playground for this man who looked so fine to me and made me feel great, but I couldn't find him anywhere. So I asked the teachers, 'Where is that man who is nine feet tall and thin with long, straight, yellow hair down to his elbows, who wears a dark brown three-piece suit, because I love him with all my heart, and he looks so fine to me that he makes me feel great?'

Unable to show empathy, some people with Asperger's have killed. However, given that they are not concerned with asserting dominance or being violent towards others, the murders occur more in the way of lethal experiments, such as the boy who was fascinated with fire and burned down his dormitory with a couple of his room-mates in it. One seven-year-old boy said, 'Mummy, I shall take a knife one day and push it in your heart, then blood will spurt out and this will cause a great stir.' He remarked that there wasn't enough blood when she cut herself and was quite excited when he was injured. Most people involved with the boy considered him sadistic, but it is more likely that he was fascinated with blood.

The intelligence of the person with Asperger's allows him or her to solve the Sally-Ann or Smarties test for Theory of Mind and many can pass higher-order tests such as the tale of Mary and John and the ice-cream van. However, over seventy per cent of those tested do not use words referring to mental states to explain a character's action. Verbal skills do influence their ability to pass

Theory of Mind tasks, but they still cannot relate to other people effectively. It's likely that they are using logical reasoning and other cognitive processes to work out Theory of Mind tasks, since they have to think carefully before replying. In their everyday life, they still appear odd and are not able to capitalise on their logical approach to solving Theory of Mind tasks in test conditions. They often show impairments in skills that require mindreading, such as taking a hint or keeping a secret, but they can learn to share and initiate routine conversations. Although these people are able to think about thinking, their handicap in relating to others means that they often need sheltered accommodation and employment. Normal children pass Theory of Mind tasks when their verbal mental age is that of a four or five year old, but people with Asperger's need a verbal mental age of a ten year old. Uta Frith comments that the absence of the ability to mindread during their development must have left some permanent scars and so it is no wonder that they don't function normally in real life and find using their hard-won Theory of Mind demanding.

People with Asperger's have a greater degree of awareness about their own plight and often understand that they don't know about other people's mental states. As one man said, 'Other people seem to have a special sense by which they can read other people's thoughts.' John, a teenager with Asperger's, didn't know how to interact with girls, so he watched them and wrote down everything they did. Sadly, his ignorance, and perhaps innocence, resulted in an indecent assault on one young woman.

Margaret Dewey, from the University of Michigan, made up stories and asked adults with Asperger's what they thought of the characters' behaviour. Their responses showed how different their reactions were from normal people's, but that they could learn specific rules about what is or is not socially acceptable. Unfortunately, rules learnt at home which applied to one set of circumstances could not always be generalised to other situations. Some of the stories Dewey made up were to illustrate to the adults that their behaviour was perceived as odd, but they did not recognise themselves in the stories. For instance, in one tale a young man got into a lift. A stranger who was already in the lift remarked that it was a nice day. The young man was on his way to an interview and, catching sight of himself in the mirror in the lift, realised that his hair was a mess. He asked the stranger if he could borrow his comb.

Dewey says the responses were as follows (the comments from the people with Asperger's are in italics, Dewey's in roman):

I never saw an elevator with a mirror in it. This is a typical pedantic, irrelevant remark.

It was eccentric for the stranger to say, 'Nice day isn't it', because you can't see the weather in an elevator. This is a typical literal analysis which misses the point that comments on the weather are common pleasantries between strangers.

Borrowing the comb is normal behaviour for him because he has to look nice for the interview. This is the most important thing because he needs very badly to get this job. Most controls [students] rated the comb incident as quite shocking. Other autistic subjects varied, as some may have learnt rules about comb sharing.

Another example Dewey gave was of a man aged twenty-two, called Roger, who was invited to dinner by a friend of the family. Roger was quite nervous and felt better if he ate every two hours. When he arrived at his hostess's house, he realised he hadn't eaten for two hours and asked her when dinner was going to be served. She said it would be ready in an hour's time, so he took out some food he'd brought with him and ate it. A little later, the hostess said that dinner was ready and when she'd served his meal, she asked him if she'd given him enough. He said it looked fine, but he was going to wait for another hour to eat as he'd just had some food.

The students were quite shocked by Roger's behaviour, but the people with Asperger's syndrome thought he behaved admirably and had got round the problem of his nervousness with skill. All of those with Asperger's took a long time to think about the answers, whereas the students intuitively recognised what they believed was eccentric behaviour.

People with Asperger's syndrome have another cognitive deficit which is related to Theory of Mind: they have weak 'central coherence'. This is the inability to draw together diverse strands of information to make a coherent whole. For example, most people can retell a story told to them by remembering the gist of the narrative and changing or embellishing the details. When you or I do jigsaw puzzles, we look at the picture as a whole and try to slot in the parts: a person with autism would examine the shapes of the pieces and many can complete jigsaws when the picture is face down.

Central coherence is perhaps best illustrated by the story of the clinician who was pointing out various parts of a doll's bed to a young boy with autism. The boy could accurately tell her that the duvet was a duvet and so on, but when she pointed to the pillow, he said it was a piece of ravioli. Indeed, the tiny pillow with its frilly edge did look like a bit of pasta, but only if taken *completely* out of context. Although most people with Asperger's syndrome and autism have weak central coherence, some are severely deficient. One boy was upset when told that a dog seen from the side at fourteen minutes past three was the same dog as one seen at fifteen minutes past three from the front. A twelve-year-old girl called Elly liked to observe shadows in the moonlight and clouds in the sky. Every mealtime she put a tall green ridged glass by her plate and filled it with green juice, pouring it up to either the sixth or the seventh level, depending on the weather and the phase of the moon. This insistence on sameness, characteristic of many with autism and Asperger's, is due to the fact that they can't see the whole and get trapped in the minutiae of the day. Elly was distressed when she travelled to a different time zone because her shadow at six p.m. was a different length.

Weak central coherence means that people with autism are good at tasks requiring localised bits of information but poor at tasks requiring the recognition of global meaning. Indeed, even when people with Asperger's are greatly talented, they approach their craft in an entirely different way from normal people. Stephen Wiltshire is a brilliant artist with an almost photographic memory. He draws incredibly detailed pictures of buildings and street scenes. When the famous psychiatrist Oliver Sacks met him, he asked Stephen if he'd like to draw his house. In his book, *An Anthropologist on Mars*, Sacks writes, 'It was snowing, cold and wet, not a day to linger. Stephen bestowed a quick, indifferent look at my house – there hardly seemed to be any act of attention – then asked to come in [. . .] Stephen did not make any sketch or outline, but just started at one edge of the paper (I had a feeling he might have started anywhere at all) and steadily moved across it, as if transcribing some tenacious inner image or visualisation.'

Later, when he got to know Stephen better and they were travelling by train to Leningrad to give Stephen some more unusual drawing opportunity, Sacks mused, 'I thought of his perception, his memory, as quasi-mechanical – like a vast store, or library, or archive – not even indexed or categorised, or held together by association, yet where anything might be accessed in an instant, as in the random-access memory of a computer. I found myself thinking of him as a sort of train himself, a perceptual missile, travelling through life, noting, recording, but never appropriating, a sort of transmitter of all that rushed past – but himself unchanged, unfed by the experience.'

Central coherence is a crucial part of Theory of Mind. As Frith explains, 'Mentalising ability can be seen as a cohesive interpretive device *par excellence*: it forces together complex information from totally disparate sources into a pattern which has *meaning*.' She adds that this ability is incredibly salient. 'As a spider is destined to weave webs, so are we programmed to weave information into coherent patterns.' By thinking about a person's actions, intentions, motives, beliefs and desires, we can build up a picture of why someone should act in the way he or she does and read meaning into it, whereas the person with autism would only see the raw behaviour itself.

Asperger's syndrome has sometimes been called 'mild autism', but in many ways this is misleading because it evokes the idea that there is no need to give these people special help. As Frith says, 'The person who has a glimmer of awareness of other minds and a dawning insight into their own problems is especially vulnerable to feelings of depression and low self-esteem. It is not surprising to read of their over-sensitivity to criticism and inability to carry lightly, or with humour, the heavy burden of their handicap.' Because many sufferers are highly intelligent yet deeply unhappy, it often takes some crisis such as a suicide attempt, or a bizarre piece of behaviour, before a person is diagnosed properly. One twelve-year-old boy was not described as having Asperger's until he tried to leap out of a third-floor window. He jumped with a smile on his face. His father took him to see psychiatrist Christopher Gillberg, from the University of Gothenburg, Sweden. Gillberg had spoken to the boy a couple of times in the school playground, but this was the first occasion the child had been to his office and, as Gillberg explains, the boy diagnosed himself.

> On meeting me, he started chatting away about various kinds of gunpowder [. . .] He told me he would start to try them out in the school-yard. He then interrupted himself, stared intensely but briefly at me and said, 'I say, you do look a lot like Christopher Gillberg!' I asked him if he could guess the reason for my looking so much like Christopher Gillberg. 'How am I to know? You just happen to look like a copy of him, that's all!' I then said: 'Well, you see, I am Christopher Gillberg.' He looked up briefly and exclaimed, 'What an extraordinary coincidence!' and then made his way into my secretary's office [. . .] He immediately asked, 'How many letters per second can you type?' My secretary said: 'Well, it used to be 1,100 in three minutes.' He then proceeded to her desk, made a quick computation and shouted: 'Six point one one one one one one in all eternity one one one.' He pointed at me and stared into thin air and said, 'He does look like Christopher Gillberg! What a coincidence!'
>
> He then entered my office and started picking out various books and papers from one of the shelves. Quite by chance, he found a Swedish leaflet for parents on Asperger's syndrome. He said: 'This is something I've never heard anybody say a word about before. I think I'll call it AS for short.' On reading the text aloud, he soon remarked, as though in passing: 'It seems I have AS! By golly, I do have AS. Wait until my father hears about this!' He went on reading and soon decided: 'My parents just might have AS too, you know, my father in particular, he too has all-

absorbing interests and . . .' He didn't seem to react emotionally to what he read. 'Now I can tell my classmates the reason why I pace the school-yard briskly ten times up and down each break all the year round is I have AS. And it will get my teacher off my back. If you have a "handicap-condition" they have to tolerate you.'

A diagnosis of Asperger's syndrome is a relief in many ways for those who for years have been aware that there is something wrong with them. Before proper diagnosis, sufferers are often prescribed drugs for schizophrenia. Although Asperger's syndrome is a different disorder from schizophrenia, some people with Asperger's also have schizoid traits. One such man, Peter, was continually carrying on litigation with local authorities for slights he felt he had received. He had several unusual beliefs. For instance, he thought that a man with red hair had attempted to assassinate him with an umbrella.

Being able to explain their often strange reactions to others as a form of handicap can save embarrassment on both sides. One young man's mother died of cancer when he was fifteen. After her death, when people asked how he was doing, he usually said, 'Oh, I'm all right. You see, I have Asperger's syndrome which makes me less vulnerable to the loss of loved ones than most people.'

Much work on Asperger's syndrome and autism has focused on childhood, but, of course, every child will eventually grow up.

It's only by logic and emotions that I get through. Hiding feelings came after I became the victim. All emotions are a sign of weakness. I'm about as flexible as a thick bar of metal in a barrel of nitrogen [. . .] I shall turn out a mechanical, inflexible person who nobody likes, nobody loves and who everybody will be glad when I'm in my grave [. . .] it's a vicious circle. 1. I get teased. 2. I make myself miserable and cynical. 3. I get teased again [. . .] The best school would be one where I spent my time working with machines – remove the human factor. If the people were very nice I could probably do very well. What I find difficult about learning, as well as the teasing, is that there's a massive great group of us and they're all unruly [. . .] I can break out of the vicious circle, but I can't take down the barriers. The clay has set – I've moulded my personality. The wall's there for good. My flexibility was one of the first things I lost – lost completely.

So wrote a twelve-year-old boy to his mother. His main worry, even at this age, is one that his parents are also very concerned about: adulthood. People with Asperger's syndrome need a lot of support but some of them can go on to lead relatively normal lives, learning over the years how to cope with the strange and bizarre behaviour of normal people.

One young man used to repeat aloud any questions directed at him. Now he hums under his breath and beneath his hum he repeats the question. He's realised that echoing others is not normal behaviour and so has found a way of dealing with his need to repeat the words that is socially acceptable. At eighteen he was achieving normal grades at school, attended an amateur acting group and wanted to go to university to study trains.

Perhaps the most famous and able person with Asperger's syndrome is Temple Grandin. A highly intelligent and articulate woman in her forties, Temple Grandin has a Ph.D. in animal science. She has published over 200 articles on her work and studies, acts as a consultant designing livestock facilities and runs her own company. Her autobiography, *Thinking in Pictures*, was released in 1996 and as she explains in this moving account of her life, she was not always as sanguine and capable as she is now.

At six months old, Temple Grandin started to claw at her mother 'like a trapped animal'. Her ears by the time she was two were like microphones transmitting everything, irrespective of relevance, at full, overwhelming volume and there was an equal lack of modulation in all her senses; she had a remarkable sense of smell. By the age of three, she'd become very destructive and violent; she painted the walls with her faeces and chewed up puzzles. She was initially diagnosed as brain damaged. However, through the love and support of her mother, aunt and teachers, she was able to go to school, high school, college and, finally, obtain a Ph.D. At school, she couldn't get on with the other children although she definitely wanted a friend. She said that there was something going on between the other children that was swift, subtle and changing; they understood the meaning behind words and perceived other people's intentions. She, like other autistic people, thought they were telepathic.

As a child, Grandin hated physical contact – she didn't like the sense of being overwhelmed or not being in control – yet longed to be hugged. From the age of five she dreamed of a machine that would squeeze her gently but powerfully and which she could control. When she was staying on one of her aunt's ranches in Arizona, she saw a squeeze shute for restraining cattle. She asked her aunt to shut her inside it. Initially, she panicked as the sides closed and the head restraint locked into place, but then began to feel serene and calm and remained in the contraption for half an hour. When she got back to college, she copied the design and built herself a 'squeeze machine' which she kept by her bed. Her device created suspicion and derision; the college psychiatrist thought she was regressive and needed to be talked out of it. Calmly, she insisted on the validity of the machine. She uses a far more sophisticated one today, again of her own design, and says it teaches her to feel empathy for others. 'From the time I started using my squeeze machine, I understood the feeling it gave me was one that I needed to cultivate towards other people. It was clear that the pleasurable feelings were those associated with love for other people. I built a machine that would apply the soothing, comforting contact that I craved as well as the physical affection I couldn't tolerate when I was young. I would have been as hard and as unfeeling as a rock if I had not built my squeeze machine.'

Grandin is now the world's foremost expert on squeeze shute designs for cattle. She writes, 'When handling cattle, I often touch the animals because it helps me to be gentle with them. If I never touch or stroke the animals, it would become easy to shove or kick them around.' She once swam through a sheep dip to find out what it was like for sheep and published an article in *Calf News* entitled 'How stressful is dipping – I jumped in to find out'.

Francesca Happé, who studied Grandin's writing, says, 'This is interesting as it suggests perhaps a lack of ability to empathise, since she felt it necessary to put herself through the same experience in order to feel the same feelings. When we empathise with another person we generally mean that we *feel with* them, despite the fact that we are not actually *suffering with* them.'

Grandin says that she can't read novels or follow plays because she can't empathise with the characters or understand their motives and intentions. 'Much of the time,' she says, 'I feel like an anthropologist on Mars.' However, she does show a high degree of sympathy for livestock. She doesn't want to shut down the meat industry, but she does object to the pain, cruelty, stress and fear that animals are subjected to before being slaughtered. Her sympathy extends to the terror a frightened animal feels, though she has no empathy for other people's states of mind or their perspective. 'When I put myself in a cow's place, I really have to be that cow and not a person in a cow costume,' Grandin says. 'I use my visual thinking skills to simulate what an animal would see and hear in a given situation. It's the ultimate virtual reality system.'

Grandin's ability to be sympathetic is aided by her weak central coherence. She notices details in the environment that other people might not be so acutely aware of, and realises what might scare cows. 'Cattle are disturbed by the same sorts of sounds as autistic people – high-pitched sounds, air hissing or sudden loud noises; they cannot adapt to these. But they are not bothered by low-pitched, rumbling noises. They are disturbed by high visual contrasts, shadows or sudden movements. A light touch will make them pull away, a firm touch calms them. The way I would pull away from being touched is the way a wild cow will pull away – getting me used to being touched is very similar to taming a wild cow.'

She adds, 'When I'm with cattle, it's not at all cognitive. I know what the cow's feeling.' People are rather different: she has to study them intensely. Fascinatingly, Grandin says that although she can *feel* the behaviour of farm animals, she can only understand the interactions of primates *intellectually*.

Like many people with Asperger's syndrome, Grandin is very visual. She says, 'I think in pictures. Words are like a second language to me. I translate both spoken and written words into full-colour movies, complete with sound, which run like a VCR tape in my head. When somebody speaks to me, his words are instantly translated into pictures.' If she receives a letter but wants to read it later, she simply looks at it and it is photocopied into her mind in the same way that Raymond, the autistic savant played by Dustin Hoffman in the film *Rain Man*, could flick through a photocopy of the phone book in his head and reel off any phone number in it.

Grandin struggled in the social arena because pictures of 'getting along with people' were hard to find. An image finally presented itself to her. At college, the students had to do jobs and one of hers was to wash the bay window in the cafeteria. It consisted of three glass sliding doors enclosed by storm windows: 'To wash the inside of the bay window, I had to crawl through the sliding door. The door jammed while I was washing the inside panes and I was imprisoned between the two windows. In order to get out without shattering the door, I had to ease it back very carefully. It struck me that relationships operate the same way. They also shatter easily and have to be approached carefully. I then made a further association about how the careful opening of doors was related to establishing relationships in the first place. While I was trapped between the windows, it was almost impossible to communicate through the glass. Being autistic is like being trapped like this.'

Grandin used her phenomenal memory and visual capacity to study how to deal with other people. She has a 'videotape collection or a CD-rom in her mind' of memories and human interactions and uses this library, based on experiences that were built up slowly and painfully over the years, to compute how a person might react and whether they might try to deceive her or sabotage her equipment. If she wants to remember something, however, she has to run through the whole clip from the start: she can't simply remember a portion of it. Although this obviously has disadvantages, the major advantage for her is that she can visualise a whole design layout in her head, imagine it from any angle, even from the cows' point of view and can play a cow's journey in her mind and see any glitches in her design before actually setting pen to paper. Drawing the blueprint for a cattle shute or a slaughter house then becomes a routine job.

Although she can operate in normal society and in the workplace, Grandin says she has built a facade of normality and learnt rules about how to behave. 'Since I don't have any social intuition, I rely on pure logic, like an expert computer program, to guide my behaviour. I categorise rules according to their logical importance. It is a complex algorithmic decision-making tree.' She adds, 'When other students swooned over the Beatles, I called their reaction an ISP — interesting sociological phenomenon. I was a scientist trying to figure out the ways of the natives [. . .] To master diplomacy, I read about business dealings with international negotiations in the *Wall Street Journal*. I then used them as models.'

She feels, she says, like Data in *Star Trek*, an emotionless android, who is curious and wistful about being human. He observes and impersonates people and longs to be one. A family with Asperger's syndrome whom Oliver Sacks visited sympathised with this view. When Sacks first walked into their house he thought that they were very normal, until he saw the trampoline which they use to jump up and down on whilst flapping their arms in order to relieve stress, a huge library of science fiction and directions for how to cook, lay the table and wash up pinned up in the kitchen. The family say that they ape being human, they learn rules and obey them. Like many people with Asperger's, they like alternative imaginary worlds, such as those of Tolkien and C.S. Lewis. The family spend hours constructing an imaginary world — computing grain production in Leutheria, designing a new flag, working out the country's currency.

Sacks visited Temple Grandin and named his book after her phrase 'An anthropologist on Mars'. In the chapter devoted to Grandin, there is a hilarious section where she smuggles him into a meat-packing plant. She'd designed the layout and wanted to show it to him, even though it was forbidden for any unauthorised persons to enter the plant. She handed him a hard yellow hat and said, 'That'll do. You look good in it. It goes with your khaki pants and shirt. You look exactly like a sanitary engineer.' The eminent psychiatrist blushed deeply, no one had ever said anything like that to him before. Once inside, she instructed him to keep his hat on, 'You're a sanitary engineer here.'

Grandin does have a couple of friends, but is celibate and has no wish for marriage; she does have sexual feelings but she can't understand what is implied or expected of her in relationships. The closest she can imagine to falling in love is the warm feeling she gets when she strokes a cow. As she said goodbye to Sacks she wept. 'I've read that libraries are where immortality lies. I don't want my thoughts to die with me. I want to have done something. I'm not interested in power or piles of money. I want to leave something behind. I want to make a positive contribution – know that my life has meaning. Right now, I'm talking about things at the very core of my existence.' Despite her handicap, Temple Grandin has said on a number of occasions, 'If I could snap my fingers and be non-autistic, I would not – because then I wouldn't be me. Autism is a part of who I am.'

There's a little bit of Asperger's in many people: the literal-mindedness, the inability fully to understand another person's point of view, the desire for the security of lack of change, the single-minded dedication to one issue. There are two old Irish jokes about getting lost which have more than a touch of Asperger's about them. In one, the lost person asks, 'Where does this road go?' The reply is, 'It goes nowhere, it stays right here.' In the second, an Irishman is asked what is the best way to get to Dublin. He replies, 'Well, I wouldn't start from here.' Many of our stereotypes – the preoccupied professor with few social graces, for example – also share traits with those who have Asperger's. Sherlock Holmes is typical of someone with Asperger's: he is eccentric, odd and highly intelligent. He is absent-minded in relation to other people, but single-minded with regard to certain issues; untroubled by the simple events of everyday life, he attends to trifles that seem insignificant to others – but usually end up being vital clues to the mystery. In true autistic fashion, Holmes has written a monograph on the ashes of 140 different types of pipe, cigar and cigarette tobacco.

In the classic film, *Being There*, starring Peter Sellers as Chance Gardener, Chance is autistic. When his parents die, he leaves his house for the first time in his life. He stops a woman laden with shopping bags and says, 'Excuse me, I'm very hungry. Could you give me some lunch?' He becomes a nationwide figure appearing on television and advises the president. He speaks simply of gardening, but the people around him read volumes into his speech and attribute intentions to him which he does not have. For example, when he is run over by Dr Ben Rand, the doctor asks him if he is going to make a claim. He replies that there's no need for a claim, 'I don't even know what they look like.' Rand thinks he's merely being humorous.

Given a room in the Rands' house, Chance, looking up from his position at the dining table to the ceiling, says that the room is all he has. Presumably, his room is directly above them. Dr Rand, who is dying, thinks Chance is talking about heaven. He says that at least Chance has his health. Chance replies, 'It's a very nice room' and Rand responds sourly, 'That's what they all say.'

The boundary between the acceptable, admirable eccentric and the disabled person is a hazy one. Men such as Wittgenstein, Kafka and Einstein may have had Asperger's syndrome, although it is obviously impossible to diagnose dead men. Einstein did not freely associate with his peers and was uninterested in personal relationships. He was very good at jigsaw puzzles and had an excellent memory. He said, 'I sometimes ask myself, how did it come that I was the one to develop the theory of relativity? The reason, I think, is that a normal adult never stops to think about problems of space and time.' Einstein thought of little else. 'Thoughts did not come in any verbal formulation,' he told psychologist Max Wertheimer. 'I rarely think in words at all. A thought comes, I try to express it in words afterwards.' He imagined himself travelling on a beam of light and translated his visions into maths. Students complained that his lectures were confusing because they were scattered and they could not see the associations between some of the specific examples he gave and his more general thinking.

Wittgenstein may also have had Asperger-like traits. He did not talk until he was four and was considered to be talentless. He had good mechanical ability and constructed a sewing-machine at the age of ten. Like many people with Asperger's syndrome, he used formal, pedantic language, and the German polite form of you, *Sie*, when talking to fellow students.

Most of the examples I have given in this chapter (with the notable exception of Temple Grandin) are of men and this is not surprising. There are four or five men to every woman who has autism and this ratio is much higher for Asperger's syndrome, where there are between nine and fifteen men for every woman. Simon Baron-Cohen and Jessica Hammer argue that Asperger's syndrome and autism are extreme forms of the male brain. Psychological studies have shown that there are differences between men and women, although this does not mean that these differences are true for every man or woman. Baron-Cohen, for instance, is no good at the 'male' skill of visualising in 3D and map reading, whereas Jessica Hammer is pretty competent at these tasks. The differences emerge when one compares the average of a group of men with an average for a group of women. The main differences are that the female brain is superior to the male brain when it comes to social relationships: women are better and quicker at Theory of Mind tests and surpass men when working out what emotion a person is feeling using only eyes as a cue. Women can also determine more easily what would be considered a social *faux pas*. The male brain is better at spatial skills and the embedded shapes task, which is where you pick out a shape that is camouflaged in a drawing. People with autism and Asperger's follow the male trend, but to a much greater extreme. They, like many normal men, collect things, focus on what seems to others to be trivial detail and have a narrow range of interests.

Robert, the central character in Nick Hornby's novel on male angst, *High Fidelity*, owns a record shop and an impressive record collection. He and his friends, Barry and Dick, believe that you can't be a decent person without at least 500 records. They continually make lists – top five singles of all time, top five Elvis Costello records, top five Monday morning hits. When he is asked to go to his girlfriend's father's funeral, Robert's response is to ask Barry and Dick for their best five pop songs on death.

Baron-Cohen and Hammer describe a continuum, with those

people who are cognitively balanced in the middle and people with Asperger's and autism at the far end of the male spectrum. They think that the variations are in part the result of biological differences in brain development. These in turn are emphasised by heritable genetic differences which alter hormone levels in the body. Even at birth, human female babies attend longer to social stimuli, such as faces and videos; while male babies attend better to spatial stimuli such as mobiles. The release of testosterone during foetal life may determine brain development, leading to male or female brain-types (in both humans and rats, spatial abilities are affected by hormonal changes), although, as I have said, the typical 'female brain' may not always be in a woman and the same applies for male traits.

Research into how the brain processes Theory of Mind is just beginning. Eye direction detection (EDD) seems to be localised in the superior temporal sulcus (STS), part of the temporal lobe. A cell assembly called MO47 in the superior temporal sulcus of monkey brains fires when an animal is looking at the eyes of another animal. The primary function of these cells is to detect whether another animal is looking at the monkey. Those people and animals who have lesions in the STS are impaired in their ability to discriminate gaze direction. Some of the cells in the STS respond to self-propelled motion (ID) – the first basic skill needed to begin to develop a Theory of Mind; others are involved with facial recognition. One autistic woman is an expert at recognising cancerous cells. Her visual ability enables her to spot an abnormal cell instantly, yet she has to meet someone fifteen times before she can recognise them.

There is evidence to show that the right hemisphere of the brain is involved in processing emotional information. Emotional cues are detected faster when they are on the left side of the visual field, and hence transmitted to the right side of the brain (the nerves from the left half of each eye are fed to the right side of the brain, those from the right half are fed to the left side). Julia Casperd and Robin Dunbar, from the Psychology Department at Liverpool University, have shown that male baboons keep their opponents on the left side in any confrontation. Their explanation of this is that it's important for the baboon to check whether their rival is bluffing, or will fight.

Keeping the rival on the left side means that the right side of the brain can process more subtle cues about his intentions.

Lesions to the STS and the frontal lobe of the brain can result in a lack of social perception — the patient fails to attach emotional significance to behaviour and shows a decrease in aggressive, fearful and affiliative behaviour. The frontal lobe could be responsible for Theory of Mind. There are several lines of evidence for this. Patients with lesions, or tumours which have to be removed from this area are said to lose their social judgement and perform poorly on Theory of Mind tests. In 1848 a man called Phileanas Gage was working on the railways. He was using an iron bar to tamp down earth over an area which was to be dynamited when a spark from the bar accidentally set off the incendiary. The bar flew up and went straight through Gage's eye and out the back of his head. Amazingly, Gage did not die. The bar wiped out part of the frontal lobe. Gage became a changed man. He was incapable of reacting normally to people and would frequently swear and grow violent. He lost all ability to react in a social fashion and, as his friends said, Gage was no longer Gage.

Rather more controlled studies have been conducted by Chris Frith and his team of researchers, who gave PET scans to healthy volunteers. A PET scan measures the flow of oxygenated blood through the brain: the part of the brain that is active will require the most oxygen. Volunteers are given a dose of radioactive oxygen and scans of the brain reveal where the radioactive oxygen has been carried in order to 'feed' that area of the brain. Frith played the volunteers stories that required either a physical understanding (that if you knock a person, they may trip) or a mental understanding, such as the Sally–Ann test. Both stories activated the STS, as well as other parts of the brain, but only Theory of Mind tasks caused blood to flow into an area known as Brodmann's 8 and 9 which is on the frontal lobe.

Brodmann's 8 has widespread connections to the rest of the cortex (the convoluted outer layer of the brain). Frith believes that the part of the brain associated with Theory of Mind might be needed to integrate information and stimuli drawn from other parts of the brain. Language comprehension, for example, is actually processed

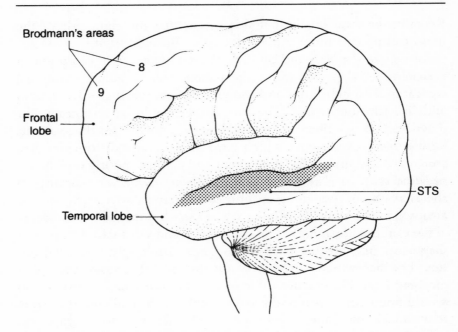

Diagram of the brain showing some of the areas associated with understanding Theory of Mind.

by the STS and lesions to this area result in deficits in comprehension and speech. But understanding Theory of Mind is more than understanding words or stories, hence the activation of a specific part of the brain that is not used when listening to a narrative that does not involve the comprehension of another person's thoughts.

A study conducted slightly earlier than Frith's, by Vinod Goel, Jordan Grafman and their colleagues from the National Institute of Health, Bethesda, in the US, gave PET scans to students while they did a Theory of Mind task. They asked them how Christopher Columbus might have categorised the function of artefacts he discovered on his travels; in other words they had to imagine what kind of knowledge a European in the fifteenth century might have had. Again, all the subjects used the medial frontal lobe: Brodmann's area 8 and 9.

Further evidence of the precise location in the brain where Theory of Mind is calculated comes from Frith, who gave a PET scan to a person suffering from schizophrenia. Some schizophrenic patients have a symptom in which they hear voices talking about them in the third person, saying, 'He is stupid', for instance. The patient believes that other people think that he, the patient, is stupid but instead of thinking in terms of beliefs, something goes wrong with the labelling so the patient experiences not beliefs but perceptions. Rather than believing that other people think he is stupid, he hears other people saying that he is stupid. The patient was hallucinating at the time of the scan, and although he thought he could hear voices, he was actually formulating a belief about himself. The area of the brain that was processing the information was Brodmann's 8, not the part of the brain that deals with perception.

So is autism caused by damage to these areas and, if so, what is the cause? In the past, people thought autism was the result of the way in which children were brought up. They blamed 'refrigerator mothers', claiming that career women who were cold and unloving turned their children into autistic individuals. We know that this is a myth and that autism is usually genetically inherited. An autistic child is between fifty and a hundred times more likely to have another sibling who has autism than a normal child. In one study on identical twins, both twins had autism in four out of eleven sets of twins and, in nearly every case, the other twin had a language disorder or an intellectual impairment or both. Christopher Gillberg studied families with Asperger's syndrome who lived in Gothenburg. He discovered that Asperger's, Asperger-like traits and autism ran in families. One girl with Asperger's syndrome who always wore the same dress (her mother had to wash it at night and then try to make it smell unwashed), had a sister, a paternal grandfather, a maternal grandfather and uncle who also had Asperger's. Her paternal aunt had autism as well as some mental retardation and both her parents had problems identifying with the feelings and perspectives of others.

Autism is often associated with other disorders, such as epilepsy, which occurs in a third of all autistic people; and nearly forty per cent suffer from Fragile X, a chromosome abnormality that causes mental retardation. These disorders are often the result of injuries to the infant, such as a delay in birth, neonatal convulsions, or a viral infection, which result in brain damage. The greater the extent of the brain damage, the more likely it is that secondary symptoms, such as epilepsy, will occur. But there might be a genetic predisposition for developmental abnormalities in these children; autism is but one of its manifestations.

There are other differences between people with normal brains and those with autism; as yet no one knows the significance of these differences. Autistic children, whether they are mentally retarded or not, tend to have lesions in a small part of the cerebellum. EEG readings of the brain-waves in autistic children aged between four and twelve produce patterns similar to a two year old. Other physical and automatic responses such as respiration, heart rate and skin conductance also show a developmental delay. Another physiological difference is that autistic children have high levels of serotonin (used in the contraction of muscles) in their blood, although levels in their spinal fluid and elsewhere are normal. The abnormality may be due to a deficiency in the uptake or storage of serotonin by blood platelets.

It is highly likely that a cluster of genes could put a person at risk of many disorders, such as autism, depression, anxiety, dyslexia, attention deficit disorder and other problems. Uta Frith explains the process that leads to autism in the following way: hazard is followed by havoc which causes harm. The hazard could be genetic, or a viral agent, or a birth defect (although problems at birth could, as we have said, be due to genetic reasons). This hazard creates havoc with the neural system and this in turn results in lasting harm to the development of specific brain systems concerned with higher mental processes. The harm may be mild or severe, but it involves a developmental arrest of a critical system at a critical point in time which leads to autism. We do not know the details of this arrest, but it is likely that it leads to damage of the frontal lobe, the part of the brain that computes Theory of Mind.

Theory of Mind is so pervasive and necessary for normal human relationships in our society that in the next chapter we are going to ask whether we can create Theory of Mind. Would it be possible to build a robot with a mind? And would that mind be capable of thinking, caring and showing empathy – would it have Theory of Mind?

9

MORE THAN HUMAN

Man is by nature a social animal; an individual who is unsocial
naturally and not accidentally is either beneath our notice or
more than human.
　　Aristotle, *Politics*

'I collected the instruments of life around me, that I might infuse a
spark of being into the lifeless thing that lay at my feet [. . .] my
candle was nearly burnt out, when, by the glimmer of the half-
extinguished light, I saw the dull yellow eye of the creature open . . .
Great God! His yellow skin scarcely covered the work of muscles
and arteries beneath; his hair was of a lustrous black and flowing;
his teeth of pearly whiteness; but these luxuriances only formed a
more horrid contrast with his watery eye, that seemed almost of the
same colour as the dun-white sockets in which they were set, his
shrivelled complexion and straight black lips.'
　　Frankenstein's monster was alive. The central theme of Mary
Shelley's novel is the danger of knowledge; there are some things,
she believes, that we ought not to know and how to create life in
our own image is one of them. Victor Frankenstein, horrified at his
creation, runs away in terror. The monster knows nothing of the
ways of men, but slowly and painfully begins to learn. He finally
confronts Frankenstein with his heart-wrenching tale of how he has
been spurned by everyone: 'Accursed creator! Why did you form a
monster so hideous that even you turned from me in disgust? God,
in pity, made man beautiful and alluring, after his own image; but
my form is a filthy type of yours . . . I am solitary and abhorred.'
　　There are some links here between high-functioning people with
autism and Frankenstein's creation. The monster has a touching

innocence and naïvety; he cannot, at first, understand the ways of people; he gradually realises that he is different and will always be alone; he says that he yearns for the love of another soul; when Frankenstein thwarts his desire for a companion creature of his own kind, he exacts a horrific revenge on his maker by murdering all his kith and kin. While by no means an exact match for autism, Frankenstein's creation symbolises the strengths, deficits, aloneness, aloofness, innocence and realisation of difference that are character-istic of high-functioning autism.

Frankenstein's monster also embodies our fascination with creating creatures in our likeness. The ancient Greeks wrote of Pygmalion, a statue brought to life to keep her sculptor company. In sixteenth-century Prague, the High Rabbi Loew created a human-like figure or golem (Hebrew for unformed) out of clay. The Rabbi gave it the name of God and so gave it life. The creature's mission was to protect the Jews from their persecutors but the monster went out of control and the Rabbi had to withdraw the divine name, thus destroying his creation.

There was no specific name for these artificial humanoid creations until 1920. This was the year that a Czech playwright, Karel Čapek, wrote a play, *R.U.R.* – Rossum's Universal Robots. Rossum ran a factory which owned robots, in effect, metal slaves, who rose up in revolt against their master. 1920 was also the year in which the grand master of robotics, Isaac Asimov, was born.

Robots, or the idea of robots, have fascinated us because of their likeness to us and yet their strange otherness. Uta Frith says, 'So many human qualities can be found in an intelligent machine, yet some elusive but essential humanness is missing.' She adds, 'As a metaphor for autism, robots serve well in many respects.' Early robots in science fiction only operated according to logical and literal principles; they had no sense of humour; their voice had a mechan-ical quality, they lacked empathy or social skills; they were specialists who concentrated on the task in hand and saw no wider implications of their work; and they had a strange gait. All of these traits could apply equally well to those with autism.

In an essay entitled 'The Sense of Humour', Asimov imagines

telling a robot a joke. He views it as a ridiculous exercise. To him, the essence of humour is the shift in perspective or point of view during the punchline. A robot with a literal frame of mind would have to have everything explained laboriously. But, as we have said elsewhere, this is a trait shared with some humans. Asimov once told his father the following joke:

> Mrs Jones, the landlady, woke up in the middle of the night because there were strange noises outside her door. She looked out, and there was Robinson, one of her boarders, forcing a frightened horse up the stairs.
>
> She shrieked, 'What are you doing, Mr Robinson?'
>
> He said, 'Putting the horse in the bathroom.'
>
> 'For goodness sake, why?'
>
> 'Well, old Higginbotham is such a wise guy. Whatever I tell him, he answers, "I know, I know," in such a superior way. Well, in the morning, he'll go to the bathroom and he'll come out yelling, "There's a *horse* in the bathroom." And I'll yawn and say, "I know, I know."'
>
> And what was my father's response? He said, 'Isaac. Isaac. You're a city boy, so you don't understand. You can't push a horse up the stairs if he doesn't want to go.'

In 1953, Asimov created an android detective, R. Daneel Olivaw. Thirteen years later, the character Mr Spock in the television series *Star Trek* became a legend of our time. Mr Spock, like Olivaw, was governed by logic and not emotions and his actions, free from the cloudiness of personal relationships, gave him a certain clarity and objectivity of thought. Both creations are similar to their human counterpart, Sherlock Holmes. To deal with his robots, Asimov devised the character of Dr Susan Calvin, robopsychologist, who has in common with her robots a sharp intellect, literalness and lack of social graces.

Robots in science fiction have grown increasingly more complex: R2D2, in *Star Wars*, for instance, has feelings programmed into him. In the film *2010*, we are given an explanation for why HAL, the supercomputer, malfunctioned at the end of the previous film. He was provided with contradictory instructions, which involved him having to lie to the human crew-members. Deception had not been programmed into him and this set up an irreconcilable conflict within his logic circuits. To avoid having to lie, he eliminated those to whom he would have had to lie – the human crew-members.

My thesis in this chapter is that real robots, if they are to work with humans and be accepted by us, would need to have a Theory of Mind, or, at least, act as if they have one (our rampant anthropomorphism would fill in any gaps in their mind). Current-day robots are extremely backward compared both to their fictional counterparts and the high hopes that were held out for robots in the fledgling stages of the new science of robotics. Would it indeed be feasible to create a robot that had Theory of Mind and, if so, would we learn anything that could be applied to the plight of people with autism which might help ameliorate their suffering?

Robots with Theory of Mind is perhaps not as bizarre a thought as it first appears. Theory of Mind allows us to establish and handle highly complex social relationships and to reflect on our own thoughts, which are skills necessary for abstract problem-solving, testing hypotheses, advance planning, creative thinking and cognitive empathy. All of these capacities would be highly useful in a machine which deals with humans.

There are quite clearly many tasks to which a thinking robot would be unsuited – work in factories, for instance – but in the future, domestic and welfare robots might be a necessity. Nowhere is the demand for robots more pressing than in Japan. There is a time-bomb ticking in the heart of the land of the rising sun. The proportion of people aged over sixty-five will double in the next three decades. By 2025, based on current predictions, a quarter of the population will be elderly. With fewer people to look after them, spiralling welfare, labour and land costs, what will the future hold for the elderly? Robotics expert, Ichiro Kato, from Waseda University, Tokyo, believes that primitive humanoid robots will assist nurses and technicians within fifteen years and that, a couple of decades later, more sophisticated androids will enter old people's homes and give them extra support. Kato says, 'Elderly people would find themselves more at ease with a personal robot than being a burden to their families.' But future welfare robots would need to be capable of adapting to human feelings. They would need to walk and talk like humans, for otherwise the elderly might find it difficult to adjust to them.

Kerstin Dautenhahn, robotics expert from the VUB Artificial Intelligence Laboratory, in Brussels, says, 'If robots have long-term contact with a person, it might be desirable to have them develop a "social skill" and individual relationships. This would enhance the performance of the robots, for example, by anticipating people's behaviour, and would be desirable for most humans who prefer being treated as an "individual" rather than an "anonymous" patient. For the development of individual relationships to humans, "social skills" cannot be defined as "rational manipulation" of others, like chess pieces, but are strongly related to individual feelings, emotional involvement and empathy.'

Our own intellectual capacities evolved because of our highly social natures, thus in order to understand us a robot with a Theory of Mind would also need to be social. Even industrial as opposed to welfare robots could benefit from some aspects of social intelligence, for it would enable them to perform co-operatively dangerous tasks, perhaps on Mars or in a nuclear reactor. Cleaning or dismantling a nuclear plant, for instance, poses specific problems: there is the obvious danger of radiation and, at present, a robot lost within a reactor cannot be retrieved except by another robot. The length of time the plant ceases to be operative is crucial, as the less time the plant is shut down, the less money is lost. Finally, radio communication does not work within nuclear plants, which means that it is difficult for human operators to keep in touch with robots and control them, unless they are attached by cables. The cables themselves are hard to deal with. Currently, separate robots have to follow the cleaning robot to disentangle its cables. A group of robots that were autonomous, worked together and were capable of understanding each other's motivation and level of knowledge would increase the ease with which tasks such as these were performed. In addition, if the robots cared about each other's survival, they could check on each other – establishing whether an individual was behaving oddly because its battery level was decreasing, for example – and make sure that members of the group returned intact.

For those machines that are made in our own image, such as future welfare robots, there is a separate name: androids. Maureen Caudill, a neural networks consultant from San Diego, California, defines androids as intelligent humanoid machines. She has a list of criteria they have to fulfil, which include several developmental stages of Theory of Mind. An android would have to understand causality – that objects will fall and can be broken or crushed. It would need to be able to communicate using language. This would involve not only comprehending the words used, but being capable of deciphering their underlying meaning. At a simple level, an android should understand that 'take the rubbish out' does not mean to the cinema.

'In addition,' says Caudill, 'the android should understand and obey basic principles of the social world. If an android is to be used for duties such as childcare or nursing, it must understand a reasonable amount of human psychology – such as the fact that children sometimes lie – and be able to judge social interactions appropriately: are the children playing, or are they really in a serious fight?'

Isaac Asimov's very first story about robots dealt with just such a scenario. In 'Robbie', the long-suffering George explains to his wife the virtues of a childcare machine. 'A robot is infinitely more to be trusted than a human nursemaid. Robbie was constructed for one purpose really – to be the companion of a little child [. . .] He just can't help being faithful and loving and kind. He's a machine – *made so.*' However, although Robbie can communicate with his small charge, he has no language, and were we ever to go down this route, I think a robot that could speak would be an absolute necessity. A generation of children that whirred, clicked, whined and nodded in response to questions would be a disaster, to say the least.

In addition, a robot should also have a socially acceptable code of behaviour – a set of 'morals'. Again, Asimov got there first with his three laws of robotics (a word that he invented):

1. A robot may not injure a human being or, through inaction, allow a human being to come to harm.

2. A robot must obey the orders given it by human beings except where such orders would conflict with the first law.

3. A robot must protect its own existence as long as such protection does not conflict with the first or second law.

'These laws,' says Asimov, 'as it turned out, proved to be the most famous, the most frequently quoted and the most influential sentences I ever wrote. (And I did it when I was twenty-one, which makes me wonder if I've done anything since to continue to justify my existence.)' Despite their fame, they would not be sufficient for the complexities of modern life. As Caudill says, 'Before androids can be turned loose on the general public, they must have some training in dealing with humans. And this means they must know that humans do not always tell the truth, that some are less than honourable and that, just perhaps, it might not be a good idea to obey the human's instructions to blow open the bank vault.'

In the real world, the Turing Test has always been upheld as the benchmark for human-like machine intelligence. Alan Turing, one of the fathers of modern computing, devised a test in 1950 which he called the imitation game. A man and a woman sit in one room and correspond via a teleprinter with an interrogator who is in a separate room. The interrogator has to work out which one is the woman. Obviously, the woman could say, 'I am the woman', but so could the man. Turing then postulated that if the man were replaced by a machine and the interrogator were no better at telling the difference between woman and machine than he or she had been at telling the difference between the man and the woman, this would be conclusive evidence of machine intelligence.

There have been several computer programs that have tried to pass the Turing Test. One program, Eliza, can hold conversations that sound very much like a psychotherapy session. Eliza picks up on key words and phrases and reformulates them into a sentence. When in doubt, the program turns the speaker's last sentence into a question. Just under fifty per cent of the people who 'spoke' to Eliza thought the program was a person. I think the whole Turing Test really says more about our own preconception of gender and how good individual people are at being empathic than it does about machine intelligence. Here's an extract from one of Eliza's conversations:

Human: I'm depressed much of the time.
Eliza: I'm sorry to hear you are depressed.
Human: It's true. I am unhappy.
Eliza: Do you think coming here will help you not to be unhappy?
Human: I need some help, that much seems certain.
Eliza: What would it mean to you if you got some help?
Human: Perhaps I could learn to get along with my mother.
Eliza: Tell me about your family.

In a twisted version of Eliza, a program called Parry was created which acted like a paranoid schizophrenic whilst the user took on the role of therapist. Then came Julia who could make polite conversation about pets and could even fool people so long as they stuck to the discussion. Julia has a large database filled with quirky sentences, such as, 'Guinea pigs are about as smart as cucumbers', which help the illusion. Racter, a software program published by Mindscape for Macintosh, could carry out long conversations and even talk aloud using the built-in speech synthesisers added to some PCs. The voice was odd, with a strange atonality, but according to Maureen Caudill, Racter definitely had a personality. She says, 'It was a bit like talking to a slightly schizophrenic literary genius who made wild leaps and connections.' Racter created bizarre stories that made sense on one level, just as Lewis Carroll's nonsense poems, such as Jabberwocky, do.

These kind of programs don't really communicate on a human level. They are programmed to respond in a certain way which can often result in mistakes that highlight their deficiencies. A story-writing program called TALESPIN produced the following story: 'Henry Ant was thirsty. He walked over to the river bank where his good friend Bill Bird was sitting. Henry slipped and fell in the river. Gravity drowned.' This bizarre ending was the result of a shortcut in the program which treated gravity as an unmentioned agent which is always present and pulls objects down. Henry had a friend who would pull him to safety and gravity didn't, therefore gravity had to drown, not Henry!

The central problem for human-like robots is the following: computers are excellent when it comes to high-level calculations conducted at speed, accessing databases and solving logical problems, but they are completely useless at common sense reasoning. In addition, it has proved well-nigh impossible to make a computer that can see and walk as well as a one-year-old child. Although there are obvious advantages to artificial intelligence, such as rapid processing, and almost instantaneous memory storage and retrieval, were we to imitate human thought processes, we might have to forgo these benefits. Two different chess-playing computers illustrate these rather different approaches.

DEEPTHOUGHT is powerful and plays chess at the grandmaster level. It can defeat all but a few hundred human players. The machine doesn't play in a human way. Instead, it explores tens of millions of options before making its choice of move. It doesn't explore every option, though; it looks at relevant sets of moves using a chess database supplied by human programmers. Its success is due to a combination of a massive memory bank unmatchable by human players and extensive, if mediocre, chess knowledge.

MATER was an earlier program which was less successful, but it operated more like a person. It was designed to exploit chess positions where immediate moves would result in a checkmate and in doing this rediscovered many of the sequences of moves that the grandmasters had used to win battles. It looks at about one hundred different sets of moves using rules of thumb, working out first those moves where its opponent would find it most difficult to retaliate.

But a thinking computer is a bit like a brain in a vat. It needs a body. Consciousness, no matter what Descartes thought, cannot be separated from bodily experiences. Animals do not simply *possess* a body, they experience everything through their body. As a result, cognition cannot be studied in isolation from the body. Having an idea of what your external body image is, as well as internal perceptions of what it feels like to be you, allows not only an indirect assessment of internal emotional states, but enables one to predict the consequences of adopting a certain external posture or expression. Autistic people can't understand how someone might perceive their actions because they are unable to mindread; in addition, some of them do not know where the boundaries between themselves and everything else lie – an autistic might bite his arm without realising it's his arm, or see his body as a series of fragments.

One of the strangest bodies imagined for a robot was dreamed up by Hans Moravec from the Carnegie-Mellon University in Pittsburgh. He had the idea of creating a robot bush some years ago and has now been awarded funding by NASA. The bush would be centred around a thick stem with lots of swivelling branches. Each branch would split into twigs and these would sprout even finer branchlets that would act as fingers. Some of the branchlets would have smaller, jointed sections which could operate on a microscopic level, others would be equipped with tools for particular tasks.

'A bush robot would be a marvel of surrealism to behold,' says Moravec. 'Despite its structural resemblance to many living things, it would be unlike anything yet seen on earth. Its great intelligence, superb co-ordination, astronomical speed, and enormous sensitivity to its environment would enable it to constantly do something surprising, at the same time maintaining a perpetual gracefulness [. . .] A trillion-limbed device, with a brain to match, is an entirely different order of being. Add to this the ability to fragment into a cloud of co-ordinated tiny fliers and the laws of physics will seem to melt in the face of intention and will. As with no magician that ever was, impossible things will simply *happen* around a robot bush.'

The data rate of a robot with one trillion fingers, each able to move a million times per second, is potentially more than a quadrillion (10^{15}) times greater than that of current robots. Such data rates imply immense co-ordination and enormous processing power. At the moment, technical obstacles make building such a machine impossible and Moravec will concentrate on devising a control system and producing a computer animation of the robot, initially with four levels of branching twigs and sixteen tools.

If a robot bush could communicate, its outlook would be very different from that of any living creature. Therefore, if we attempt to build a robot with Theory of Mind, as well as needing to be a social machine, it would be preferable if it had an anthropoid (ape-like) or humanoid body. It is conceivable that it could be given another shape and still have Theory of Mind (or a version of it). For instance, a robot which could not drink would not understand that you could become thirsty, but it might compare 'thirst' to the uncomfortable sensation it felt when its batteries were running down; thus, such a robot might be able to empathise vaguely with us, but not sympathise. A robot that is a brain in a computer could have conversations about philosophy with you, even give you psychotherapy sessions, but the robots that will have the closest approximation to Theory of Mind should, at the very least, have mammal-like bodies. They would also need a sensory modality that allowed them to share joint attention: vision would, obviously, be the best. Apart from anything else, we would be much more anthropomorphic about such robots, attributing motives, desires and beliefs to them.

As for current robots, many are adequate for the task they need to perform, but they can't operate in an environment that's even slightly different or complete a job if it is marginally altered. They're not smart. The most intelligent robot we've built so far probably has an IQ similar to a slug's. However, using principles from animal behaviour, a new breed of robots has been designed. These robots will never be able to play chess, noughts and crosses, or calculate differential equations on demand. But they can be completely autonomous – in other words, instead of being connected to a computer by an umbilical cord of cables which downloads precise instructions, the robots are able to explore and navigate round their environment by themselves.

The first of these robots borrowed heavily from biological work on insects, particularly insect locomotion. Max has six legs, each with three joints. Possessing the eerie creepiness of a giant metal spider, it inches slowly over the ground. Given an instruction to speed up, the robot automatically edges from a gait that is wave-like, with five legs supporting its body, to a tripodal scuttle with only three legs on the ground at any one time. As the terrain becomes increasingly rough, the legs extend, allowing the body to remain flat at all times. Each leg takes note of what all the other legs are doing; like a real insect, there is no overall central unit giving commands to each leg individually; the central control system simply determines the speed of movement. The robot, once built, automatically showed a smooth transition between the two gaits, although, when pressed beyond its normal speed, 'It goes into a Friday evening epileptic fit,' says one of its creators, David Barnes, of the Robotics Department at Salford University, Manchester.

One of the first and most elaborate robo-insects was a cockroach constructed by Randall Beer from the Case Western Reserve University in Cleveland, Ohio. The cockroach had a neural net so it could learn about its environment. When its energy levels got low, its primary aim was to top them up. Beer released the 'hungry' cockroach into a holding pen with an energy source at one end which was obscured by a curved barrier extending three-quarters of the way into the room. The cockroach scented the 'food' and started to head towards it only to be pulled up short by the barrier. With its left antenna touching the barrier, its follow-the-edge behaviour took over and it trundled along the barrier away from the food. By this stage it had lost the scent of the food. At the end of the barrier it continued in the same direction and found itself surrounded by open space. Its walking behaviour took over until it regained the scent of the food and made a bee-line towards the energy source where it recharged itself. The behaviour of the insect shows the classic 'bottom-up approach': a series of behaviours are processed in parallel and whichever type of behaviour is most appropriate to the situation takes over. Like a real insect, the cockroach is not totally predictable. Using these principles derived from animal behaviour, simple reaction-based systems can generate quite complex behaviour in robots.

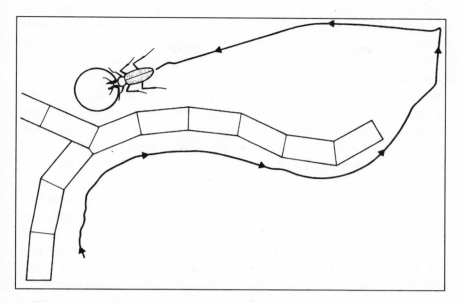

Randall Beer's 'hungry' insect robot attempting to locate its energy source.

Barbara Webb, from the Artificial Intelligence Research Group at Nottingham University, created an artificial cricket out of lego. Female crickets listen to the calls of males and head towards the one they have chosen. Webb thought that this behaviour might have a very simple neurological basis. Cricket song is composed of a series of chirps; Webb hypothesised that once the chirps reached a given intensity, a set of neurons fired in one of the female cricket's ears (crickets' ears are on their legs) and made the female turn towards the male singing to the side of that leg. The mechanical cricket had microphones for ears and electronic circuits that evaluated the chirps. Once the chirps had reached a certain level, the circuit prevented the wheel on that side of the cricket from turning so the robot would head towards the male's song. This led to unpredictable cricket-like behaviour: when two male crickets were singing identical songs, the robot would 'choose' one.

It may seem a huge waste of resources to build a mechanical

cockroach or cricket (Barbara Webb's latest grant was £100,000), but advanced models could explore the moon or other inaccessible places. A giant eight-legged robotic crab called Dante has already been used to explore active volcanoes. Built by the Carnegie-Mellon Robotics Laboratory, Dante is three metres tall, three metres wide, weighs almost 800 kilos and can traverse any incline from horizontal to vertical. His last outing was in 1994 when he descended into the active volcano, Mt Spurr, in Alaska, taking gas and temperature readings. The trip was a success, although rather ironically Dante was buried – not by lava, but by a mud-slide on his way out – and had to be winched to safety by helicopter.

Today's robots behave like very simple animals – real cockroaches, spiders and crickets are still much more complex than anything we have created. To say that these robots have the IQ of a slug, as I said earlier, is perhaps pushing it. 'If you accept that a slug should have slug-like intelligence for behaving sensibly in a slug-environment, looking for slug-food, slug-mates, avoiding slug-predators, then I haven't seen a robot one per cent as robot-intelligent as a slug is slug-intelligent,' says Inman Harvey from the School of Cognitive and Computer Sciences at Sussex University. 'I have a lot more respect for slugs than any robot I've seen.' They also have another major fault: according to Kerstin Dautenhahn, our robots are like 'Kaspar Hauser animals'. Kaspar Hauser was discovered in 1828 when he walked into the Unschlittplatz in Nuremberg. He could barely speak, liked darkness and walls, would only eat bread and water and at first had problems with vision – he thought distant objects were really small toys. He was made a ward of the town; the local people concluded that he must have been locked up in a dungeon until his release at the age of sixteen. Robots behave, says Dautenhahn, as if they too have been socially deprived and have grown up in isolation. Robotics needs to take account of social dynamics if Theory of Mind, or at least some kind of social intelligence, is ever to be witnessed.

Dautenhahn suggests that one way of facilitating social intelligence would be through the use of imitation. Copying another person's or animal's behaviour is only seen in whales, dolphins, parrots, primates and people – the animals we consider most cognitively advanced. At the highest levels, imitation involves changing your behaviour according to how you know another person will perceive you; in other words, being consciously self-aware and aware of the other's perspective. For instance, suppose your teenage daughter is imitating your best friend. In spite of yourself, you start to laugh and in response she exaggerates her imitation even more. At a much lower level, young children imitate parents and peers as a way of learning socially relevant gestures and probing the reactions of others to themselves.

To test out her theory, Dautenhahn built a fleet of mini-robots that had to navigate a Hügellandschaft – a hilly surface. As the robots travel uphill, they slow down and use up more energy but, unluckily for them, the recharger is at the top of the steepest hill. Even worse, the robots can't get there by themselves, but if they don't charge themselves back up in time, they 'die'. In the Hügellandschaft there are two kinds of robots, both of which have an inherent (pre-programmed) desire to search for and approach lights (all the robots and the recharger are fitted with lights) and look for bodily contact. The M-robots perform ritualised movements which are like social bonding in animals – the equivalent would be touching beaks and cooing in some birds. The I-robots try to imitate the movements of the M-robots. If two M-robots meet they will immediately lose contact as each individual performs its own behaviour. If two I-robots meet they stop and keep contact (eventually an 'avoid-light' behaviour will take over for a short time to enable the robots to escape from each other). If an I- and an M-robot meet, they dock with each other. The I-robots cannot climb up the recharging hill by themselves, whilst the M-robots cannot 'see' the hills. Once an I-robot and an M-robot have docked, however, the I-robot acts as a 'seeing-eye' for the M-robot, which turns into a tug, pulling the I-robot along. The two robots can now search for and climb up the steep hill to the recharger.

Both types of robots are self-interested: they need to recharge their energy levels. Yet this self-interest: combined with a set of basic behavioural traits and pre-programmed motivations, can develop into co-operative behaviour. Dautenhahn wants to enhance the robots' sensory capacities so that they will be able to watch and imitate other robots without having to dock with them first – a learning-from-a-distance approach which is more like the observational learning seen in chimpanzees.

Borrowing from biology textbooks on animal behaviour and loco-motion is a crucial first step towards designing autonomous robots that will show some degree of socially motivated intelligence. However, because we, as humans, are intensely anthropomorphic, we are likely to ascribe feelings and motivations to a robot. This may not be a bad thing, according to Hans Moravec. He describes a robot which has the task of fetching a cup. It has to go down a corridor, past two doors and into a third room. But it doesn't recognise the second door as a door because it is covered with posters and when it approaches what is actually the fourth door it finds itself at the top of a stairwell. Since a robot that falls down stairs would end up in a rather less than healthy state, the makers have programmed in a circuit to override all other behaviours – an avoid-cliff-edges behaviour. The robot backs off and circles round. A person watching this might offer the following interpretation: 'First, the robot was determined to go through the door, but then it noticed the stairs and became frightened and preoccupied so it forgot what it had been doing.' The actual processes going on inside the robot are different, but as Moravec says, 'The robot came by its foibles and reactions as honestly as any living animal; the observed behaviour is the correct course of action for a being operating with uncertain data in a dangerous world [. . .] As the complexity of mobile robots increases, their similarity to animals and humans will become even greater.'

To facilitate this similarity to animals, robots might need to have emotions. Suppose a robot could learn to recognise spoken words. A module might generate a 'pleasure' signal on hearing the word 'good' and a 'pain' message on hearing the word 'bad'. It might be possible to train the robot to stop hoovering when a room is in use by saying 'bad' to it, rather than writing a long and convoluted program giving instructions on hoover etiquette. Such a robot might get pleasure from picking up rubbish and pain from seeing piles of trash scattered around. It would also be possible to make a robot grow bored (not always an advantage) by supplying it with a feedback loop telling it that it had repeated a task several times. For instance, if no one answered a door on which the robot was knocking, eventually the robot would grow bored and desist.

Autonomy and motivation are deeply linked. A robot will only be truly autonomous if it can plan, set goals and have desires. According to Michel Aube from Sherbrooke University in Canada emotions could be used to regulate motivation and help planning, as they do in animals. He divides things that animals need into two classes: first-order resources are those an animal or a robot can get by itself; second-order resources are those that the animal or robot acquires from others. Needs such as those associated with states of hunger and thirst are the motivational processes that regulate first-order resources; emotions might regulate commitments for second-order resources. A commitment is the promise of a resource. For instance, a commitment between a parent and child is that the parent will look after the child. What the parent actually gives the child, such as food, could be given by anyone and could count as a first-order resource. The emotion that regulates this commitment is affection or love. Emotions act upon commitments and regulate them just as physical needs regulate first-order resources. Aube gives the example of anger, which would, in this context, make a robot register that another robot or person was breaking a commitment. Sadness might be felt by a robot that incurred a loss or did not gain a resource when no one was at fault. 'The function of sadness,' says Aube, 'is to switch to "economy mode" and call for help and support from a possible ally. On the other hand, "having your resources fulfilled" by another robot would rather lead to gratitude or liking or attachment: it would create or strengthen a commitment (one consequence of which will be a tendency to reciprocate at some other time).'

In general, positive emotions act as amplifiers: they would make the robot keen to persist in pursuing its goal and to strengthen commitments to other robots. Negative emotions would act as regulators, motivating robots to repair damaged commitments or to ask for help. Emotions, because they are linked to motivations and commitments, should be related to the robot's goals and could be triggered by an anticipated loss of resources or an anticipated gain. The anticipation of either outcome, as well as the actual result, could make the robot alter its behaviour. An example of where emotional robots might work together is in a company where a community of robots, each with different goals, is faced with some tasks requiring co-operation between the robots. Aube says, 'If each robot is designed so as to maximise their production (as most companies expect), they might try to profit from one another so as to achieve the best of their own goals with the limited resources allotted to them. There are risks that some robots will be exploited by some of the more "ambitious" robots. Hence the need for a mechanism to regulate those commitments and ensure optimal co-operation. If this co-operation is mediated by the robots themselves, what kind of built-in control structure could ensure optimal interaction? My contention is that this is precisely what emotions are for – even in real life.'

At the Artificial Intelligence and Cognitive Science Department in Birmingham, Aaron Sloman is simulating emotions in the mind of a computer. Complex emotions, such as humiliation and guilt, clearly need a Theory of Mind component: to feel humiliated you need to know, 'who was involved, what happened, what they thought about you, why they thought it, why you wish they hadn't, and so on,' says Sloman. 'We know we have these emotional states because we can monitor them in ourselves in a rather primitive fashion, but we don't know about the chemical and functional states our brains are in. Making a computer feel these same emotional states is far more complex than anything we can do right now.' The project is currently focusing on the process of feeling emotional. However, one key factor about emotions is that they are usually out of our control: no one chooses to feel utterly depressed or enraged. Sloman thinks that the ability to 'lose it' occasionally might be a vital part of being emotional and could well be a by-product of creating an emotional robot.

Neuro-Baby is a computer which does occasionally 'lose it'. Created by artist Naoka Tosa and researchers from the University of Tokyo, Neuro-Baby is outwardly deceptively simple: a round blob of a face with huge eyes which interacts like an infant with humans. Throughout a session with the simulated infant its eyes remain locked on yours. Two video cameras track the eyes of both human and Baby, so the simulation is always staring at the speaker. Neuro-Baby expresses emotions that range from stubborn and introverted to cute. It analyses stress patterns in the speaker's voice to determine his or her mood and responds accordingly. However, if you ignore Neuro-Baby's synthesised voice, it can get irritating by asking things such as, 'Do you know any tongue-twisters?' before proceeding to recite all the ones it knows. And if you snap at it, it goes red, looks angry and shouts, 'Stop it! Stop it!' Tosa took an early version of the Baby to an American conference. Unfortunately, the computer started to behave as if it were deranged. Tosa finally realised that American intonation was too strong for it – the Baby was used to Japanese monotone – and so she has now developed a US version of Neuro-Baby.

But how exactly does one build an emotional robot? The same outward behaviour in a robot could be achieved in two different ways. One approach is to run a series of behaviours in parallel with a central processor controlling the whole thing, which is how robot insects work. As we learn more, we could build up the complexity of our robot animal. An alternative approach is to evolve the behaviour in the same way as we have evolved. Eventually, this approach would lead to the creation of a feeling robot – or one that acted as if it felt pleasure or pain.

Inman Harvey from the School of Cognitive and Computer Sciences, at Sussex University, explains how behaviour that looks as if it is prompted by pain or pleasure could emerge. 'Under evolutionary pressures over generations, individual control systems emerge which promote the survival and well-being of a robot. The robot can then be seen to have goals, to display purposive behaviour; the evolved mechanisms through which this is achieved are just the robot equivalent of flesh and blood – silicon and wires – with no magic essence needed! Typically, one would expect, if the evolution took place over generations in which occasionally a robot put its limb into a fire (which would harm it if it left its arm in), pain responses would be appropriate and would be favoured by selection.'

Harvey and his colleagues have adopted a strategy modelled on evolution. They evolve virtual robots who live, breed and die in their computer before one survivor is then downloaded into a robot's body. Of course, real evolution has no God hanging around determining the task for which animals are to be designed. In Harvey's world it is as if God constructed a body that would be brilliant for a being that built skyscrapers, watched as virtual brains in virtual bodies practised building skyscrapers in a virtual world, then placed the end product of years of evolution in the builder's body, which twitched, came alive and set off, inhabited by its brand-new brain.

The genes of the robots are codes for the design of their 'brains' or control system and initially the robots' genes will be completely random. Each virtual robot has ten attempts at a set task, such as getting round a maze. Those who score highest are kept and bred with each other. As in real evolution, fifty per cent of each of the set of genes from the two parent robots are combined. A random mutation of the genes is also introduced, which may result in a completely inept robot or one that is smarter than both of its parents. Typically, after between 2,000 and 5,000 generations, a set of genes – a program – evolves which can do the designated task (although some very simple tasks only take fifty generations). It is then downloaded into the waiting robot body. The Sussex robots can perform tasks that would be difficult to program, but their behaviour is still rudimentary in comparison with even very simple animals.

Perhaps the most innovative form of evolved artificial life are 'the Creatures'. Created by Cyberlife at Millennium Interactive in the UK, the Creatures are intelligent, they have rudimentary language and can learn simple tricks. They are two-dimensional animated bundles of fluff with saucer-eyes and floppy ears, yet each Creature is a complex mathematical model designed to be an accurate mimic of a simple biological organism which can be run on a home computer. Dave Cliff, from the School of Cognitive and Computer

Sciences at Sussex University was asked to investigate Millennium's claim that the Creatures were a form of artificial life. Millennium said that the Creatures eat, drink, sleep, have sex, learn to speak and are as unpredictable as a gerbil; like every child's favourite pet, they also die. Cliff says, 'When I was first told what they'd done, I must admit, I didn't believe it.' What convinced him was the Creature's make-up: each one contains an individual neural net, a sophisticated piece of computer programming containing 3,000 neurons, which act as a rudimentary brain, allowing the Creatures to learn.

The software pack consists of between four and six eggs and an environment that's twelve computer screens wide and three screens high. The Creatures hatch from their eggs: their maximum lifespan is forty hours of computer time (when the PC is switched off, they go into suspended animation). Owners have to grow plants for them, which they eat, and try to stop them from tucking into toxic toadstools. They have a metabolism which borrows heavily from simple biology: their food is converted into starch and then broken down into glucose and then glycogen. If they overeat, the glycogen is stored as fat and they become obese; if they don't eat enough, they get hungry and will eventually starve. They can also get drunk.

After they've been alive for between four and six hours they start to show an interest in the opposite sex and will breed. The females are pregnant for two hours and then lay eggs and although there is little parental care, they do play more with their offspring and other relatives than non-related Creatures. Breeding is like true genetic evolution. When two biological organisms mate, half the genes from each sex are passed on to the offspring; in addition, some of the genes mutate. In the same way, each Creature passes on half of its 'genes' – parts of its program – and some sections of the program mutate. There is a familial resemblance between offspring and parents: basic body design is a constant but physical features – gait and various poses (such as the one adopted whilst sleeping) – are genetically determined and will be inherited from the parents. 'You could do selective breeding,' says Cliff, 'by taking two individuals which have traits that you like in the hope that the offspring will also show those characteristics, but you have no more guarantee that they will turn out to be better than their parents than if you were a dog breeder.'

As well as having a primitive metabolism, the Creatures have biochemical reactions which can affect their neural net (their brain). Biochemicals, such as toxins and alcohol, cause whole clusters of neurons in the Creatures' brains to be stimulated (whereas in humans neurons signal only to one other neuron at a time). Millennium calls this a hormonal system – for example, particular genes are switched on after the Creatures have been running for a certain amount of time, and this creates sex hormones which flood through the Creatures, altering the net and making them become sexually active. The exact time at which these genes are turned on is genetically inherited and hence will vary slightly between individuals. The combination of hormones and their metabolic drive allows them to have simple emotions such as hunger, thirst, unhappiness and so on. Their emotions are not completely predictable because they are dependent on the interaction of up to eighty different chemicals.

The Creatures speak (in speech bubbles), understand simple words and will learn tricks, but, like any pet, there's no certainty that they will perform on request. It's this very unpredictability that is special. The Creatures have been caught playing and chasing each other, behaviour that was neither programmed nor predicted and no one knows what to expect from the Creatures after they've been breeding for a few hundred generations.

The idea of evolution in action is exciting for biologists. It will be possible to release the Creatures into the Internet, sending them out to other Creature owners. For Tom Ray this must be a dream come true. Ray, who is currently at the Advanced Technology Research Centre near Osaka, was the first pioneer of artificial life. A biologist who worked in the Costa Rican rainforest, he became frustrated by the fact that he couldn't see the process of evolution. He was determined to model life on his computer screen, but soon realised that creating various habitats and a multitude of species – a veritable 'digital game reserve' – would take more power than a supercomputer possesses. Ray has just handed out one hundred versions of a program called Tierra to computers linked by the

Internet. In Tierra there are tiny software creatures that can determine how much memory and processing capability their host computer has and they then duplicate themselves until they have used up all the available memory. This may be life, but it is not as we know it: the Tierrans are as complex as bacteria. In contrast, the Creatures are much more sophisticated. If even a small proportion of them are allowed into the Internet, who knows what the result would be – Cliff predicts the emergence of rudimentary language and culture in the absence of human intervention and believes new species might evolve.

Apart from the Creatures and Neuro-Baby, who are both two-dimensional, the kind of robots described above use what's known as a bottom-up approach. Low-level behaviours are programmed into the robot; once they are running, higher-level properties emerge or at least appear to emerge. Randall Beer's cockroach may have only been a collection of low-level behaviours, but when these ran together the machine acted a little like a real cockroach. The top-down approach, in contrast, is one where a central controller delegates tasks to specific parts of the machine, thus imposing its will rather than allowing behaviour to emerge. One such example is Fumio Hara's face. Hara, who is from the Tokyo University of Science, has created a humanoid face that can read the facial expression of a person and copy it. A top-down controller 'tells' the face what facial expression to adopt. The human face can make forty-four different movements, twenty-four of which are related to expression. Hara has combined the learning power of a neural net with a series of gadgets that operate using air pressure and which change the face's expression so that it can show anger, sadness, fear, surprise and disgust. He hopes eventually to create a robot that can talk and make appropriate expressions in conversation, so, for example, if a person is angry, the robot will look apologetic. In future, it may be possible to marry Hara's design for expressing emotion to a robotic device that 'feels' the emotion. Both bottom-up and top-down approaches are becoming increasingly sophisticated and it is possible that in future these two could meet.

How advanced are the best humanoid robots? The two most

famous and well-developed robots are in America and Japan. Wabot-2, built by Ichiro Kato and his colleagues at Waseda University in Japan, can recognise music, both heard and seen, and play the piano to concert standard. Its delicate piano-playing fingers contain fifty pneumatic joints controlled by eighty microprocessors. So finely tuned is it, that it flinches when it touches something hot. It's learnt to play music, but it can't do anything else.

Cog, the brainchild of Rodney Brooks from MIT at Massachusetts, in contrast, can do little, but he's learning fast. Cog is humanoid, modelled on the proportions of a small graduate student. Brooks believes that body shape is important. 'The fact that we have bodies matters. It both constrains and enables the way we interpret the world.' Cog has the same range of movement in the hip and neck region as a person, but he's slower. He has arms (but the hands are not capable of fine motor control), two cameras for eyes that see in black and white and three ears.

Brooks was inspired by Arthur C. Clarke. 'When I was a teenager, the movie *2001* came out. In the movie Hal was turned on at 12 January 1992 and that date came by and I realised we didn't have a Hal or anything like that on the horizon. In fact, I had a birthday party for Hal at my house and all my students came by and we had cake and champagne and I got to thinking, maybe I should try and make Hal, and that was the inspiration for Cog.' Brooks's approach is to try to emulate biology. He has abandoned the traditional notion that the brain consists of two tiers – a high- and a low-level processor. The old view was that information was gathered and stored using a low-level processor and intelligence was generated by the high-level part of the brain. He believes that intelligence is created by storing knowledge by category (madeleines in the cake category and so on) as well as by how the knowledge was acquired (the scent of lime makes you think about eating your first madeleine beneath an avenue of lime trees). According to Brooks, it is out of the combination of these different low-level processes that intelligence emerges.

Cog's brain is a neural net, an artificial nervous system that can learn. It is layered and each layer produces a behaviour in its own right, but each implicitly relies on the presence of other pieces of the network. For instance, the 'explore environment' layer doesn't need to say explicitly 'avoid obstacles when exploring' because another layer tells Cog how to avoid obstacles. A basic value system, emotional responses and positive feedback loops for reinforcing behaviour have been built in. At the moment, Cog is attached to his brain (a massive parallel computer system that is stacked up in banks at the other side of the room) by a very long brain stem (heavy-duty cables).

The idea is that Cog will play with toys, pass items and generally act like a baby – but one that doesn't cry or wet its nappy – and learn as a baby does through interacting with its environment and other people. Brooks's colleague, Lynn Stein, hopes that Cog will eventually recognise faces. 'I don't know whether this ability will emerge or will have to be built in. It's important. I want Cog to know who we are, or at least that I'm the same person I was yesterday.' Three years into the project, Cog can track movements with his eyes, catch a ball, grasp someone's hand and flinch if they touch him on the outside of his arm. Because his eyes follow movement and he can turn his head, he appears remarkably human, glancing from a person's mouth if she is speaking to another researcher as she walks into the room. He can't hold objects very well but when he drops whatever he's holding, he looks down. If someone points at a ball, he will follow the pointing finger but, like an autistic child, looks at the person's hand and not the ball. At the moment he's being trained to follow eye gaze and research on his speech is underway.

'Thought and consciousness are epiphenomena of the process of being in the world. As the complexity of processing to deal with that complex world rises, we will see the same evidence of thought and consciousness in our systems as we see in people,' says Brooks optimistically. He adds, 'We'll be able to build robots that are as intelligent as humans and interact with us as humans do and are indistinguishable from humans. I don't think this is going to take place in a very short time, but eventually this is going to happen.' However, Nicholas Humphrey, a psychologist at the University of Cambridge, disagrees: 'The quality of human experience is based on our ancestral history. Unless you repeat that evolutionary history in the construction of an artificial brain, you won't replicate the quality of human experience.' Humphrey has support from an unusual area: the School of Cognitive and Computer Sciences at Sussex. 'We haven't got a chance of designing a human-like robot, either by hand or by evolution in our lifetime,' says Inman Harvey. 'Currently, we can't get robots to do the simplest of things, so we will have to evolve them. And if you want a robot to pass the Turing Test satisfactorily, it could take about a hundred million years of evolution and it would have to be done on a human time-scale – the robot would have to evolve in an environment with humans. It's no problem in principle, but in practice we won't be alive to see it happen.'

Horst Hendrik-Jansen, formerly also from Sussex University, says, 'I think it will be an awfully long time before we can produce a robot that has the skills subsumed under Theory of Mind. The robot would need to be "born" with species-typical activity patterns; it would need a human mother so that interactions could be set up to shape those patterns into intentional acts.'

Does this mean that we are doomed to failure? Well, not quite. It might in future be possible to combine a top-down with a bottom-up approach in robotics. We might not get full-blown Theory of Mind, but we may get some aspects of it. In ten to twenty years' time, it should be possible to have a humanoid robot that can sell tickets at train stations, deal with queries and carry out a simple conversation, acting as if it understood the desires and intentions of others. In practice, its scope would be very limited and removing the robot from its booth would highlight these deficiencies. It might also be possible, in a similar time-scale, to create animal-like robots that have rudimentary desires, goals and motivations, which could help in simple tasks, such as clearing up rubbish or cleaning out nuclear reactors.

There are those who are less pessimistic. 'Within fifty years there should be machines that are comparable in intelligence to the largest vertebrates, including human beings,' says Hans Moravec. 'After that, they'll be moving into new territory and there'll be super intelligent

machines able to do things that nothing on earth can do today.'
Moravec's prophesy comes from a simple calculation: 'Current computers are approximately a factor of a million short of being able to
match the human nervous system, but computers are evolving at
the rate of a thousand-fold every fifteen years and at that rate we
have only approximately thirty years to catch up that factor of a
million, which means that by 2030 there'll be computers capable of
[. . .] doing the job of the human nervous system.' And Maureen
Caudill adds, 'The mind of an android, like the mind of a human,
will emerge only when enough of the individual subsystems begin
communicating among themselves to institute this mysterious
quality. In its own way, the birth of an android mind will be as
mystical and awe-inspiring as the birth of a baby – and just
as perplexing to philosophers and scientists alike.' As for that doyen
of science fiction, Arthur C. Clarke: 'Hal isn't realistic for the year
2001, but he's certainly realistic for the year 2101 – if not before.'

So it might, in the near future, be possible to build robots that
have a simple version of Theory of Mind, or more complex androids
like the ticket-seller that appear to act as if they have Theory of
Mind in a very limited context. Will any of this future research help
us to understand the deficiencies suffered by a person with autism?
The short answer is that we don't know because robotics has not,
as yet, advanced terribly far. I stressed earlier the importance of body
shape in generating intelligence: even if a robot is developed which
has a version of Theory of Mind, it will still be relatively alien to
us if it does not have the same body build as we do. If we can
manage to make an android with Theory of Mind, we may learn
some important lessons.

The computers most likely to help people with autism are animal–
like robots which could be used as 'pets'. A robot, unlike a person
or an animal, won't, after an encounter with an autistic person, end
up both psychologically and physically bruised and could help teach
children rudimentary Theory of Mind skills such as desire and simple
belief comprehension. The Cyberlife Creatures might also prove
invaluable. The fact that they need to be fed could, at the very least,
instil a sense of responsibility in a child. It may be possible to show

autistic children how a Creature can suffer pleasure and pain by praising or punishing it, and its large eyes and capacity to engage in triadic joint attention could help make this concept clearer to them. If it is possible to teach rudimentary Theory of Mind skills to autistic children with computers, what better tool to use than a computerised Creature that acts as if it can think, feel, and have desires and beliefs?

THE MORAL MIND

With such a book
Before our eyes, we could not choose but read
Lessons of genuine brotherhood, the plain
And universal reason of mankind,
The truths of young and old.
>   William Wordsworth, *The Prelude*, Book VI, 'Cambridge
>   and the Alps'

Although ethical systems differ from country to country, there is a basic code of conduct, a concept of good and evil, which most people adhere to most of the time. The basis of this moral system is Theory of Mind.

To make valid moral judgements we need to be able to view things from several perspectives and to do this we need to have developed a Theory of Mind, which enables us to understand others' beliefs, emotions and expectations and therefore to empathise with them. A code of ethics could not have evolved if we did not have the ability to mindread or understand another's point of view.

Morality begins early. Unlike people with autism and psychopaths, young children have some idea about moral rules from a very young age. From around the age of four, children think it is worse to break a moral rule (stealing or lying, for instance), that will affect other people, than a conventional rule, such as calling the teacher by her first name or shouting out in class.

In chapter six I discussed research which suggested that women report feeling empathy for others and express their emotions more frequently than men. Even though both sexes are perfectly capable of assessing other people's feelings, women are often more affected by the plight of others; they tend to be more imaginative in terms of being able to visualise suffering and several studies indicate that girls do better at Theory of Mind tasks where the emotion of the characters has to be assessed.

If men and women do have slightly differing empathic skills, does this mean they have a different approach to morality? According to Carol Gilligan, an American psychologist and author of *In a Different Voice*, there is a gender difference when it comes to moral issues. She believes that men tend to have a more rights-based philosophy of morality, which depends on authority and rules. Women think more in terms of attachment, intimacy and responsibility to others. The bible stresses these apparent differences between men and women. For example, Abraham offers to sacrifice his son as proof of the strength of his faith, yet the woman faced with the prospect of seeing Solomon slice her child in two preferred to give up all claim to her baby than see the child killed.

It would be incorrect to say that men are unable to empathise; it would be fairer to say that they are often empathic in a more detached and clinical way. Neither are women adverse to framing moral issues in terms of rights. Moreover, a rights-based morality requires an abstract sense of caring and does go hand-in-hand with the acceptance of duties, social relationships and responsibilities.

There does appear to be a sex difference in the way in which teenagers solve moral problems. In one study, a group of adolescents were told some of Aesop's fables and asked what solutions were possible to the dilemmas posed. For example, one tale told of a porcupine who stumbled into a moles' burrow one dark, cold night. He asked if he could share their home for the winter. The moles agreed but soon regretted their decision as the porcupine's quills scratched them. When they finally gathered the courage to ask the porcupine to leave, he said no, their home suited him very well. In general, most of the boys preferred solutions to the fables based on rights – they said the porcupine has got to go, it's the moles' hole – whereas many of the girls tried to choose mutually agreeable solutions. They suggested wrapping the prickly animal in a towel or making the hole bigger. There were a fair number of children who suggested both kinds of solution and most were able to swap from a rights view to a compromise or vice versa.

It is possible that any male-female differences could be culturally inherited. However, there is one example of a male-female difference which has little to do with upbringing. From their first day of life, babies will cry if they hear another child crying. However, female babies react more strongly and more often to a baby's cries than male babies. This indicates that, at the very least, many female children are more predisposed to become personally distressed by emotion in others and will cry in sympathy.

One caveat should be added at this point. Even if morality does rely on Theory of Mind, being highly skilled at mindreading can often be used to one's own advantage – and to the disadvantage of others. The stereotype of bullies both in school and at work as unintelligent social inadequates is not highly accurate. Jon Sutton, from Goldsmiths University, London, has shown that children aged between seven and ten who are bullies are also skilled at a wide variety of Theory of Mind tasks which encompass understanding another person's point of view, what they think, how they feel and how one ought to behave in order not to make a social *faux pas*. Sutton's study did not find that there were more female than male bullies, but other research has shown that female bullies tend to target their friends in over fifty per cent of cases, whereas boys bully their friends only a third of the time. Schoolgirls' intimate, one-to-one relationships often emphasise empathy and sensitivity towards one another, but this understanding can be used in a more Machiavellian way. As Sutton says, 'We spend a lot of time thinking about what other people think and it may not be a great step from this understanding of what other people are thinking to actually manipulating these minds, which is a very useful skill in certain types of bullying.'

My belief is that, biologically, males are more predisposed to violence than females. Most male mammals concern themselves with fighting for females and for territories; males care directly for infants in fewer than one per cent of mammalian species. The image of a male animal, such as a red deer, roaring, fighting and mating, rather than protecting and suckling infants reflects the predominant mammalian pattern. Most wars are fought by men, most murders are committed by men, most government leaders who lead countries into war are men. (It is interesting also to note that most people with Asperger's syndrome or autism are male; they lack Theory of Mind to some degree and show an obsessive desire for rules and regulations. In addition, they lack empathy.) Female animals, on the other hand, have been selected by evolution to give birth, care for and raise offspring.

This does not mean that all men are war-mongers and all women are would-be mothers. Although we share a biological legacy with other mammals, what is true for one species of animal will not necessarily be the case for ourselves. Nevertheless, it seems quite likely that there is a biological disposition towards authoritarian rules, the desire for status and power and violence in men and a more caring, compassionate and sympathetic nature in women. Even if there are only slight differences between the sexes, in most cultures these are likely to be exacerbated.

Morality is a trait which we consider to be uniquely human. It is highly likely to be a by-product of our big brains and our propensity for social living. These are traits that we share with our closest living ancestor, the chimpanzee. Scientists have recently argued that gorillas and chimpanzees are so close to us genetically that we should be classified in the same group. On the basis of similarity of DNA, the molecule that determines our genetic code, there is only a difference of 1.6 per cent between us and chimps and 1.7 per cent between humans and gorillas. This has led Simon Esteal (amongst others), from the John Curtin School of Medical Research in Canberra, to argue that humans and the other two apes should all be classified in the genus *Homo*.

Apes are by far the cleverest animals that we have come across. Their ability to manipulate others, and their high level of adaptability and problem-solving skills are unmatched in the animal kingdom. As the previous chapters showed, great apes can recognise themselves in mirrors. Chimpanzees can use joint attention, the brightest of them appear to understand that seeing leads to knowing, they are capable of responding better than a four-year-old child to a false belief task, they are able to show empathy and deception. Many apes have learnt our own language through signs and symbols and can, to a limited extent, communicate with us. If any animal is likely to show the beginnings of morality, it is the chimpanzee.

As I mentioned, chimpanzees can show empathy to some extent. They travel more slowly as a group if one of their number is injured and will carefully clean each other's wounds. But unselfish behaviour is not enough: one of the essential features of morality is that it is a system based on rules that we have internalised. To a limited extent, chimpanzees also have a set code of conduct and their rules are enforced by the group. This was seen at Arnhem Zoo in the Netherlands where the keepers have a policy of not feeding the group unless all the chimps come into their indoor enclosure at night. One summer night two adolescent chimps refused to go indoors. The keepers spent two hours trying to persuade them to co-operate; when they did, they were given a separate enclosure. But the next morning, as soon as all the chimps were let out, the whole group chased the pair and beat them.

The internalisation of rules is not something which other animals seem to do. If a rat is trained to take only four pieces of food, it will happily eat more when the experimenter is not present. Even dogs, who are capable of obeying rules in the absence of their owners, usually treat the rule as a simple association between an object and an outcome. A dog who was told off for shredding paper showed typical expressions of submission and guilt whenever she saw torn paper, regardless of whether she was the culprit or not.

A moral system will not work if every individual is motivated by purely selfish reasons. A concern for others and for the community is essential. Frans de Waal, from Emory University in Atlanta, described the following incident which took place amongst the Arnhem Zoo chimps: 'A high-ranking female, Puist, took the trouble and risk to help her male friend, Luit, chase off a rival, Nikkie. Nikkie, however, had a habit after major confrontations of singling out and cornering his rivals to punish them. This time Nikkie displayed at Puist shortly after he had been attacked. Puist turned to Luit, stretching out her hand in search of support. But Luit did not lift a finger to protect her. Immediately after Nikkie had left the scene, Puist turned on Luit, barking furiously. She chased him across the enclosure and even pummelled him.' De Waal adds that if Puist was angry because Luit had failed to help her, then 'reciprocity in chimps may be governed by obligations and expectations similar to humans'.

Chimpanzees frequently bark if a fight breaks out. The particular bark used, a 'woaow' bark, is commonly associated with aggressive displays between group members who are threatening to harm social relationships. The bark might symbolise a mutual recognition of rules that operate within the group and an indication that they are being infringed. Chimpanzees, whilst capable of savagely beating each other on occasion, have an overwhelming desire for harmony. After a fight, the two warring parties must make up. Those who are reluctant to do so are often encouraged by a third party, usually a female. Females will also remove rocks from the hands of males who are threatening others and groups gang up on the physically more powerful males to prevent them from fighting. The dominant male of the group plays the role of mediator, splitting up conflicts without taking sides. The idea of reconciliation after discord and punishment followed by appeasement has much in common with human moral contracts.

De Waal, commenting on 'peace and reconciliation' in the primates that he watches says that as a human observer he feels that 'there is some moral order upheld by the community. We cannot help but identify with a group that we watch day in and day out [. . .] our own values of order and harmony are so similar.'

Chimpanzee rules are imposed from above by the dominant individuals in the group. Not every rule is enforced aggressively, but coercion does play an important role. Humans, too, have a respect for authority, for strong leaders and for the enforcement of law and order. An animal such as a cat has no respect for authority; cats have evolved as solitary hunters and as such are firmly outside the human moral realm. Not only do they have no conception of crime and punishment, they have no desire to fit in, to belong to a group.

That chimpanzees show the beginnings of morality and of empathy does not make them angelic. Chimpanzees have frequently been noticed enticing birds such as chickens and ducklings to the bars of their cage, only to poke them with a stick or worse. In some cases a pair of chimps will act in concert, one baiting, the other taking the role of the hit man. This is empathy – both chimps appear to have some understanding of the other's goal and motives – but it is empathy combined with indifference, which is just as people often act. The wild chimpanzees at Gombe in Tanzania caught polio from humans. Their group shunned them, frightened by their odd gait and the way they dragged their limbs. At first they displayed at the crippled chimps, then they attacked them. Jane Goodall, who spent years studying these chimps, described how one male with polio, Pepe, met with the following reaction: '[The others] stared for a moment and then, with wide grins of fear, rushed for reassurance to embrace and pat each other, still staring at the unfortunate cripple. Pepe, who obviously had no idea that he himself was the object of their fear, showed an even wider grin of fright as he repeatedly turned to look over his shoulder along the path behind him.' It is of little surprise how characteristically human this story sounds.

We evolved from apes and there is some evidence that our ancestors, the hominids, had an emotional life that we could recognise. Some of our hominid ancestors were disabled yet they lived to the same age as their peers. It is well-nigh impossible to read morals from fossils, but the age and handicap of these Neanderthals reveal that tolerance was extended towards those who could not contribute effectively to a primitive food-gathering society. If we share a common biological heritage, not only with proto-humans but with other animals, it would be arrogant to assume that our ethical skills and our Theory of Mind are unique. Our minds and hence our ability to reason morally must have evolved as we evolved as a species. But is it possible that our Theory of Mind will continue to evolve?

The short answer is that Theory of Mind will only advance if there is a selection pressure for it, in other words, if those people who are better at Theory of Mind become more desirable and hence attract partners more easily, give birth to more children who are even more skilled at Theory of Mind and even more desirable and successful. This scenario invites two questions: will it happen and, if it does, what effect might it have on our Theory of Mind? It could be argued that Theory of Mind will atrophy in the future. After all, our society is becoming increasingly dependent on technology. More of us can work or will be able to work easily from home, we are tending to devote a greater percentage of time to work, we spend increasing amounts of time communicating by phone, e-mail, the web and the internet and we can even shop from home via the net. People meet, have affairs and end relationships electronically. The result of this change in society is that face-to-face contact is decreasing. However, I would argue that this could make us more, rather than less dependent on Theory of Mind. Spending less time seeing the people with whom we communicate ought to force us to become more adept at detecting subtle changes of tone in a person's voice. As we start to network globally, the ability to deal with people from other cultures sensitively and assess their thoughts and beliefs will be essential. In addition, the style of e-mail and internet communications is such that shorthand is favoured, which is open to misinterpretation. We will have to become better at inferring meaning when there are no gestures, facial expressions or even voice tone to help us decode what others mean or think. I predict that we will go through a period where rude behaviour on the net proliferates – it is especially easy to write what one would never dream of saying to a person's face for there is no fear of retaliation and it is possible to communicate anonymously. There will be electronic conflict and misunderstanding before a fully fledged 'netiquette' develops and we become both more careful of other people's feelings and better able to comprehend them in this new and initially distancing medium. Those people who are the most successful in society (and this will mean skilled at communicating electronically and with more developed interpersonal skills) may end up being the most attractive to the opposite sex.

I think we could evolve a more sophisticated Theory of Mind as I have outlined; in addition, we might be able to pick up subtle cues more readily, not just over the internet or on the phone, but by becoming better at mindreading, recognising emotional states and deciphering gestures. We might also develop a greater understanding of higher levels of intentionality.

One further way in which we could advance morally and mentally is not through our own development, but through the creation of a robot that has Theory of Mind. I believe that at the present time it would be possible to build a 'morality machine', a computer capable of making ethical decisions. Unfortunately, this machine would only be able to use a rights-based utilitarian philosophy. Utilitarianism is the code of ethics that believes in the greatest good for the greatest number. Computers can perform rational, emotionless calculations with ease and this kind of philosophy thrives on sums and rules. One could imagine a computer that could solve typical dilemmas posed to philosophy students, such as the transplant scenario (in which there are five men in a room, one is about to have a heart attack, another is suffering from failure of the liver, a third has kidney stones and the fourth has ruptured his intestine. The fifth is healthy, so healthy, in fact, that, were it medically feasible, he could donate his heart, his liver, his kidneys and his intestine to the other four, thus satisfying the criteria of the greatest good for the greatest number.) A more practical use for a moral computer would be to allocate scarce resources, such as hospital beds, according to who has the greatest need, or to decide who could be allowed an operation in any financial year. Such a computer would be an invaluable tool – and I stress 'tool'. As long as there were people making decisions based on the computer's summary, people who were able to make exceptions to the rule and weigh up the pros and cons in a less clinical way, a moral machine could help sift the data used for complex moral questions of this nature. Creating a computer that could work out the sum total of another person's happiness, or one that could bend rules without having a rule to tell it how to bend them, will take a very long time.

In Isaac Asimov's short story, 'Evidence', Stephen Byerley is a lawyer who is standing as a political candidate. His opponent, Francis Quinn, asks the robot psychologist Dr Susan Calvin to vet Byerley in the hope that she can prove he is a robot and thus eliminate him from the competition.

'As a matter of fact, Mr Quinn, I have looked into Mr Byerley's career since you first brought this matter to our attention. I find that he has never demanded the death sentence in his closing speeches to the jury. I also find that he has spoken on behalf of the abolition of capital punishment and has contributed generously to research institutions engaged in criminal neurophysiology. He apparently believes in the cure, rather than the punishment of crime. I find that significant.'

'You do?' Quinn smiled. 'Significant of a certain odour of roboticity, perhaps?'

'Perhaps. Why deny it? Actions such as his could come only from a robot, or from a very honourable and decent human being. But you see, you just can't differentiate between a robot and the very best of humans.'

I would prefer to disagree. If we ever managed to create an android with a Theory of Mind and raised it in human society, any moral and ethical decisions it made would be just as flawed and unsatisfactory as most of our own.

APPENDIX

This book is clearly not a self-help guide for people with autism or parents with autistic children. However, I hope that the information I have provided will help in some small way towards furthering the understanding of autism by those who are affected by this disorder. For more practical help and advice, the following organisations can be contacted:

The National Autistic Society,
276 Willesden Lane,
London,
NW2 5RB,
UK

0181–451–1114

The Autism Society of America,
7910 Woodmount Avenue,
Suite 650, Bethesda,
Maryland, 20814,
USA

301–657–0881

Bundesland Hilfe für das Autistische Kind,
Bebtl Alle 141,
D-22297 Hamburg,
Germany

40–511–5604

Whatever the rights or wrongs of animal exploitation, it seems clear to me that animals such as the great apes (chimpanzees, bonobos, gorillas and orangutans) which are highly intelligent and closely related to ourselves should not be ill-treated, deprived of their freedom, used for illegal trading, eaten, experimented upon, nor should they lose their natural habitat. These organisations are dedicated to safeguarding the rights of the great apes:

Das Great Ape Projekt – Germany,
Postfach 616234,
D-22450 Hamburg,
Germany

The Great Ape Project – UK,
PO Box 6218,
London,
W14 0GD,
UK

The Great Ape Project – Netherlands,
Haarlemmer Houttuinen 45 A,
1013 GM,
Amsterdam
Holland

The Great Ape Project – USA,
c/o National Alliance for Animals,
PO Box 77591,
Washington, DC,
USA

World Society for the Protection of Animals (WSPA) – UK
2 Langley Lane,
London,
SW8 1TJ,
UK

WSPA – USA
29 Perkins St,
PO Box 190,
Boston,
Mass, 02130
USA

BIBLIOGRAPHY

Basic academic text books used throughout the book:

Collections of academic papers:

Baron-Cohen S., Tager-Flusberg H. and Cohen D.J. (eds), *Understanding other minds: Perspectives from autism*, Oxford University Press, Oxford, 1993.
Byrne R.W. and Whiten A. (eds), *Machiavellian intelligence: Social expertise and the evolution of intellect in monkeys, apes and humans*, Oxford University Press, Oxford, 1988.
Frith U., *Autism and Asperger syndrome*, Cambridge University Press, Cambridge, 1991.
O'Connell S.M., Theory of Mind in Chimpanzees (unpublished manuscript), Liverpool University, Liverpool.
Whiten A., *Natural theories of mind*, Basil Blackwell, Oxford, 1991.

Academic text books:

Baron-Cohen S., *Mindblindness: An essay on autism and Theory of Mind*, MIT Press/Bradford Books, Cambridge, Mass., 1995.
Frith U., *Autism: Explaining the enigma*, Basil Blackwell, Oxford, 1989.
Happé F., *Autism: An introduction to psychological theory*, UCL Press, London, 1994.
Wellman H.M., *The child's theory of mind*, MIT Press/Bradford Books, Cambridge, Mass., 1990.

Chapter one: A person is a person through other people

Calvin W.H., 'The emergence of intelligence', *Scientific American*, issue 79–85, October 1994.

Dennett D.C., 'The intentional stance in theory and practice', in *Machiavellian intelligence: Social expertise and the evolution of intellect in monkeys, apes and humans*, Byrne R.W. and Whiten. A. (eds), Oxford University Press, Oxford, 1988.

Dennett D.C., *The intentional stance*, MIT Press/Bradford Books, Cambridge, Mass., 1987.

Hale R.J., *Machiavelli and Renaissance Italy*, English University Press, London, 1961.

Smith U. (ed.), *Folktales from Australia's children of the world*, Paul Hamlyn, Sydney, 1979.

Wing L., 'Diagnosis, clinical description and prognosis', in *Early childhood autism*, Wing L. (ed.), Pergamon Press, Oxford, 1976.

Chapter two: Out of the armchair

St Thomas Aquinas, selected and translated by Gilby T., Oxford University Press, Oxford, 1951.

Dennett D.C., 'The intentional stance in theory and practice', op.cit., pp. 180–201.

Dennett D.C., *The intentional stance*, op.cit.

Dennett D.C., *Brainstorms*, Bradford books, Montgomery, VT, 1978.

Descartes R., *A discourse on method: Meditations on the first philosophy, Principles of philosophy*, Veitch J. (trans), Everyman's Library, London, 1978.

Descartes R., *Philosophical writings*, Anscombe E. and Geach P.T. (eds), Nelson University Press, Sunbury-on-Thames, 1970.

Dunbar R. *The trouble with science*, Faber and Faber, London, 1995.

Fodor J.A., *Psychosemantics: The problem of meaning in the philosophy of mind*, MIT Press/Bradford Books, Cambridge, Mass., 1987.

Griffen D.R., 'Progress toward a cognitive ethology', in *Cognitive ethology*. Ristau C.A. (ed.), Lawrence Erlbaum Ass., New Jersey, 1991.

Griffen D.R., *Animal thinking*, Harvard University Press, Cambridge, Mass., 1984.

Griffen D.R. (ed.), *Animal mind – human mind*, Springer-Verlag, Berlin, 1982.

Griffen D.R., *The question of animal awareness: Evolutionary continuity of mental experience*, William Kaufman Inc., California, 1981.

Griffen D.R., 'Prospects for a cognitive ethology', *Behaviour and Brain Science* 4:527–38, 1978.

Griffen D.R., *Listening in the Dark*, Yale University Press, New Haven, Conneticut, 1958.

Hume D., *Enquiries concerning the human understanding and concerning the principles of morals*, Selby-Bigge L.A. (ed.), Clarendon Press, Oxford, 1902.

Hume D., *Treatise on human nature*, Selby-Bigge L.A. (ed.), Clarendon Press, Oxford, 1988.

Leibniz W.G., *New Essays on human understanding*, Remnant P. and Bennett J. (eds), Cambridge University Press, Cambridge, 1981.

Locke J., *An essay concerning human understanding*, Dover Press, New York, 1959.

Midgley M., *Beast and man: The roots of human nature*, Harvester Press, Sussex, 1979.

Nagel T., 'What is it like to be a bat?', *Philosophical Review* 83: 435–450, 1974.

Plato, *The Republic*, Waterfield R. (trans.), Oxford University Press, Oxford, 1993.

Popper K.R., *Conjectures and refutations: The growth of scientific knowledge*, (Fourth edition), Routledge and Kegan Paul, London, 1972.

Popper K.R. and Eccles J.C., *The self and its brain*, Springer International Press, Berlin, 1977.

Ryle G., *The concept of mind*, Hutchinson, London, 1949.

Schopenhauer A., *On the fourfold root of the principle of sufficient reason and on the will in nature*, Hillebrand K. (trans.), G. Bell, London, 1915.

Schopenhauer A., *The world as will and idea*, Haldane R.B. and Kemp. I. (trans.), Kegan Paul, Trench, Trubner, London, 1883.

Searle J.R., *Speech acts, an essay in the philosophy of language*, Cambridge University Press, London, 1969.

Wittgenstein L., *Philosophical investigations*, Anscombe G.E.M. (trans.), Basil Blackwell, Oxford, 1976.

Chapter three: Windows to the soul

The quote by Ralph Emerson at the beginning of this chapter appeared in Simon Baron-Cohen's book *Mindblindness* and he has been kind enough to let me reproduce it.

Arduino P.J. and Gould J.L., 'Is tonic immobility adaptive?', *Animal Behaviour* 32(3):921–923, 1984.

Bakeman R. and Adamson L.B., 'Co-ordinating attention to people and objects in mother–infant and peer–infant interaction', *Child Development* 55:1278–1289, 1984.

Baron-Cohen S., (in press) 'EDD and SAM: Two cases for evolutionary psychology', in *Joint attention: Its origins and role in development*, Moore C. and Dunham. P. (eds), Lawrence Erlbaum Ass., New Jersey.

Baron-Cohen S., 'The relationship between SAM and ToMM: The "lock and key" versus the "tadpole and frog" hypotheses', Proceedings of Theories of Theory of Mind Conference, Sheffield, 1994.

Baron-Cohen S., 'From attention-goal psychology to belief-desire psychology: The development of a theory of mind and its dysfunction', in *Understanding other minds: Perspectives from autism*, op.cit.

Baron-Cohen S., 'Perceptual role-taking and protodeclarative pointing in autism', *British Journal of Developmental Psychology* 7:113–127, 1989a.

Baron-Cohen S., 'Joint attention deficits in autism: Towards a cognitive analysis', *Development and Psychopathology* 1:185–89, 1989b.

Baron-Cohen S., Campbell R., Karmiloff-Smith A., Grant J. and Walker J., 'Are children with autism blind to the mentalistic significance of the eyes?', *British Journal of Developmental Psychology* 13:379–398.

Burghardt G.M., 'Cognitive ethology and critical anthropomor-

247

phism: A snake with two heads and hognose snakes that play dead', in *Cognitive ethology*, Ristau C.A. (ed.), Lawrence Erlbaum Ass., New Jersey, 1991.

Carpenter M., Tomasello M., Savage-Rumbaugh S., (in press) 'Joint attention and imitative learning in children, chimpanzees and encultured chimps', *Social Development*.

Gergely G., Nadasy Z., Csibra G., Biro S., 'Taking the intentional stance at 12 months of age', *Cognition* 56:165–193, 1995.

Landau B. and Gleitman L., *Language and experience: Evidence from the blind child*, Harvard University Press, Harvard, 1985.

Leekam S., Baron-Cohen S., Perrett D., Milders M. and Brown S., (in press) 'Eye-Direction Detection: A dissociation between geometric and joint attention skills in autism', *British Journal of Developmental Psychology*.

Miller P.H. and Aloise P.A., 'Young children's understanding of the psychological causes of behaviour: a review', *Child Development* 60:257–85, 1989.

Pepperberg I. and McLaughlin M.A., (in press) 'Effect of avian-human joint attention on allospecific vocal learning by grey parrots (*Psittacus erithacus*)', *Journal of Comparative Psychology*.

Phillips W., Gomez J.C., Baron-Cohen S., Laa V. and Riviere A., 'Treating people as objects, agents of "subjects": How young children with and without autism make requests', *Journal of Child Psychiatry* 36(8):1383–1398, 1995.

Povinelli D.J. and Eddy T.J., (in press) 'What young chimpanzees know about seeing', *Monograph for Child Development*.

Scaife M. and Bruner J.S., 'The capacity for joint visual attention in the human infant', *Nature* 253:265, 1975.

Chapter four: Heart's desire

Baron-Cohen S., 'Do people with autism understand what causes emotion?', *Child Development* 62:385–395, 1991.

Baron-Cohen S. and Hammer J., 'Is autism an extreme form of the "male brain"?', *Advances in Infant Research*, 1996.

Baron-Cohen S., Riviere A., Fukishima M., French D., Hadwin J.,

Cross P., Bryant C. and Sotillo M., 'Reading the mind in the face: A cross-cultural and developmental study', *Visual Cognition* 3(1):39–59, 1996.

Darwin C., *On expressions of emotion in man and animals*, John Murray, London, 1872.

Ekman P. and Friesen W., 'Constants across cultures in the face and emotion', *Journal of Personality and Social Psychology* 17(2): 124–129, 1971.

Ekman P. and Friesen W., 'Pan-cultural elements in facial displays of emotion', *Science* 164:86–88, 1969.

Goodall Jane, *The chimpanzees of Gombe*, Harvard University Press, Harvard, Mass., 1986.

Gopnik A., 'How we know our minds: The illusion of first-person knowledge of intentionality', *Behavioural and Brain Sciences* 16: 1–14, 1993.

Hobson R.P., 'The autistic child's appraisal of expressions of emotion', *Journal of Child Psychology* 27(5):321–342, 1986a.

Hobson R.P., 'The autistic child's appraisal of expressions of emotion: A further study', *Journal of Child Psychology* 27(5):671–680, 1986b.

Hobson R.P., Ouston J. and Lee A., 'Naming emotion in faces and voices: Abilities and disabilities in autism and mental retardation', *Journal of Developmental Psychology* 7:237–250, 1989.

Mallon B., *Children Dreaming: Pictures in my pillow*, Penguin, London, 1989.

Povinelli D.J. and Perilloux H., (in prep.) 'A preliminary note on young chimpanzees' reactions to intentional and accidental behaviour'.

Savage-Rumbaugh S. and Wilkerson B., 'Socio-sexual behaviour in Pan paniscus and Pan troglodytes: A comparative study', *Journal of Human Evolution* 7:327–344, 1978.

Sorce J.F., Emde R.N., Campos J. and Klinnert M.D., 'Maternal emotional signalling: its effect on the visual cliff behaviour of one-year-olds', *Developmental Psychology* 21(1):195–200, 1985.

Tager-Flusberg H., 'Autistic children's talk about psychological states: Deficits in the early aquisition of a Theory of Mind', *Child Development* 63:161–172, 1992.

Chapter five: True belief

Avis J. and Harris P., 'Belief-Desire reasoning among Baka children: Evidence for a universal conception of mind', *Child Development* 62:460–467, 1991.

Baron-Cohen S. and Goodhart F., 'The "seeing-leads-to-knowing" deficit in autism: The Pratt and Bryant Probe', *British Journal of Developmental Psychology* 12:397–401, 1994.

Cheney D.L. and Seyfarth R.M., 'Précis of *How monkeys see the world*', *Behavioural and Brain Sciences* 15:135–182, 1992.

Cheney D.L. and Seyfarth R.M., *How monkeys see the world: Inside the mind of another species*, University of Chicago Press, Chicago, 1990.

Clements W.A. and Perner J., 'Implicit understanding of belief', *Cognitive Development* 9:377–395, 1994.

Corcoran R., Mercer G. and Frith C., (in press) 'Schizophrenia, symptomatology and social inference: Investigating Theory of Mind in people with schizophrenia', *Schizophrenia Research*.

Dunn J., Brown J., Slomkowski C., Tesla C. and Youngblade L., 'Young children's understanding of other people's feelings and beliefs: Individual differences and their antecedents', *Child Development* 62:1352–1366, 1991.

Flavell J., Green F. and Flavell E., 'The development of children's knowledge about attentional focus', *Developmental Psychology* 31(4):706–712, 1995.

Flavell J., Everett B., Croft K. and Flavell E., 'Young children's knowledge about visual perception: Further evidence for the level 1–level 2 distinction', *Developmental Psychology* 17:99–103, 1981.

Freeman N.H., (in prep.) 'The learnability of intentional relations'.

Frith C. and Corcoran R., (in prep.) 'Exploring Theory of Mind in people with schizophrenia'.

Gagliardi J., Kirkpatrick-Steiger K., Thomas J., Allen G. and Blumberg M., 'Seeing and knowing attribution versus stimulus control in adult humans (*Homo sapiens*)', *Journal of Comparative Psychology* 109(2):107–114, 1995.

Hesse H., *The Glass Bead Game*, (first published 1943) Picador, London, 1987.

Leslie A.M. and Frith U., 'Autistic children's understanding of seeing, knowing and believing', *Journal of Developmental Psychology* 6:315–324, 1988.

Perner J. and Ogden J.E., 'Knowledge for hunger: Children's problem with representation in imputing mental states', *Cognition* 29:47–61, 1988.

Perner J., Leekam S.R. and Wimmer H., 'Three-year-olds' difficulty with false belief', *British Journal of Developmental Psychology* 5:125–137, 1987.

Povinelli D.J. and Eddy T., (in press) 'What young chimpanzees know about seeing', monograph for *Child Development*.

Povinelli D.J. and deBlois S., 'Young children's (*Homo sapiens*) understanding of knowledge formation in themselves and others', *Journal of Comparative Psychology* 106:228–238, 1992.

Povinelli D.J., Nelson K.E. and Boysen S.T., 'Comprehension of role reversal in chimpanzees: Evidence of empathy?', *Animal Behaviour* 43(4):633–40, 1992.

Povinelli D.J., Parks K. and Novak M.A., 'Role reversal in rhesus monkeys, but no evidence of empathy', *Animal Behaviour* 44: 269–281, 1992.

Povinelli D.J., Parks K. and Novak M.A., 'Do rhesus monkeys (*Macaca mulatta*) attribute knowledge and ignorance to others?', *Journal of Comparative Psychology* 105:318–325, 1991.

Povinelli D.J. and Nelson K.E., 'Inferences about guessing and knowing in chimpanzees', *Journal of Comparative Psychology* 104: 203–210, 1990.

Pratt C. and Bryant P., 'Young children understand that seeing leads to knowing (so long as they are looking into a single barrel)', *Child Development* 61:973–981, 1990.

Premack D., 'Mind with and without language', in *Thought without language*, Weiskrantz L. (ed.), Oxford University Press, Oxford, 1988.

Swettenham J., 'Can children be taught to understand false beliefs using computers?', *Journal of Child Psychology and Psychiatry* 37(2):157–165, 1996.

Swettenham J., Baron-Cohen S., Gomez J.C. and Walsh S., 'What's inside someone's head? Conceiving of the mind as a camera helps children with autism acquire an alternative to a Theory of Mind', *Cognitive Neuropsychiatry* 1(1):73–88, 1996.

Whiten A., 'Evolutionary and developmental origins of the mind-reading system', in *Piaget, evolution and development*, Langer J. and Killen M. (eds), Lawrence Erlbaum Ass., New York, 1996.

Yuill N. and Perner J., 'Intentionality and knowledge in children's judgements of actors' responsibility and recipients' emotional reaction', *Developmental Psychology* 24:358–365, 1988.

Chapter six: Someone else's shoes

Batson C.D., 'How social an animal? The human capacity for caring', *American Psychologist* 45:336–346, 1990.

Batson C.D., Bolen M.H., Cross J.A. and Neuringer-Benefiel H.E., 'Where is the altruism in the altruistic personality?', *Journal of Personality and Social Psychology* 50(1):212–220, 1986.

Blair R.J.R., (in prep.) 'Morality in the autistic child'.

Blair R.J.R., 'A cognitive developmental approach to morality: investigating the psychopath', *Cognition* 57:1–29, 1995.

Blair R.J.R., (unpublished manuscript) 'The absence of empathy in the psychopath', University College London.

Blair R.J.R., Sellars C., Strickland I., Clark F., Williams A.O., Smith M. and Jones L., (in prep.) 'Theory of mind in the psychopath'.

Blair R.J.R, Jones L., Clark F. and Smith M., 'Is the psychopath "morally insane"?', *Personal Individual Differences* 19(5):741–752, 1995.

Blair R.J.R., Sellars C., Strickland I., Clark F., Williams A.O., Smith M. and Jones L., 'Emotion attribute in the psychopath', *Personal Individual Differences* 19(4):431–437, 1995.

Borke H., 'Interpersonal perception of young children: Egocentrism or empathy?', *Developmental Psychology* 5:263–269, 1971.

Casey R.J., 'Children's emotional experience: Relations among expression, self-report and understanding', *Developmental Psychology* 29(1):119–129, 1993.

Chisholm K. and Strayer J., 'Verbal and facial measures of children's emotion and empathy', *Journal of Experimental Psychology* 59: 299–316, 1995.

Eddy T.J., Gallup G.G. and Povinelli D.J., 'Age differences in the ability of chimpanzees to distinguish mirror-images of self from video images of others', *Journal of Comparative Psychology* 110(1):38–44, 1996.

Eisenberg N., Fabes R.A., Miller P.A., Fultz J., Shell R., Mathy R.M. and Reno R.R., 'Relation of sympathy and personal distress to prosocial behaviour: A multimethod study', *Journal of Personality and Social Psychology* 57 (1):55–66, 1989.

Eisenberg N., Schaller M., Fabes R.A., Bustamante D., Mathy R.M., Shell R. and Rhodes K., 'Differentiation of personal distress and sympathy in children and adults', *Developmental Psychology* 24(6): 766–775, 1988.

Eisenberg N. and Lennon R., 'Sex differences in empathy', *Psychological Bulletin*, 94:100–131, 1983.

Gallup G.G. 'Self-awareness and the emergence of mind in primates', *American Journal of Primatology* 2:237–248, 1982.

Gergeley G., 'From self-recognition to Theory of Mind', in *Self-awareness in animals and humans: Developmental perspectives*, Taylor Parker S., Mitchell R.W. and Boccia M.L., (eds.) Cambridge University Press, Cambridge, pp. 51–60, 1994.

Gopnik A. and Slaughter V., 'Young children's understanding of changes in their mental states', *Child Development* 62:98–110.

Heyes C.M., 'Reflections on self-recognition in primates', *Animal Behaviour* 47:909–919, 1994.

Hobson R.P., 'On acquiring knowledge about people and the capacity to pretend: Response to Leslie (1987)', *Psychological Review* 97(1):114–121, 1990.

Kavanaugh R.D. and Harris P.L., 'Imagining the outcome of pretend transformations: Assessing the competence of normal children and children with autism', *Developmental Psychology* 30(6):847–854, 1994.

Lillard A., 'Young children's conceptualisation of pretence: Action or mental representational state?', *Child Development* 64:372–386, 1993.

O'Connell S.M., 'Empathy in Chimpanzees: Evidence for Theory of Mind?', *Primates* 36(3):397–410, 1995.

Patterson F. and Linden E., *The education of Koko*, Holt, Rinehart and Winston, New York, 1981.

Pepperberg I.M., Garcia S.E., Jackson E.C. and Marconi S., 'Mirror use by African grey parrots (*Psittacus erithacus*)', *Journal of Comparative Psychology* 109(2):182–195, 1995.

Perner J., Baker, S. and Hutton D., 'Prelief: The conceptual origins of belief and pretence', in *Children's early understanding of mind: Origins and development*, Lewis C. and Mitchell P. (eds), Lawrence Erlbaum Ass., New Jersey, 1994.

Povinelli D.J., 'The unduplicated self', in *The self in infancy: Theory and research*, Rochat P. (ed), Elsevier Science, Amsterdam, Holland, 1995.

Povinelli D.J., 'How to create self-recognising gorillas (but don't try it on macaques)', in *Self-awareness in animals and humans: Developmental perspectives*, op. cit.

Povinelli D.J., Landau K. and Perilloux H.K., (in press) 'Self-recognition in young children using delayed versus live feedback: Evidence of a developmental asynchrony', *Child Development*.

Povinelli D.J., Nelson K.E. and Boysen S.T., 'Comprehension of role reversal in chimpanzees: Evidence of empathy?', *Animal Behaviour* 43(4):633–640, 1992.

Povinelli D.J., Parks K. and Novak M.A., 'Role reversal in rhesus monkeys, but no evidence of empathy', *Animal Behaviour* 44: 269–281, 1992.

Swartz K.B. and Evans S., 'Not all chimpanzees (*Pan troglodytes*) show self-recognition', *Primates* 32(4):483–496, 1991.

Wimmer H. and Perner J., 'Beliefs about beliefs: Representation and constraining function of wrong beliefs in young children's understanding of deception', *Cognition* 13:103–128, 1983.

Wispé L., 'The distinction between sympathy and empathy: To call forth a concept, a word is needed', *Journal of Personality and Social Psychology* 50(2):314–321, 1986.

Yirimiya N., Sigman, M.D., Kasari C. and Mundy P., 'Empathy with cognition in high-functioning children with autism', *Child Development* 63:150–160, 1992.

Chapter seven: The tangled web

Adang O.J., 'Teasing in young chimpanzees', *Behaviour* 88:98–122, 1984.

Baron-Cohen S., 'Out of sight or out of mind? Another look at deception in autism', *Journal of Child Psychology and Psychiatry* 33(7):1141–1155, 1992.

Byrne R. and Whiten A., 'Cognitive evolution in primates: Evidence from tactical deception', *Man* (N.S.) 27:609–627, 1992.

Corcoran R., Cahill C. and Frith C., (in prep.) 'The appreciation of visual jokes in people with schizophrenia: a study of mentalising ability'.

Fouts R.S. and Fouts D.H., 'Chimpanzees' use of sign language', in *The Great Ape Project: Equality beyond humanity*, Cavalieri P. and Singer P. (eds), Fourth Estate, London, 1993.

Lang A. (ed.), *The Blue Fairy Book*, Dover Publications Inc., New York, 1965.

Meissner H-O., *Magda Goebbels: A biography*, Sidgwick and Jackson, London, 1978.

Mestel R., 'Behind the mask', *New Scientist* supplement, 27 April 1996, pp. 10–13.

Miles H.L., 'How can I tell a lie? Apes, language and the problem of deception', in *Deception: Perspectives on human and nonhuman deceit*, Mitchell R.W. and Thompson N.S. (eds), University of New York Press, Albany, 1986.

Patterson F. and Cohn R., 'Self-recognition and self-awareness in lowland gorillas', in *Self-awareness in animals and humans: Developmental perspectives*, op. cit.

Ristau C.A., 'Aspects of the cognitive ethology of an injury-feigning bird, the piping plover', in *Cognitive ethology*, Ristau C.A. (ed.), Lawrence Erlbaum Ass., New Jersey, 1991.

de Waal F.B.M., 'Deception in the natural communication of chimps', in *Deception: Perspectives on human and nonhuman deceit*, op. cit.

Whiten A. and Byrne R.W., 'Tactical deception in primates', *Behavioural and Brain Sciences* 11:233–273, 1988.

Wimmer H. and Perner J., 'Beliefs about beliefs: Representation and constraining function of wrong beliefs in young children's understanding of deception', *Cognition* 13:103–128, 1983.

Woodruff G. and Premack D., 'Intentional communication in the chimpanzee: The development of deception', *Cognition* 7:333–362, 1979.

Chapter eight: The water lilies have opened their eyes

Bailey A., Phillips W. and Rutter M., 'Autism: Towards an integration of clinical, genetic and neuropsychological and neurobiological perspectives', *Journal of Child Psychology and Psychiatry* 37(1): 89–126, 1996.

Baron-Cohen S. and Hammer J., 'Is autism an extreme form of the "male brain"?', op. cit.

Bishop D.V.M., 'Annotation: Autism, executive functions and Theory of Mind: A neuropsychological perspective', *Journal of Child Psychology and Psychiatry* 34(3):279–293, 1993.

Bowler D.M., 'Theory of Mind in Asperger's syndrome', *Journal of Child Psychology and Psychiatry* 33:877–894, 1992.

Brothers L., 'Neurophysiology of the perception of intentions by primates', in *The Cognitive Neurosciences*, M. Gazzaniga (ed.), MIT Press/Bradford Books, Cambridge, Mass., 1995.

Brothers L., 'A biological perspective on empathy', *American Journal of Psychiatry* 146(1):10–19, 1989.

Brothers L., Ring B. and King A., 'Response of neurons in the macaque amygdala to complex social stimuli', *Behavioural Brain Research* 41:199–213, 1990.

Fletcher P.C., Happé F., Frith U. et al., 'Other minds in the brain:

A functional imaging study of Theory of Mind in story comprehension', *Cognition* 57:109–128, 1995.

Frith U., (in press) 'Social communication and its disorder in autism and Asperger's syndrome'.

Frith U., Happé F. and Siddon F., 'Autism and Theory of Mind in everyday life', *Social Development* 3(2):108–124, 1994.

Frith U., Morton J. and Leslie A.M., 'The cognitive basis of a biological disorder: Autism', *Trends in Neurological Sciences* 14(10):433–438, 1991.

Goel V., Grafman J., Sadato N. and Hallett M., 'Modelling other minds', *Neuroreport* 6:1741–1746, 1995.

Happé F.G.E., 'The role of age and verbal ability in the Theory of Mind task performance of subjects with autism', *Child Development* 66:843–855, 1995.

Leslie A.M. and Frith U., 'Prospects for a cognitive neuropsychology of autism: Hobson's choice', *Psychological Review* 97(1):122–131, 1990.

Smith C., 'Trapped in worlds of their own', *Independent on Sunday*, 8 January 1995, p. 73.

Sparrevohn R. and Howie P.M., 'Theory of Mind in children with autistic disorder: Evidence of developmental progression and role of verbal ability', *Journal of Child Psychology and Psychiatry* 36(2):249–263, 1995.

Wolff S. and McGuire R.J., 'Schizoid personality in girls: A follow-up study – what are the links with Asperger's syndrome?', *Journal of Child Psychology and Psychiatry* 36(5):793–817, 1994.

Chapter nine: More than human

Asimov I., *Robot Visions*, Victor Gollancz Science Fiction, London, 1991.

Caudill M., *In our own image: Building an artificial person*, Oxford University Press, Oxford, 1996.

Cliff D., 'Artificial intelligence or artificial insects', *Cognitive Science Research Papers 305*, University of Sussex, 1993.

Concar D., 'Can robots come to care for us?', *New Scientist*, 2 October 1993, pp. 40–42.

Curry A., Clayton R., 'Remote through-wall sampling of the Trawsfynydd reactor pressure vessel: an overview', *British Nuclear Energy Society*:27–32, 1995.

Dautenhahn K., 'Getting to know each other – Artificial social intelligence for autonomous robots', *Robotics and Autonomous Systems* 16:333–356, 1995.

Dautenhahn K., 'Trying to imitate – a step towards releasing robots from social isolation', in *Proceedings from Perception to Action Conference, Lausanne, Switzerland*, Gaussier P. and Nicoud J.D. (eds), The Institute for Electrical Electronics Engineers, Computer Society Press, Los Alamitos, California, 1994.

Dautenhahn K. and Christaller T., 'Remembering, rehearsal and empathy – Towards a social and embodied cognitive psychology for artifacts', *Arbeitspapier der GMD 956*, Sankt Augustin, Germany, 1995.

Ford K.M., Glymour C. and Hayes P.J. (eds), *Android epistemology*, MIT Press, Cambridge, Mass., 1995.

Moravec H., *Mind Children: The future of robot and human intelligence*, Harvard University Press, Cambridge, Mass., 1988.

Rossney R., 'Oh look, he's brought me a present', *New Scientist*, 16 September 1995, pp. 38–42.

Webb B., 'Robotic experiments in cricket phonotaxis', in *Proceedings of the Third International Conference on the Simulation of Adaptive Behaviour*, Cliff D., Husbands P., Meyer J.A. and Wilson S.W. (eds), MIT Press, Cambridge, Mass., 1994.

Chapter ten: The moral mind

Freeman N.H. and Lacohée H., 'Making explicit three-year-olds' implicit competence with their own false beliefs', *Cognition* 56: 31–60, 1995.

Freeman N.H., (in prep.) 'The learnability of intentional relations'.

Gilligan C., *In a different voice: Psychological theory and the women's movement*, Harvard University Press, Cambridge, Mass., 1982.

Rivers I. and Smith P.K., 'Types of bullying behaviour and their correlates', *Aggressive Behaviour* 20:359–368, 1994.

Sutton J., Smith P.K. and Swettenham J., 'Bullying: Perspectives from social cognition', Paper presented to the 1996 British Psychological Society London Conference.

de Waal F., *Good natured: The origins of right and wrong in humans and other animals*, Harvard University Press, Cambridge, Mass., 1996.

INDEX